TRY NOT
TO BE
STRANGE

MICHAEL HINGSTON

Try Not To Be Strange

THE CURIOUS HISTORY *of* THE KINGDOM *of* REDONDA

BIBLIOASIS | WINDSOR, ONTARIO

FIRST EDITION

Library and Archives Canada Cataloguing in Publication
Title: Try not to be strange : the curious history of the Kingdom of Redonda / Michael Hingston.
Names: Hingston, Michael, 1985– author.
Description: Includes bibliographical references and index.
Identifiers: Canadiana (print) 20220251355 | Canadiana (ebook) 2022025138X | ISBN 9781771964159 (softcover) | ISBN 9781771964166 (ebook)
Subjects: LCSH: Redonda (Antigua and Barbuda) — History.
Classification: LCC F2035 .H56 2022 | DDC 972.974 — DC23

Edited by Daniel Wells
Copyedited by Rachel Ironstone
Indexed by Allana Amlin
Text and cover designed by Natalie Olsen

Published with the generous assistance of the Canada Council for the Arts, which last year invested $153 million to bring the arts to Canadians throughout the country, and the financial support of the Government of Canada. Biblioasis also acknowledges the support of the Ontario Arts Council (OAC), an agency of the Government of Ontario, which last year funded 1,709 individual artists and 1,078 organizations in 204 communities across Ontario, for a total of $52.1 million, and the contribution of the Government of Ontario through the Ontario Book Publishing Tax Credit and Ontario Creates.

PRINTED AND BOUND IN CANADA

In memory of Etheline Hingston
(1922–2021)

CONTENTS

"Islands can
get a bit
claustrophobic."

– SO SAY BANANA BIRD –

PROLOGUE |
PERPETUATING
the FRAUD

ON THE evening of November 24, 2009, an email appeared in Michael Howorth's inbox.

It had been a crisp, windy Sunday in Downton, the village in Southern England where Howorth lived with his wife. Michael and Frances had made their home in Downton for many years and had raised a family there. But now that their youngest daughter had moved out, the couple used the village mainly as a landing pad between assignments as travelling freelance journalists covering the yachting industry. They were a team: Michael wrote the stories, and Frances took the photos. Over the years, their work had appeared in dozens of maritime-related publications and had taken them everywhere from Africa to the Galapagos to the Maldives. Just that month, the couple had been to both Amsterdam and Fort Lauderdale, Florida, attending trade shows and taking notes on local accommodations. One overly cozy Dutch establishment had, Howorth wrote on his blog, "the smallest elevator known to mankind, that is far from kind to men of ample girth!"

Now, Michael and Frances were back in England, airing out their suitcases and making plans for the remainder of the year. One of the biggest events in the yachting world, for instance, was coming up in mid-December. The Antigua Charter Yacht Show attracted brokers from around the globe, who gathered to view boats on display in multiple harbours all around the island; they also came to have a good time under the Caribbean sun. Howorth had spent enough time in the industry to know that these parties and liquid lunches were the perfect places to find a good story. But he also felt the quality of the Antigua show was on the decline, and the price to fly him and Frances across the Atlantic and back was not insignificant. Like any good freelancer, Howorth was weighing his upfront costs against the potential profits that would come with a well-placed article or two.

But that evening in front of his computer, Howorth's eye was immediately drawn to the subject line of his new email. He clicked on it and saw the message in full:

Dear Michael

An old sea chest was found in the bilge of King Bob the Bald's naval flagship, the *Great Peter*. Within this sea chest were some water damaged papers including one assigning the Kingship upon his demise. I attach a copy of the document. I have the original.

Regards

John Duffy

P.S. I am just helping to perpetuate the whole fraud.

Attached was a scanned copy of a smudged single-page royal proclamation. At the top of the page was a tricoloured flag with a crest containing a crown sitting atop a castle turret; instead of hand-written calligraphy, the main text appeared in a cursive typeface that came standard on Microsoft Word. At first glance, Howorth wasn't sure what to make of the document, but he did recognize a few key words and names — especially the one confidently signed in actual handwriting at the bottom of the page: his old friend Robert Williamson, who was also known in certain circles as King Bob the Bald.

All at once, the pieces clicked into place.

"Frances!" Howorth called to his wife in the next room.

"Yes? What is it?"

Howorth stared at his computer screen in disbelief. "I think I'm the new King of Redonda."

AN ENCOUNTER
on the PRAIRIES

1

THE FIRST TIME I heard about the Kingdom of Redonda was during a chance encounter in a used bookstore in Edmonton, Alberta. It was the summer of 2013, during a period of professional restlessness. For the past five years I'd been trying to establish a career for myself as a writer, while also enduring eight-hour cubicle stints at a series of unfulfilling day jobs. Now I was approaching a delicate yet critical point in the process. While trying to generate enough freelance journalism work to justify quitting my current cubicle, I'd ended up doing the equivalent of two full-time jobs at once. My writing assignments were interesting enough, but the ones that paid on time didn't pay well, so I needed to do a lot of them. I also had a partner and two young kids at home, and my first book, a gleefully foul-mouthed novel about a university student newspaper, was about to be published that fall. I could tell my life was about to change; I just couldn't predict exactly how.

While in many ways a fine place to live, Edmonton is not known as a book mecca. There are reasons for that: the city is fairly young, mid-sized (though growing), and located not just in the sparsely populated prairies but also hundreds of kilometres farther north than every other major centre in the country. Edmonton has had its share of stalwart indie bookstores over the decades, but its supply of used books just can't compete with that of larger, more established cities. As a result, readers here develop leonine instincts. When something interesting or unusual catches our eye, we grab it right away. Because we don't know when we might see it again.

That's what happened when I was browsing Alhambra Books one afternoon and came across a copy of Javier Marías's novel *All Souls*. Marías is a Spanish novelist who had recently been added to my mental list of writers to look out for, even though at that point I knew him mostly by reputation. His work was discussed, both in print and on social media, in awed, almost-reverential terms; plus, his North American publisher was New Directions, a press whose taste in translated fiction I had quickly come to trust. A few months earlier, I'd bought a copy of the ND edition of a stand-alone story by Marías called *Bad Nature, or With Elvis in Mexico*, and had been charmed by the author's plummy style, as well as the way he populated his story with real-world figures and events. So when I saw that used copy of *All Souls* on the shelf, I pounced.

The copy itself was nothing special: a well-thumbed paperback with flecks of sticker grease on the back cover and a remainder line drawn in permanent marker across the bottom of the text block. On the cover was a black-and-white photograph of a silhouetted couple, and the typefaces were pure '90s, in that they were abrasive and there were too many of them. Still, I knew a lucky find when I saw one. I shelled out $10.50 and brought the book back home, where I placed it next to *Bad Nature* in my library.

I buy books in mad flashes of optimism, but they rarely end up getting read in the same calendar year they're acquired. This is partly because I don't keep a formal TBR pile and so never have to face up to my neglected purchases every time I walk past my desk or bedside table. And partly it's because the thrill of acquisition is so potent that actually reading the book becomes a secondary task that can wait for later. I tend to work through my library from the opposite direction: when looking for a new book to read, the question I ask myself is not, "What do I feel like reading?" but "What's something I've owned forever but haven't gotten to yet?" In reading, as in life, guilt is a powerful motivator. But Marías's novel proved so intriguing that I snuck it to the front of the line anyway.

I picked up *All Souls* in late July. In addition to being conducive to quiet freelancing off the side of my desk, my day job also allowed for reading time that was reliable, if piecemeal. I got fifteen minutes on my morning commute, riding the train downtown; fifteen minutes during my morning coffee break; thirty minutes during lunch; another fifteen minutes during the afternoon coffee break; and a final fifteen minutes on the train back home. More than an hour in total, and I used it all on reading. Anything that might get between me and my book had to be kept ruthlessly to the perimeter. Unnecessary socializing with co-workers was out, save the occasional hockey venting; lunch I could eat at my desk, or balanced on my lap at a park bench, my hands occupied by a fork and a paperback.

The day I squished my way into a train car and opened *All Souls*, however, I realized that Marías's novel was going to pose a problem. For one thing, there were few obvious places to stop and bookmark. Marías's paragraphs casually looped and spiralled for entire pages at a time. It was easy to get lost in the narrator's languid, almost conversational inner monologue and surprisingly difficult to pull myself back out again, even when the train pulled up to my station and the doors slid open: I needed to see the thought resolved before I could stop. Yet no sooner would I reach the end of a paragraph than I would greedily glance at the beginning of the next, and the entire process would repeat itself. Despite having three different freelance deadlines that week, in addition to my actual cubicle work, I ended up reading the book straight through over forty-eight hours.

Though *All Souls* was Marías's sixth novel, it was his first to be translated into English. (The translation was done by Margaret Jull Costa, who would go on to translate many of his subsequent works.) First published in Spanish as *Todas las almas* in 1989, the book is narrated by an unnamed Spanish man, reflecting on his time as a visiting professor at the University of Oxford. The narrator is a bemused figure in an unfamiliar land, observing the school's rigid traditions while trying to ingratiate himself with the gossip-hungry faculty. Early on, he attends a comically ritualistic high-table dinner and begins an affair with the wife of one of his colleagues, both signs that he is a quick study in how to fit in.

If the plot of the novel sounds simple, its execution is anything but. *All Souls* confounds expectations by floating along on the narrator's train of thought as he reflects—in long, winding, luxurious sentences—on pretty much anything that comes to mind: the elderly porter who can't remember what decade it is, the symbolic power of the garbage bag, and the recurring rumour around campus that Oxford and Cambridge are recruiting grounds for spies. ("Oxonians have sharper ears," he notes, "Cantabrigians fewer scruples.") For readers used to straightforward A-to-B narrative engines, it is an unusual reading experience, but also an addictive one, in large part because of the narrator's idiosyncratic style of storytelling. For instance, despite the fact that the affair is one of the novel's driving forces, the attraction between the narrator and his colleague's wife is never fully explained or even dwelled upon. Instead, he finds himself happily distracted by the various exotic minutiae that stand out to a foreigner in a city as storied as Oxford — including his discovery, in one of the city's many rare bookshops, of a forgotten English poet named John Gawsworth.

As a young man, Marías's narrator tells us, Gawsworth was energetic and ambitious, and widely regarded as a rising star in the English poetry world. He edited anthologies, advocated for his fellow authors, and went on to serve in the Royal Air Force in World War II. Yet he died, homeless and neglected, at the age of fifty-eight. In *All Souls*, the narrator finds a signed copy of one of Gawsworth's first books, and finds himself wondering

what had happened in between, betwixt his
precocious, frenetic literary and social beginnings
and that anachronistic, tattered end; what could have
happened during (perhaps) those visits and journeys
of his to half the world, always publishing, always
writing, wherever he was? Why Tunis, Cairo, Algeria,
Calcutta, Italy? Just because of the war? Just because
of some obscure and never recorded diplomatic
activity? And why did he publish nothing after 1954 —
sixteen years before his pathetic end — a man who
had done so in places and at times when finding
a publisher must have verged on the heroic or the
suicidal?

Gawsworth's death mask.

To emphasize this transformation, Marías includes two photographs on successive pages of the novel. The first shows Gawsworth as a wily young man in his RAF uniform. The second is the poet's bloated and sombre death mask.

Swaying inside the train car, and later hunched over at my fluorescent-lit desk, I was transfixed. The writing was impressive, but so, too, was the author's audacity. Marías was so confident in his talents that he was willing—even eager—to abandon his storyline whenever a suitably intriguing detour presented itself. He simply had faith his readers would stay with him. And his style was so elegant and sprawling that at times it actually made me woozy, like the feeling I got halfway into a third beer. Yet the most interesting thing about *All Souls* was Gawsworth, and in particular one detail that Marías mentions with a difficult-to-decipher mixture of jocularity and seriousness: this ailing, alcoholic poet was also a king.

The way Marías's narrator tells it, in 1947, with his career still on the ascent, Gawsworth was named heir to something called the Kingdom of Redonda, which had previously been ruled over by a science-fiction writer named M.P. Shiel. Redonda is described as "a tiny island in the Antilles," and officially the property of the British government. But that doesn't stop Gawsworth from spending the ensuing years theatrically walking the streets of London as King Juan I and naming other writers, including Dylan Thomas and Lawrence Durrell, to his royal court as Redondan admirals and dukes.

What? I looked up from the book and frowned at the flickering daylight as my train barrelled into a tunnel headed downtown. I was barely a hundred pages into the novel, and my grasp on the reality of its premise was slipping. Throughout, Marías seemed to be daring readers to conflate truth and fiction, to have us conclude that *he* was the book's narrator and that its events actually happened to him — for instance, the real-life Marías taught at Oxford at roughly the same time his narrator claimed to — while also maintaining plausible deniability by publishing the book as fiction. But a secret island kingdom with a court full of writers? That was too outlandish to take seriously. In fact, it was such a cartoony claim that it made me rethink a bunch of other assumptions I'd made up to that point. If Marías invented Redonda, then what else did he make up? Was Gawsworth a fictional creation, too? What about the rest of the story of the narrator/Marías? And to what end? Doubt began to creep in everywhere.

When I arrived at my cubicle, I threw my bag down, booted up my desktop computer, and took to the internet in search of answers. The initial results didn't seem very official or reliable, and the following ones even less so. I went through page after page anyway, clicking on link after link, to make sure. Eventually, the outlines of a story came into focus. Redonda, it seemed, was a real island. Gawsworth was a real person, and a real poet. And the kingdom itself was apparently real, too — so real that, following the publication of *All Souls* in English, *Marías himself* had been named the latest king and was currently ruling over the realm as King Xavier I.

That morning, I got even less real work done than usual. And so began my trip down a rabbit hole that I still haven't emerged from, nearly a decade later.

GUANO *and* GUNPOWDER 2

WHEN MARÍAS referred to Redonda as "a tiny island in the Antilles," he wasn't exaggerating. Not only will you not find it labelled on your typical globe—odds are the island won't be represented at all, unworthy of even the most minuscule dot of pastel pink or yellow. Online tools like Google Maps aren't much more helpful. Even once you've zoomed in far enough to spot Montserrat, Redonda's closest neighbour, you have to click that same button another *five* times before Redonda reluctantly appears. ("No wifi," notes one cheeky Google reviewer.)

Redonda is located in a part of the Antilles called the Leeward Islands, midway between the nearby islands of Nevis and Montserrat; politically, it belongs to the slightly more-distant two-island nation of Antigua and Barbuda.↓ Redonda is a mile long and about a third of a mile wide, with a ring of sheer cliff that makes it difficult for humans to access, then and now. The island is the product of ancient volcanic activity in the area, and to all appearances is pretty well

> Technically, it's a three-island state: Antigua, Barbuda, and Redonda. But nobody refers to it that way, and even the official government website makes no mention of its littlest sibling.

empty. In all, it's the kind of place you'd half-notice on your way somewhere more interesting—which is exactly what Christopher Columbus did during his second voyage in 1493, dubbing it Santa María de la Redonda, or Saint Mary of the Round, after a church in Logroño, and then sailing on. Had Columbus taken the time to look more carefully, he would have realized that the island isn't round at all, but rather pill-shaped, with a steep summit in the centre that rises to nearly one thousand feet above sea level. Redonda's inhospitable cliffs, at least, were spotted easily and accurately enough from afar, prompting one of Columbus's sailors to record that the whole island "appears to be inaccessible without ladders or ropes let down from above." For centuries, Indigenous Caribs in the area knew the island as Ocanamunru and are thought to have used its shores as a resting stop between larger islands; sailors in the 1700s would later refer to it as Rock Donder. But when maps of the area began to circulate among Europeans, Columbus's name was the one that stuck.

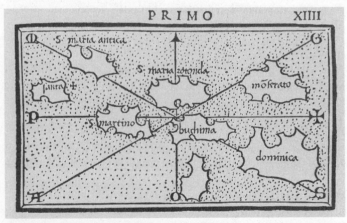

Detail of Benedetto Bordone's "Isole del Mondo" (Venice, 1529), possibly the first map of Redonda, shown here as "S. Maria Rotonda."

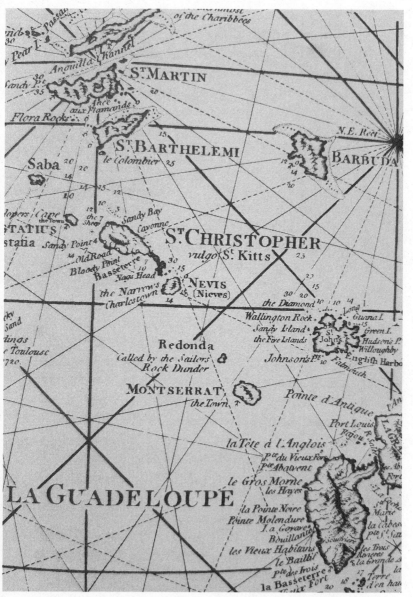

Detail of L.S. De la Rochette's "A Chart of the Antilles" (1784), showing Redonda, "Called by the Sailors Rock Dunder."

Owing to the difficulty of scaling its cliffs, Redonda has been almost entirely untouched by humans. Instead, the island's terrain of coarse grasses and prickly cacti were home to an abundance of wildlife, including lizards, hermit crabs, pelicans, moths, and burrowing owls. It wasn't until the nineteenth century that some enterprising locals realized that large sections of the island's difficult-to-access plateau were covered in thick layers of guano, deposited by untold generations of seabirds. This guano could be harvested and sold at a profit, its high-quality calcium phosphates used as a crucial ingredient in fertilizer. Later, it was discovered that underneath the calcium-rich guano lay aluminium phosphate, which was equally in demand for its role in making gunpowder. It lacked the glitz of a gold rush, but the discovery of phosphates on Redonda brought mass human activity to the island for the first time in its history.

This whiff of profit quickly made its way to the nostrils of the British, who already controlled the nearby island of Antigua. Worried that rival imperial nations might smell it, too, the British government sailed over to Redonda in 1869, planted a flag on the neglected island, and then went about the familiar business of making money off of it. They leased the mining rights to a newly formed American outfit called the Redonda Phosphate Company, which employed groups of locals brought over from Montserrat. To service these workers, the company built several permanent stone structures on the island, including barracks-like worker residences, a separate manager's building, water cisterns, and even a post office. The key to the entire operation was a large pulley system that allowed workers to easily transport guano from the plateau to the shoreline, hundreds of feet below. Workers would break off chunks of guano-spattered rock from the shafts and caves on the northern half of the island, then carry them, balanced on their heads, back to the plateau, where they were then placed inside metal buckets attached to a cable and slowly lowered down to the shore. From there, the rocks were loaded onto barges and carried out to larger cargo ships anchored farther offshore. At the island's commercial peak, around the turn of the twentieth century, a permanent population of more than a hundred men was mining and exporting more than seven thousand tons of phosphates per year.

For workers on Redonda, there was little to distract them from their labour. Accommodations were minimal, and most of their food arrived, in bulk, from nearby islands. If supplies ran low between shipments, the cook would take a group of workers out to tackle one of the sheep or goats that could also be found around the island, usually in areas inaccessible by humans. Native fresh water, meanwhile, came exclusively from rainfall—a scant nineteen inches' worth per year. As Dorothy Harding cheerfully wrote in the *Wide World Magazine* in 1901, "In seasons of drought, we take instead a dry rub with sand." Harding may hold the distinction of being the only person who actually grew up on Redonda, as she spent eleven years there with her mother and father, the latter of whom managed the mine. Her status also gave her the luxury of recreation. Harding passed the time surveying the sky for potential hurricanes and studying the local wildlife, including cockroaches, which, she wrote, "attain a very high state of physical development, destroy the bindings of our favourite books, eat the black off our boots in patches, till they look as if they were afflicted with leprosy, and consider the piano the most suitable place in which to rear their young families." (Harding may hold a second distinction, then, as one of the only people to have ever played a *piano* on Redonda.) She admitted that her particular kind of island life was not for everyone. "But," she added, "given a contemplative disposition and a fondness for one's own society, one might be very happy, even at Redonda."

Despite its isolation and natural inaccessibility, Redonda held a fascination for visitors passing through the area. In 1885, a journalist named William Drysdale spied the island from the deck of a passing steamship and was so struck by the sight that he grabbed the captain's telescope and charged up to the bridge to get a better view. "It is not hard to imagine what a dreary, desolate place Redonda must be for anyone to live on," he wrote in the *New York Times*. "It is enough to give one the blues to look at it. I think I should rather take up quarters and build a house and garden in the main crosstrees of some ship." Despite this assessment, Redonda left an impression on Drysdale, if only as a place so remote that the details of its reality could be safely altered. A few years later, Drysdale published what was likely the first piece of fiction ever set on the island. His romance novel *The Princess of Montserrat* reimagines Redonda as an oasis of forests and fresh water. It was a fantastical counterbalance to the stark rock Drysdale had spied from the deck of the steamship, but it would not be the last time the island was commandeered to suit the whims of its passing observers.

Mining on Redonda continued until 1914, when the outbreak of World War I rendered Germany, the Redonda Phosphate Company's largest and best customer, no longer suitable to do business with. Technological advances in gunpowder production, meanwhile, meant that labour-

intensive practices like mining had become too expensive, and shortly thereafter the mine was wound down. The Redonda Phosphate Company continued to retain a small staff to look after the existing machinery, but in the late 1920s a hurricane blew through the area and destroyed most of what was still in operation. The following year the site was abandoned for good.

IN 1929, the same year that the Redonda mine was left to crumble, a pamphlet began to circulate thousands of miles away, on the streets of London, containing a curious story about the island, written by a man who had grown up in its shadow.

M.P. Shiel was an imaginative and prolific author who had managed over the course of his thirty-year career to make a name for himself in two different genres: first as a member of the infamous English Decadence movement at the turn of the century, and then as a pen for hire in the less prestigious (but more profitable) world of commercial serial adventure novels. No matter the genre, the Caribbean-born writer was relentless, averaging better than a book per year for most of his working life. And even if he hadn't been able to achieve the wider recognition of which he'd always dreamed, he was confident that he had nonetheless produced works of wild imagination that were as likely to be read by future generations as anything produced by his peers. One of them, H.P. Lovecraft, wrote: "Shiel has done so much better than my best that I am left breathless and inarticulate."

But the path to canonization isn't so simple. Even within his own lifetime, Shiel had watched his reputation wax and wane. By the 1910s he'd fallen out of favour with serial audiences, who were fed up with the way he kept stuffing highfalutin digressions about math, science, and philosophy into the fluffy adventure stories they wanted to read. A mysterious jail sentence hadn't helped. As World War I sent shockwaves through Europe, and a new artistic movement called modernism rewired poetry and fiction alike, Shiel published nothing at all for nearly a decade.

There were signs, however, that Shiel's literary reputation was beginning to improve. It began an ocean away, when readers in the United States became interested once more in the works of other Decadents, including his friend Arthur Machen. The American writer Carl Van Vechten then talked Shiel up to publisher Alfred Knopf, describing him as "an important artist" whose work was "much more than a commercial proposition," capable of charming not just critics, but mainstream audiences, too. A few years later, Shiel's tentative return to the page became his bestselling American novel to date with 1928's *How the Old Woman Got Home;* at the same time, Paramount Pictures purchased the film rights to *The Purple Cloud*, his last-man-on-Earth novel published more than twenty years earlier.↓

The best sign of all was when Victor Gollancz proposed reissuing a series of Shiel's older novels, including *The Purple Cloud*, through his recently formed press in London. Both parties recognized the opportunity. For Gollancz, a marketing whiz who would soon become the first British publisher of writers like George Orwell and Daphne du Maurier, Shiel was a useful addition to what was then still a fledgling publishing list. For Shiel, the arrangement was another chance to showcase his strengths as a novelist, which he felt had not always been apparent in the stretched-out versions of his stories that ran in serial form. It also provided the opportunity to introduce himself to a new generation of the British reading public. To that end, Gollancz asked Shiel to write something that could be used to drum up interest in the reissues.

As it happened, Shiel had just such a document already prepared: a short autobiographical essay that he'd first published years earlier. But as he looked it over, the aging writer realized the essay was missing something about his childhood in the Caribbean. Something important. He decided the time was right, at last, to tell the world the truth.

It was time to admit that he was royalty.

> It would, however, take another three decades to make it to the screen, eventually being used as one of the sources for 1959's *The World, the Flesh and the Devil,* starring Harry Belafonte.

TRY NOT *to* BE STRANGE 3

UNLIKE the daughter of the mine manager, Matthew Phipps Shiell (he dropped the second "L" when he started writing) did not grow up on Redonda. He was born on July 21, 1865, and we don't know exactly how many siblings he had because the number fluctuated over time — sometimes he claimed to be the youngest of eight, and others the youngest of nine. But he was, indisputably, the first son born to Matthew Dowdy Shiell and Priscilla Ann Blake, and that Y chromosome automatically gave him exalted status in the eyes of Matthew Sr. The family grew up together on Montserrat, another piece of volcanic rock in the West Indies with a tempestuous climate.

Like Antigua, Montserrat had long been conquered by the British, but the makeup of Shiel's family reflected its actual on-the-ground demographics. His mother was part of a family of freed African slaves (slavery not being fully abolished on the island until Priscilla was six years old), and his father was descended from the initial group of Irish servants exiled to the island in the seventeenth century by Oliver Cromwell. Like many Montserratians, Matthew Sr. was likely of mixed heritage himself, though he was light-skinned enough to pass as white. Matthew Jr., on the other hand, was noticeably darker, a fact that would become more significant when he attempted to navigate the overwhelmingly white publishing world in England.

When it came to lineage, however, no detail was more important in Matthew Sr.'s mind than his belief that his family was also descended from a line of ancient Irish kings. He carried this royal conviction—deeply felt, if not genealogically sound—everywhere, through his life as a husband and father as well as in his various shifting careers as a tailor, merchant, ship owner, and Methodist lay-preacher. It wasn't until young Matthew Jr. was born that his father's royal aspirations finally found their outlet. The elder Shiel was so excited to have a male heir that he decided to claim the nearby island of Redonda, which was visible from Montserrat's shores, as a birthday present for his infant son. Matthew Sr.'s annexation predated the British claim to Redonda by several years and went unreported, and therefore unchallenged, for more than a decade. It wasn't until the summer of 1880, on the morning of Matthew Jr.'s fifteenth birthday, that the gift was finally revealed. That was the day that Matthew Sr. gathered up his son, the local bishop, and a group of well-wishers to set out by boat and finally crown Matthew Jr. as Felipe I, king of Redonda.

THIS WAS THE story that Shiel revealed in the new version of "About Myself," which was distributed as a promotional pamphlet in 1929, in advance of his reissued novels with Victor Gollancz. Here is the relevant section:

On my fifteenth birthday, July 21st, 1880, [my father] had me crowned King of Rodundo—a day of carousal, of a meeting of ships (he was a ship-owner), and of people, to see the palm of the Rev. Dr. Semper, of Antigua, daub me with the balm of anointment; and this notion that I am somehow the King, King of Kings, and the Kaiser of imperial Caesar, was so inveterately suggested to me, that I became incapable of expelling it. But to believe fantasies is what causes half our sorrows, as not believing realities causes half, and it would have been better for me if my people had been more reasonable here; nor can I forgive myself now for the solemnity and dignity with which I figured in that show. For what is a king without subjects? Certainly if I am a king, my kingdom is "not of this World": Rodundo is a rock-island of scarcely nine square miles, and my subjects were troops innumerable of boobies deciding to swoop with sudden steepness into the sea like streams of meteors streaming, together with eleven poor men who gathered the boobies' excrement to make "guano" (manure). And these were *American* people! Moreover, not long after my coronation the British Government, apprehensive that America might "annex" the rock, "annexed" it itself, i.e., stuck a little flagstaff on it; and though my parent irked heaven and earth with his claim of "priority," there the flagstaff remains, if it has not now gone to heaven on some gale's gallop; there it may ever remain.

Secure in the knowledge that even the most thorough fact-checker in London would not have access to his little corner of the Caribbean, Shiel casually stretched a few facts: overestimating Redonda's area by a factor of twenty, while also diminishing the size and robustness of the guano mine at the time. His date of the British annexation is also off by more than a decade. But what's really noteworthy about this anecdote, given all that would follow, is that Shiel's account of his coronation isn't exactly celebratory. The spirit of playfulness that would come to define the kingdom for the next century was, here, nowhere to be found. On the contrary, Shiel, who at this point was in his sixties, presents himself as an unwilling accomplice, forced to go along with his father's joke even though he didn't find it very funny. But — how much of it was a joke, really? Redonda was truly unclaimed territory at the time of Shiel's birth, and stories have circulated for decades that Matthew Sr. petitioned Queen Victoria herself to have his claim to the island formally recognized. From the beginning, it seems that the Kingdom of Redonda was a concept that floated somewhere in between fantasy and reality. Whatever his father's intentions, Shiel found himself in an impossible position: stuck with a title he didn't want but was "incapable of expelling," and finding the prospect of ruling over an empty kingdom ridiculous, yet also being unable to fully dismiss it, lest he spoil the fun of their afternoon excursion. Accordingly, his retelling of the story neither endorsed nor rejected the terms of Matthew Sr.'s birthday gift. In place of a definitive answer, Shiel left an ambiguous hole into which readers could project their own assumptions about the kingdom's existence.

Five years after his coronation atop Redonda, Shiel decamped for a new life in London, and in the subsequent half-century would barely mention his island home on the page. Before leaving, his father had given him some double-edged advice: "Try not to be strange." But now, with the publication of the Gollancz pamphlet, the kingdom of Shiel's childhood was released onto the English reading public, where it would enjoy a new life that was very strange indeed.

SHIEL FIRST LANDED in England in the spring of 1885. An intelligent and precocious child—he read voraciously in Greek and Hebrew, completed his first full-length novel at the age of twelve, and hand-wrote and -distributed a weekly newspaper to a few indulgent subscribers—he stepped off the boat and into the streets of London fuelled by teenaged bravado. The nineteen-year-old planned to complete his education while soaking in life in the big city, then begin a no-doubt-illustrious career as a doctor or academic. But there were complications from the start. Shortly after his arrival, Shiel's financial support from back home dried up alongside Matthew Sr.'s latest business venture, and finding steady income of his own proved challenging. Shiel's first job was at a grammar school in Devonshire, a county in South West England, but he contracted the measles and was immediately fired for fear that he might infect his students as well. Subsequent teaching jobs didn't last much longer. Sometimes this was due to more bad luck, and other times because of Shiel's growing appetites. He admitted in a letter that he had to discreetly leave one such job after impregnating a local girl named Mary—the first documented instance of what would become a troubling pattern. There followed a brief stint at King's College back in London, but Shiel found the literature classes boring while also discovering he was squeamish around blood: as he wrote later, his dreams of becoming a physician wilted the day he observed his first eye surgery.

Shiel grew frustrated with how quickly his plans had gone awry. Unemployed and broke, he was reduced to selling his personal library on the streets of London to earn some quick cash. Back on Montserrat, things were becoming worse. Shiel's beloved sister Ada died near the end of 1886, likely of cholera; his father, meanwhile, suffered two separate strokes, then bombarded Matthew Jr. with detailed letters describing his suffering. It all weighed heavily on young Shiel's mind. In the summer of 1887, he wrote to another of his favourite sisters to complain, and in response Augusta (whom he called "Gussie") suggested that perhaps the former child novelist should try writing prose again. Shiel was initially thrown by Gussie's suggestion, but not for long. "You have kindled a strange fire in me," he wrote to her. "I have begun writing, writing, writing. Most strange!"

Fuelled by his sister's encouragement, Shiel started composing short stories, which he submitted to a variety of magazines and periodicals around the city. His first published piece of fiction, "The Doctor's Bee," won a contest and appeared in the magazine *Rare Bits* in 1889, netting him a sorely needed twenty shillings in the process. During these years, Shiel is thought to have largely lived off of the financial kindness of Gussie and her husband, a wealthy Saint Kitts businessman. But he also made use of his linguistic skills, finding work as a translator and interpreter when an international conference of statisticians came through London in 1891. On the side, Shiel took on whatever he could to inch his way into the publishing industry: doing secretarial work for a weekly publication called *The Messenger*, translating short jokes and stories, and writing anonymous celebrity portraits for the recently launched *Strand Magazine*. More short stories appeared over the next few years. "Guy Harkaway's Substitute" is about a woman who disguises herself as a man in order to deliver a last-minute sermon in lieu of her absent preacher husband, while "The Eagle's Crag" is an adventure story set in the mountains of Italy. Given Shiel's financial situation, it may not have been a coincidence that both of these pieces feature characters who yearn for inheritances kept tantalizingly out of reach—nor, given his childhood encounter with Redonda, the fact that the titular crag is an intriguing, nearly impossible-to-access island located just offshore.

When it came time to assemble his first full-length book, Shiel turned to two of his biggest literary inspirations: Arthur Conan Doyle, whose popular Sherlock Holmes stories were running monthly in *The Strand*, and Edgar Allan Poe, who had set the template for the modern detective story a half-century earlier. The result was 1895's *Prince Zaleski*, a collection of three stories, each built around a case for Shiel's detective character to solve. Parallels between Zaleski and Holmes—who by that point Conan Doyle had killed off, creating a clear market opportunity—were particularly hard to miss. Both detectives had superior minds, unorthodox and opaque methods of detection, a wealth of arcane knowledge, and a taste for recreational drugs. Yet when it came to excess, Shiel's hero surpassed even Conan Doyle's. Zaleski draped himself in flamboyant Asian clothing and surrounded himself with opulent tapestries and artifacts from cultures around the world, including an open sarcophagus containing an actual mummified Egyptian. These flourishes were extreme compared to a typical Sherlock Holmes tale, but they fit right in with the Decadence movement, which was then on the rise in London. Decadent writers took pleasure in imbuing popular genres like the detective story with extravagant language and over-the-top phrasing; they also made a point of cocooning their heroes away from the natural world, instead letting them revel in emotional numbness and intentionally artificial surroundings. Shiel knew all about the Decadents and was eager to join their ranks.

Prince Zaleski was released by The Bodley Head as part of its Keynotes series, which, along with the *Yellow Book* magazine, was a central platform of Decadent publishing. Both were overseen by John Lane, who pushed for Bodley Head to become even more subversive — ironically, in part due to the conservative book market. Without the resources to lure away England's most well-known authors, Lane instead went hard the other way, publishing misfits, rebels, unknowns, and other writers who had been rejected by the mainstream but whose works nonetheless generated their own illicit mystique. By the time Shiel was shopping *Prince Zaleski*, The Bodley Head's credentials in this area were well established.

Even though he had already published stories in the more buttoned-down *Strand*, Shiel decided to align his first book with the Decadents in the hopes of giving it some added rebellious cachet. Presenting Zaleski as an edgier, more literary Holmes was a savvy business strategy, and it wasn't lost on reviewers, either: one wrote, helpfully, "As is the *Yellow Book* to the *Strand Magazine*, so is *Prince Zaleski* to Sherlock Holmes." Yet despite obvious similarities between their characters, Shiel privately bristled at any comparisons between the men who created them — not because the comparisons flattered him, but because Shiel believed they flattered *Conan Doyle*. In Shiel's mind, he was creating something new and exciting, infusing paint-by-numbers Holmes stories with baroque language, heady digressions, and dense poetic and philosophical underpinnings. Any comparisons between them were thus indications that he'd failed in his efforts. After she read *Zaleski*, Gussie made the mistake of mentioning her brother's competition by name. "But why do you insist on comparing me to Conan Doyle?" Shiel shot back. "Conan Doyle does not pretend to be a poet. I do."

Comparisons to Poe, on the other hand — a writer who *had* successfully reached both critical and commercial audiences — brought Shiel great joy. He once called Zaleski the "legitimate son" of Poe's Dupin, which made Sherlock Holmes, logically, the "bastard." Unfortunately, there weren't as many of these comparisons as he would have liked. Most reviewers admired *Prince Zaleski* but felt that it skewed too far to the high-art end of the spectrum, best suited, as one put it, for "the select few who can appreciate delicate work, and who are not bored by a touch

First edition of Prince Zaleski *(Bodley Head, 1895).*

of metaphysics." Others disapproved of Shiel's overly tangled plots and excess of detail. The most vicious review came from no less than H.G. Wells, who wrote: "This, we sincerely hope, is the low water-mark in 'Keynotes.' We doubt if Mr. John Lane in his short but brilliant career has ever published anything half so bad before." Still, the book was successful enough that Shiel was allowed to follow it up with *Shapes in the Fire*, a story collection that appeared under the same Keynotes aegis in 1896. The supernatural writer Arthur Machen especially admired the collection and wrote in his review that Shiel's stories "tell of a wilder wonderland than Poe dreamed of in his most fantastic moments." In a span of less than two years, Shiel had gone from a struggling unknown to a working Decadent, with multiple books under his belt and a career that held nothing but promise.

Then the Oscar Wilde trial came along and ruined everything.

ONE OF THE REASONS M.P. Shiel has been largely forgotten today is due to an error in taxonomy. By working across multiple genres, he was thereby excluded from the basic histories of each. With a vocabulary and aesthetic sense too lofty for the pulps, and plots too outrageous for the intelligentsia, Shiel seemed doomed to perennially split the difference.

Decadence as a literary movement originated in France and rejected all that was simple and practical. Writers like J.K. Huysmans embraced rococo language, morbid (even perverse) subject matter, and a vision of life as a constant battle against ennui, which pursued their characters at every turn. This was art for its own sake, not just freed from commercial expectations but also working in active defiance of the endless intellectual mush on offer to the public. The quintessential Decadent work was Huysmans's 1884 novel, *À rebours* (translated into English as *Against Nature* or *Against the Grain*), in which his hero rejects society in order to focus on artificial pleasures like sticking precious gems onto the shell of a live tortoise. Decadence proved popular enough that it was soon imported to England, first in poetry and then via fiction—where it reached its apex, in 1890, with the publication of *The Picture of Dorian Gray*.

Originally published in *Lippincott's* magazine, Oscar Wilde's novel-length story of a pleasure-loving dandy who makes a Faustian bargain to stay forever beautiful crystallized many of the movement's principles, while also introducing them to the English reading public for the first time. Wilde even subtly alluded to *À rebours*, one of his favourite books, by having Gray fall under the spell of an unnamed, "poisonous" French novel, which convinces him to try out a suite of new vices. The magazine's editor, J.M. Stoddart, did his best to tamp down what he found to be the text's most objectionable elements by censoring references to homosexuality, as well as the Huysmans-esque novel. But Stoddart's fears about impressionable women being exposed to Wilde's text came to pass regardless. *Dorian Gray* quickly became a hit, and just as quickly a topic of national debate. Journalists found the story immoral, not to mention a blatant advertisement for Wilde himself, who had been a national celebrity since his days as an undergraduate. When the book version was published the following year, the retail chain W.H. Smith declared the entire thing "filthy" and refused to carry it. "Whether the Treasury or the Vigilance Society will think it worth while to prosecute Mr. Oscar Wilde or [publisher] Messrs. Ward, Lock & Co.," wrote one anonymous reviewer, "we do not know."

Thanks to *Dorian Gray*, the entire Decadence movement briefly became a topic of grave national importance, flattened and caricatured in the press as pundits fretted over how its lurid subject matter would corrupt innocent minds. At the same time, several Decadent writers saw their personal reputations smeared, as they were often equated with the very worst of their fictional creations. Luckily, presses like The Bodley Head knew how to take advantage of the charges being made against them, and before long Decadence's dangerous reputation became the new banner under which the movement rallied. The media's accusations of moral degeneracy turned out to be the best free publicity the Decadents could have asked for — and at the front of the procession was Wilde himself, defending *Dorian Gray* in typically dazzling style. "[The book] is poisonous if you like," he wrote in a letter to one editor, "but you cannot deny that it is also perfect, and perfection is what we artists aim at."

On April 6, 1895, Wilde was arrested for "gross indecency" — more specifically, sodomy. The charge was a recent one, introduced just a decade earlier as part of sweeping changes to the English criminal code intended to protect young women and suppress brothels, but which also included a last-minute provision that outlawed homosexual acts of all kinds. Wilde pled not guilty to the new charges and defended himself eloquently in court, but to no avail. The trials were a national sensation, and the media all but unanimous in condemning the man one paper had nicknamed "the High Priest of the Decadents." On May 25, Wilde was sentenced to imprisonment and two years' hard labour.

Shiel followed the Wilde trial with interest. For one thing, *Prince Zaleski* had been published that March, and as a newcomer to the world of Decadence Shiel would have been all too aware of the ripple effects the trial's verdict could have on their shared field. But he also had strong personal opinions about Wilde himself, which he shared in a letter to Gussie. "Poor chap!" Shiel wrote. "I am sorry for him. It is not his fault: he is not well made: he is a *moral idiot*: he was born so: his mother made him so. *God will straighten him out*" (emphasis in original).

As soon as Wilde was behind bars, the English Decadence movement dissolved. What had been, up to that point, a controversial but undeniably popular literary scene was now fatally tainted by its association to an actual criminal conviction. One of Decadence's central tenets was a belief in a fundamental gap between the brilliant artist and the public that can never truly understand them. To this end, the book version of *Dorian Gray* opened with a preface in which Wilde scorned small-minded readers who "find ugly meanings in beautiful things." This kind of sentiment irritated conservative pundits, who were sick of being lectured to by a small group of cultural provocateurs. They used Wilde's prison sentence as an excuse to argue that Decadence and movements like it had led society astray and that now was the time to clamp back down and establish stricter borders on taste and decency. "The Wilde scandal," writes academic Kirsten MacLeod, "provided moralists with the opportunity to re-assert a bourgeois cultural hegemony and to take pride in rather than be ashamed of their philistinism."

Decadence had, of course, from the beginning built its reputation on a certain amount of public outrage. But with its high priest behind bars, other members of the movement now grew worried about being linked too closely to it. To save their careers, some switched genres. Others found new lines of work entirely. Publisher John Lane decided to wind down the *Yellow Book* in 1897 after just thirteen issues. The critic Arthur Symons, meanwhile, was already halfway through his book about Decadence when the Wilde verdict came down; he quietly changed the title from *The Decadent Movement in Literature* to *The Symbolist Movement in Literature* and hoped nobody would notice. Decadence was a sinking ship, and no one wanted to go down with it.

For Shiel, the decision to distance himself from Decadence was bittersweet. While his early books hadn't become the genre-transcending hits he'd hoped, they had nonetheless earned him the admiration of many writers in and around the movement. But in the end, he had no choice. The good news was that Shiel was still early enough in his career to be able to change tack without too many readers noticing. Following the tepid response to *Shapes in the Fire*—one of the final entries in the Keynotes series—Shiel would abandon his highbrow aspirations and instead learn to embrace a new life as an unlikely, full-time scribbler of adventure serials for the masses.

CITATION NEEDED 4

BACK AT MY DESK in Edmonton, I leaned back from my computer screen, blinking, and tried to make sense of what I'd been able to figure out so far.

The kingdom was real. Or at least real enough to merit a lengthy Wikipedia entry. But what did that really mean? In the early 2010s, online research had an even greater air of unreliability around it. Wikipedia's open, anonymous editing process in particular raised fears ranging from subtle pranks to outright malfeasance, and out-of-the-way entries like this one seemed to be especially ripe for misinformation, where readers were as rare as actual experts, and oftentimes the same people.

In my head, I went through every contact I had in the publishing world, trying to think of anyone who might be able to offer me a way into the story. The best I could come up with was an online acquaintance I knew through the blogging platform Tumblr, and who briefly went on to work for New Directions. I dashed off an email: "What do you know about Javier Marías and the Kingdom of Redonda?" (She did not respond.)

Javier Marías © Roger Parkes / Alamy Stock Photo.

With no better options available, I went back through the Wikipedia entry one line at a time. There was no shortage of information. But every section left me with more questions than answers. After a brief overview of the island's size and location, for instance, there was this:

Redonda also is a micronation which may, arguably and briefly, genuinely have existed as an independent kingdom during the 19th century. The title to this supposed kingdom is still contested to this day in a half-serious fashion. The "Kingdom" is also often associated with a number of supposed aristocratic members, whose titles are presented by whomever is currently the "King". Currently there are a number of different individuals in several different countries who claim to be the sole legitimate "King" of Redonda.

Multiple claimants to the throne? That was worth looking into. So was the suggestion that Redonda was once its own country, though the phrase "arguably and briefly" didn't exactly fill me with confidence.

I did, at least, know a little about micronations. The term referred to a lighthearted political entity (typically a single person) that claims jurisdiction over a piece of land so small that it would be silly for the nation that actually owns it to even respond. Micronations were a harmless bit of fun that stayed jokey enough to avoid having the military called in. A few months earlier, I'd happened to look up a map of Canadian micronations and found one just a few minutes from my office: a tiny, half-submerged island in the North Saskatchewan River that I saw through the train window each morning. On my lunch hour I'd even tried to get down to it, just to see whether there were any real-life signs of its status as a breakaway state. But the water level was too high, my coordination too low, and I ended up sitting through an afternoon's worth of meetings in mud-spattered dress pants.

Over the years, a few micronations have achieved mainstream notoriety. In 1966, a British pirate-radio operator named Paddy Roy Bates seized an abandoned naval platform off the coast of Essex and declared it an independent nation called the Principality of Sealand. Initially, the British government contested Bates's claim but has since moved to a position of bemused tolerance. A fourteen-year-old in Milwaukee founded the Kingdom of Talossa, whose borders happened to match the exact dimensions of his bedroom, drawing the attention of the *New York Times* and *Wired*. Other micronations have been conceived to make a specific political statement, such as the Glacier Republic, founded by Greenpeace activists in 2014 in an effort to protect Chile's glaciers from private mining interests. For a more literary example, consider the Welsh town of Hay-on-Wye, which became an international hub for readers when a man named Richard Booth starting buying up second-hand books by the thousands and used them to fill a half-dozen storefronts in the 1960s. His quixotic mission to shore up rural economies and preserve the identity of market towns attracted other like-minded people to the area, and at its peak the town was home to fewer than two thousand people but more than thirty bookshops. Hay-on-Wye's turn towards micronationality came on April Fool's Day in 1977, when Booth marched down the high street in a homemade crown and declared the town an independent kingdom, and he its new king. (His horse was named prime minister.)

If there is a golden age for micronations, then we are currently living in it. The internet has single-handedly made it possible for every uninhabited corner of the planet to become knowable, viewable, and conquerable, all without leaving the comfort of one's laptop. There are now thousands of documented micronations scattered all around the world. The vast majority, however, rise and fall along with their founder's level of interest. It's rare for a given micronation to survive more than a few years, which puts Redonda in rare company: with its intergenerational handoffs and continuous 150-year history, this kingdom appeared to leave all of its competition in the dust.

Further down the Wikipedia entry, another section seemed promising. "The history of the 'Kingdom' of Redonda," I re-read, "is shrouded in doubt and legend, and it is difficult to separate fact from fiction." At the end of this sentence was a footnote, which directed me to an essay called "Of Dreams and Shadows," written by one John D. Squires and published on a website that collected essays about the life and work of M.P. Shiel (who at that point I'd never heard of, save for a brief mention in *All Souls*). In the essay, Squires attempted to lay out the history of the Kingdom of Redonda, along with, as the subtitle put it, "Some Notes on Various Claimants to its Uncertain Throne."

Squires's piece was illuminating—the best lead I'd found so far. To hear him tell it, the Redondans were a loose assortment of merry men running around London in the 1940s and '50s, throwing spirited parties, knighting their friends, and tossing off royal proclamations to an alternately confused and delighted press corps. At times the piece had the feel of a sort of secret history, with cameos from better-known literary figures like Thomas and Durrell sprinkled into the story in one convoluted capacity or another. That theatricality became even more apparent when it came time for the kingdom to be passed down, Squires wrote. Redondan succession, it seemed, was a messy affair full of blood pacts, front-page newspaper ads, and signatures on beer-soaked napkins.

I wanted to believe it all, but something still seemed off. Squires's essay was careful and orderly, but it was hosted on a personal website—not even Squires's—with no external checks or balances in sight. Plus, all of the piece's sources were either out of print or held, supposedly, in special-collections libraries across North America and England. As with *All Souls*, I had no way of double-checking any of the claims. A note at the top of the essay made me even more skeptical. It said that in addition to being an amateur Shiel scholar, Squires also published books—and when I clicked over to a different webpage listing all of the titles, it was full of books *he'd* written or edited about Shiel, often in bizarrely short print runs:

M.P. Shiel and the Lovecraft Circle: A Collection of Primary Documents, Including Shiel's Letters to August Derleth, 1929–1946, Edited with Notes by John D. Squires, Kettering, Ohio: The Vainglory Press, December 2001, 35 copies.

Some Comments on Shiel, Gordon Holmes, and Louis Tracy Dustwrappers, Compiled with Notes by John D. Squires, Kettering, Ohio: The Vainglory Press, February 2004, 5 copies.

Shiel and His Collaborators: Three Essays on William Thomas Stead, Louis Tracy, and John Gawsworth, by John D. Squires and Steve Eng, Kettering, Ohio: The Vainglory Press, October 2004, 15 copies.

Thirty-five copies? Fifteen? *Five?* What was the point? The press being named after a synonym for excessive vanity also seemed a little too on the nose. Further down the page there was mention of a foundation that at one time published official-looking maps of Redonda, but had since renamed itself after the artist Salvador Dalí, for equally inscrutable reasons. As I continued clicking around the website, I kept seeing the same handful of names repeated. Or maybe I was just getting confused. There was so much information to digest, and almost none of it meant anything to me; without a reliable foundation, I wasn't building knowledge so much as gathering it into a formless pile. Eventually, after trying and failing one more time to cross-reference one of the outlandish facts of Redonda's history with the sources cited by

Squires and his colleagues, my thoughts turned conspiratorial. *What if these guys are all in on it?* I wondered. *What if they made the whole thing up? This could all be some big joke — a bunch of fake names and essay titles with nothing at the centre.* It would certainly fit the pattern that Wikipedia skeptics had been warning us about: make a fake claim, back it up with a fake secondary source that you also wrote, then sit back, hope nobody looks too closely (they won't), and watch the confusion spread.

Just then, there was a knock on my cubicle wall. It was one of my co-workers, holding out a manila envelope containing a birthday card for another woman on our floor. "Can you sign this and pass it on?" she said, discreetly eyeing my computer screen, which was now stuffed with so many open tabs and windows that the fan inside the desktop tower had turned on.

"Sure," I said. "No problem."

The trance had been broken. I looked around my surroundings, then took a breath and shut everything related to Redonda, Shiel, and his weird obsessive superfans. I was frustrated, and a little embarrassed, at having sunk so much time into a corner of the internet where the facts were being obscured by what seemed like an intentional fog of misinformation. If there really was truth to the Kingdom of Redonda, I wasn't going to be the one to muck around deep enough to find it. The next day, I finished reading *All Souls* on the train home and filed it away on my bookshelves, where it could safely be ignored.

The HUNGARIAN CURE 5

COULD IT BE? M.P. Shiel—*pulp novelist?* After making such a calculated attempt to break into the upper echelons of literary society, it's difficult to imagine Shiel having a positive reaction to his new reality. But he was willing to learn and recognized an opportunity when he saw one. That's what happened in the spring of 1897, when Shiel was asked by *Pearson's Weekly* to fill in for the prolific serial writer Louis Tracy, who had fallen ill with a fever midway through the publication of a story called *An American Emperor*. Shiel stepped up and, based on a provided outline, penned the next eleven chapters of the story while Tracy recuperated.

For the next two years, Shiel found a new gear in his work, relentlessly filling pages for what would become *eight* new novels. Despite how easily the words came, however, Shiel struggled to adjust to life in the world of commercial fiction. In what is no doubt a generous paraphrase, Shiel claimed that Tracy once told him, "[Y]ou could make as much money as Bernard Shaw and Edgar Wallace put together, but you persist in casting your pearls before swine-herds, who know not pearls." Shiel was determined to earn enough from his writing to live comfortably, but he found it difficult to commit fully to the chameleon act. Even when he was firing off tens of thousands of words about the court of Henry VIII (*Cold Steel*) or a kidnapping plot involving Napoleon and the Duke of Wellington (*The Man-Stealers*), Shiel couldn't resist adding lengthy digressions about topics he found personally stimulating, like land ownership, religion, or the English class system. Some of the novels produced in this period were able to strike a balance between their competing interests. Others began to test the patience of Shiel's burgeoning readership.

The most successful of these was a story that came directly from the headlines. Inspired by a surge of British interest in China during the "scramble for concessions" at the end of the Opium Wars, *The Empress of the Earth* was written in 1898 without the benefit of an outline of any kind, as Shiel filled each instalment with details pulled from news articles published just that morning. Readers were transfixed by the real-life story that threatened to send Europe into war and became equally absorbed in Shiel's fictionalized version. The story was stretched, at his editor's insistence, from its original length of 70,000 words to 150,000; it proved so successful that Shiel was hired to write another topical story, *Contraband of War*, instalments of which started running in a different magazine two months before the first story had concluded. An abridged version of *The Empress of the Earth* was published in book form that summer as *The Yellow Danger*, where it spent several weeks on England's bestseller lists.[↓]

> *The Yellow Danger* survives today, albeit indirectly, through its villainous Dr Yen How, who was one of the primary inspirations for Sax Rohmer's own supervillain character, Fu Manchu.

Shiel was opportunistic in his personal life as well. While on vacation in Paris one winter, he spotted a beautiful Spanish teenager at a skating rink and prayed to God that he might be able to woo her. Carolina Garcia Gomez (or Lina, as she called herself) was sixteen years old and likely still in convent school when she met Shiel, who was by then in his mid-thirties. Shiel's feelings for her were genuine, but not exclusive. At the same time that he travelled back and forth to Paris to seduce Lina, Shiel was also sleeping with an Englishwoman named Nellie Seward, who was the model for the female lead in *The Yellow Danger*. Shiel's biographer, Harold Billings, is confident there were other flings around this time as well.

Shiel and Lina's relationship progressed quickly, and the couple was married in an Italian church in Holborn on November 3, 1898. The wedding was joyful, with many of Shiel's peers from the writing world in attendance. But the cost was an added burden onto what, for the groom, was an already-precarious financial situation. In the hours before the ceremony, Shiel wrote to Grant Richards, his publisher for *The Yellow Danger*, asking for an advance on the forthcoming paperback edition. These fears were shared by his new extended family. Lina's mother was so worried about her son-in-law's ability to provide for her daughter that she began lobbying for Lina to leave London — where she couldn't speak the language — and return home to the comforts of France.

Shiel's problems were compounding, and they were about to get even more complicated. In the same month he got married, Shiel's mistress Nellie Seward gave birth to a daughter she named Ada.

SOME OF THE BOOKS Shiel wrote during this burst of creativity were forgettable. But it was during this time that he also produced the trio of novels that would become the high-water mark of his career, including the one title of his that has survived into the twenty-first century.

The Purple Cloud was Shiel's energetic take on the last-man-on-Earth genre. In his story, a massive cloud appears out of nowhere, poisoning and killing the entire human population—with the exception of a man named Adam Jeffson, who at the time was sailing to the North Pole, and who survived by fluke as the frigid Arctic air converted the gas into millions of crystals that fell harmlessly to the ice. The truth of the situation only dawns on Jeffson when he returns to a port in Norway and discovers scores of people, of various nationalities and cultures, all dead in a heap, awaiting a rescue boat that never arrived. "If now a wave from the Deep has washed over this planetary ship of earth," Jeffson thinks, "and I, who alone happened to be in the extreme bows, am the sole survivor of that crew? ... What then, my God, shall I do?"

In addition to its inventive language and frenetic pace, *The Purple Cloud* includes a framing device that features the real-life author as a character.[*] In the book's foreword, Shiel claims to have received a series of four notebooks in the mail, each crammed to the margins with an inscrutable shorthand. Accompanying the notebooks was a letter from a hypnotist friend, who claimed they were transcriptions of

This was actually the second time Shiel had used such a meta-fictional tactic: each of the cases in *Prince Zaleski* is brought to the fictional detective not by a member of the public, but by Shiel himself, who as narrator then sits around the apartment listening to Zaleski solve them, one by one.

hallucinations experienced by one of his patients while under his trance. The text of *The Purple Cloud*, readers are told, is nothing more than the cleaned-up contents of "Notebook III."

First edition of The Purple Cloud *(Chatto & Windus, 1901).*

This was all part of a larger plan on Shiel's part. The material from "Notebook II" had appeared in book form a few months earlier as *The Lord of the Sea*, and "Notebook I" would become the religious novel *The Last Miracle* a few years later. As for the fourth notebook? The Shiel character in *The Purple Cloud* says that he hasn't quite finished going through it yet, but "so far [does] not consider it suitable for publication." (It isn't clear whether a real manuscript was ever attached to this fourth notebook, but if so, it has never seen its way to print.) Numbering the notebooks this way suggested a preferred reading order as well as a timeline, with each subsequent novel-notebook taking place further into the future than the last, leading some critics to argue that this makes Shiel's trilogy the first recorded instance of a literary "future history."

Like many of his books, *The Purple Cloud* first appeared in serial form — in this case, over six issues of the *Royal Magazine* from January to June 1901. But where Shiel's editor for *Empress of the Earth* had encouraged him to add more and more material, this time his story drew the opposite response. At times, Shiel submitted more than a hundred pages of prose only to have fewer than a dozen make it to print. This chopping was likely done on the fly, after a lukewarm response from the magazine's readers, and even the publication of the full-length book several months later did little to improve Shiel's mood towards it. The first edition of *The Purple Cloud* was full of typos and other printing errors, and received minimal promotion from its publisher, Chatto & Windus. Reviewers, at least, tended to be positive, if overwhelmed by the book's maximalism: the *Sunday Times* declared it "an unconventional and horribly fascinating romance—one which I would not recommend for perusal just before going to bed."

If he was frustrated at how this particular story was received, Shiel was at least too busy with other work to stay that way for long. Over the next decade he would publish an average of one new novel every year, so even he may not have even noticed when *The Purple Cloud* soon went out of print.

THE FIRST DECADE of Shiel's career was defined by the breakneck pace he maintained, churning out weekly serials for the public, revising previously serialized work for expanded book versions, and negotiating (and renegotiating) financial terms with his publishers. But this pace had its risks, too. Chief among them was Shiel's constant need for material, which led him to scour his real life for anything that could be repurposed for the page. He had a habit, for instance, of taking lines from letters written to family members and dropping them, word for word, into his latest manuscript. Parts of *The Yellow Danger* went a step further, heavily borrowing from Villiers de l'Isle-Adam's story "A Torture by Hope," which Shiel had translated for the *Strand* several years earlier. Other times Shiel's transgressions on the page were simply a matter of poor taste, as when he wrote Arthur Machen into *The Purple Cloud* just a few years after his wife Amy's death from breast cancer. In Shiel's novel, Jeffson visits the author's bungalow by the sea, and inside comes across not just Machen's dead body, but also that of a fictional second wife — a "very beautiful" eighteen-year-old Spanish girl — and their infant child. It's not known how Machen reacted to Shiel fictionally gifting him a double of his own new bride, but not long afterwards the two writers had a falling out that would last the rest of their lives. Machen later described Shiel as "an inveterate liar" and a man to whom "'right' and 'wrong' were words entirely without meaning."

Shiel's tactic of seeing how far he could stretch himself without snapping extended, again, into his personal life. Having a child out of wedlock with Nellie Seward created havoc in his marriage to Lina, made worse still when Shiel insisted on making regular trips to Gloucester to visit Nellie and baby Ada. In response, Lina made semi-regular trips of her own back to France to be with her mother and sisters.

Soon afterwards, Lina, too, became pregnant with Shiel's child, and Dolores Katherine Shiel (nicknamed "Lola") was born on July 21, 1900. Even though Shiel later estimated he earned £2,000 per year during this period, a lucrative income for a writer, his mounting expenses kept him desperate for money wherever he could find it. In that same month, Shiel had one novel (*The Man-Stealers*) published, another (*Cold Steel*) reprinted, and a third (*The Yellow Danger*) serialized for a second time — but it wasn't enough, in part because of how much of his free time and funds were dedicated to pursuing other women. To save money, Shiel repeatedly downsized his family's accommodations, eventually moving them out of the city entirely. He tried pawning individual pieces of furniture, and even, at one point, his wife's umbrella.

It was around this time that the first version of "About Myself" was published, in response to an anonymous

Woodcut of Shiel by Henry Glintenkamp.

newspaper article that speculated at length on Shiel's ethnicity. The article praised Shiel's talents as a novelist but noted "his race is as great a mystery as his birthplace," adding that while those who knew him agreed that Shiel was of mixed heritage, "they differ utterly as to which two or three of the great races culminate in him." Shiel's defiant response appeared in the same newspaper that August. For the first time in print, he clarified that he was born in Montserrat, "a very great and holy place, full of passionate woes, the very apex and hub, it seems to me, of the world." But there was no mention of Redonda. Not yet.

IN THE SPRING of 1902, one of Grant Richards's office boys arrived at Shiel's apartment in Bloomsbury to retrieve a manuscript. His name was Arthur Ransome, and he would go on to achieve his own distinction as author of the Swallows and Amazons series of children's books. At the time, however, Ransome was still a teenager finding his footing in the literary world, and he was excited to meet an author as experienced as the man behind *Prince Zaleski*. But the circumstances of their meeting made him uneasy. As Ransome later wrote in his book *Bohemia in London*, Shiel "was so well known that it was a little surprising to find him in Bloomsbury at all." Ransome had assumed that a writer of Shiel's stature would be able to live comfortably, and was shocked to find that he instead lived in the most rundown house on the block. Shiel's single-room flat was, Ransome wrote, "the most dishevelled room it is possible to imagine," containing a large unmade bed, a bunch of broken chairs, and a washing-stand "with a basin out of which someone had taken a bite."

Shiel himself was stationed at his desk, wearing a dressing-gown and writing furiously. When he completed a page, he would toss it to the floor, where it was then gathered and shuffled into place by Lina, who sat on the ground while also trying to entertain their screaming toddler, Lola. Ransome was taken aback by the scene before him, and Shiel noticed. "Aha!" he said. "You are thinking that it is not worth while to be a success, if this is all it leads to. Eh! What? Yes. I am right. I can always tell. That is the curse of it."

Over the next few years the pair became friends, and on future visits Ransome noticed the same compulsive work ethic on Shiel's part — and the same larger-than-life personality behind it. The pair discussed literature, as well as whatever grandiose ideas popped into Shiel's head. On one occasion, a solo Shiel kept a glass of sour milk on the table between them, and kept interrupting their conversation to take small, pained sips from it. He explained that scientists believed this was why people lived so long in Hungary. "He loved theories above everything else," Ransome wrote, "and went on sipping heroically till he finished the glass. Then he jumped to his feet, and arched his biceps, and smote proudly on his chest. 'Ah!' he cried, 'it was worth it. I feel better already. Let's have supper.'" At the table, however, Shiel's mood suddenly changed, and he leaned in to tell Ransome: "I say, my wife is dying in Dublin this week. Pass the toast." Ransome was too shocked to respond, but Shiel re-brightened just as quickly, going on to explain his new theory that everything in the universe was a brain, from individual molecules to the Earth itself. "He could think of nothing else till supper was done," Ransome wrote.[↓]

AS THE FIRST YEARS of the twentieth century continued, Shiel's fiction took another unexpected turn. He kept publishing at a rapid clip but surprised his readers by shifting away from fantastical adventure stories to more realistic fare, set in the present day and concerned with the lives of everyday people. He also kept up his pulp collaborations with Louis Tracy, publishing together under at least two different pseudonyms, Gordon Holmes and Robert Fraser.

> At first, Ransome kept his encounter with Shiel anonymous, referring to him in *Bohemia in London* as simply "A Novelist" and changing certain identifying details—such as describing Shiel's wife as Irish, rather than Spanish. Later, in his autobiography, published posthumously in 1976, Ransome admitted the reason he didn't name Shiel was because he was worried about his reaction. But when Shiel found out about the essay, the elder writer took it in stride. "Dedicate the book to me," Shiel told Ransome, "and libel me as much as you please."

But this time, Shiel's prolificacy was causing him more problems than it solved. His constant wheeling and dealing between presses — playing publishers off of one another in an attempt to eke out a few extra pounds — ended up costing him his relationship with Grant Richards, his most loyal and long-suffering publisher. (In his memoir, Richards wrote that *The Yellow Danger* was the only one of Shiel's books he worked on that actually turned a profit.)

At the same time, his marriage to Lina fell apart for good. During another period of separation in May 1903, Shiel ended things in a letter in which he placed the blame largely on the ongoing interference of Lina's mother, whom he referred to as "the Spanish Squall." Shiel also brutally washed his hands of any future involvement in his daughter's life. "You must remember, darling," he wrote to Lina, "that I have my own little life to live, which is no longer than any other, and it would be silly for me to spend it messing around with a group of amusing little women from Seville." It's believed Lina died not long after the divorce was finalized.

Despite spending countless hours at his writing desk, Shiel struggled to find another commercial hit. Without any new ideas, he tried returning to the "yellow peril" material that had led to what was still his most successful book. After several such attempts, culminating in 1913's poorly received *The Dragon*, it appeared that Shiel's creative wick was finally reaching its end.

Then he disappeared. For more than a year, the public heard nothing at all from Shiel. Nor did his colleagues and peers in the publishing industry — several of whom were actively looking for him. For a long time it was thought that from late 1914 to early 1916, Shiel was in jail, perhaps for fraud. The truth, when it finally came out, was worse.

THE LIGHT *of* OTHER SUNS 6

AFTER YEARS of keeping his unruly personal and professional lives in a tenuous balance, 1914 is when everything collapsed. Shiel's latest novel, *The Dragon,* had been a flop. His income, meanwhile, had shrunk to less than a tenth of what he'd earned in earlier years. That September, Shiel applied for relief to the Royal Literary Fund, a British charity that supported writers who'd fallen on hard times. In response, he received a paltry £10.

Desperate to avoid bankruptcy, Shiel abandoned even more of the unspoken moral code that governs all working writers. He'd already proven himself willing to borrow ideas; now he crossed over into outright plagiarism. Shiel took a piece by a relatively unknown American writer named Stewart Edward White, swapped in a new name for its cowboy protagonist, and submitted it as his own work. The story was published in the *Red Magazine* in January 1915, and right away spotted as a forgery. But, strangely, nobody could get hold of Shiel to demand answers, not even the editor who had purchased the work. They couldn't have suspected that Shiel was then behind bars for having sex with a twelve-year-old girl.

For years, Shiel had been close with the family of John and Martha Price, who lived in Chepstow, on the River Wye. Their relationship dated back to the turn of the century, when Shiel began vacationing along the England–Wales border; he had inscribed a copy of his 1904 novel *The Evil that Men Do* to the eldest Price daughter, Kate. Shiel continued to spend extended periods of time in the area, during which he struck up affairs with at least one of the Price daughters. The exact details aren't clear, but in 1908, the youngest, Mary, who was then eighteen, wrote to Shiel in the aftermath of what is thought to be either a suicide attempt or a self-administered abortion. "I was so pleased to get your letter for I thought you had turned against me since I done the foolish act," she wrote. Mary added that her parents had forbidden her from any further communication with Shiel. "But," she wrote, "we will see about that wont we." Shiel later began an affair with Lizzie, the middle Price daughter, following her separation from the father of her two children, and she soon became pregnant again, this time with Shiel's child. In response, Shiel moved in with her and her daughters, Dorothy and Eileen, and Lizzie gave birth to Caesar Kenneth Shiel on March 13, 1914. But when their son was still an infant, Lizzie filed charges against Shiel for having obtained "carnal knowledge" of Dorothy, who was not yet a teenager. He was arrested a few days later.

From the moment he arrived in jail, Shiel was outraged. But not about his conviction, about which he maintained his innocence, perhaps in an attempt to preserve his relationship with Dorothy's mother. Rather, Shiel was upset that having sex with a twelve-year-old was illegal in the first place. In a letter written from jail to Grant Richards, the forty-nine-year-old dismisses the case against him as "making mountains out of molehills and crimes out of love-toyings," and claims that, as someone who is "wildly non-English," he has "copulated, *as a matter of course*, from the age of two or three with ladies of a similar age in lands where that is not considered at all extraordinary" (emphasis in original).[↓]

Another shocking fact from this period of Shiel's life was that throughout his arrest, trial, and imprisonment, he was in a committed relationship — with a different woman. Lydia Furley was an outspoken left-wing organizer who belonged to several socialist groups, as well as a fierce advocate for women's rights. The two had met in 1908, and Shiel pursued her even as he shared a home with Lizzie Sircar (née Price) and her children. When he was released from prison, in February 1916, Shiel and Furley's relationship carried on much as before. Three years later, they got married and moved to London together.

Shiel's story continues from here, but little is known about what happened to the other people he entangled in this period of his life. His involvement with the Price family appears to have concluded with his prison sentence. Yet it was Mary who had to deal with the after-effects of "the foolish act," whatever it was, and Lizzie who was now tasked with raising three children on her own. The only other known information about Dorothy, meanwhile, comes from a letter Kenneth wrote to his father in 1946. At one point, Kenneth mentions that the two half-siblings are still living together as adults.

This belief in the sexual availability of very young women translated into a significant portion of Shiel's fiction. The academic Kirsten MacLeod found that of his twenty-nine published works, nineteen of them included female protagonists in their teens, and noted that the author repeatedly "fixes on the girl budding sexually into womanhood."

"She is still the same as ever," he writes of the sister he called Dolly, adding, "I doubt that she will ever change, but then I think she is quite happy." Shiel held on to this letter until his death, a year later. But there is no record of a reply.

BEGINNING WITH his incarceration in 1914, Shiel spent most of the next decade away from the publishing world. Instead, he experimented with other media, adapting five of his earlier novels into screenplays and also writing several new plays for the stage. He also spent more time pursuing the socialist politics he shared with his new wife. As the Russian Revolution dominated headlines following the end of the Great War, Shiel translated at least one pamphlet for the Workers' Socialist Federation; he and Lydia also spent hours discussing education reform and at one point considered opening their own private school. When the British Parliament debated sending troops into Russia to support the Tsar-affiliated White Guard in 1919, Shiel and Lydia sat in the gallery and openly heckled the members below. "You have not settled the last war, and you are leading the workers into another," they yelled as they were escorted out of the building, according to the *Times*. "You are a gang of murderers." Shiel came away with a black eye for his troubles.

Now well in his fifties, Shiel continued his longstanding interest in unusual exercise and diet trends. He enjoyed mountain climbing, but only if he could do it barefoot. And he swore off of sugar entirely, instead following a diet that included prunes he kept soaking in a chamber pot underneath his bed. Friends remember him keeping unusual hours, sleeping through the day and then staying up all night to write and to go on long starlit runs. (By way of explanation, Shiel said, "I like the light of the other suns even better than ours.") Arthur Ransome, who had first met Shiel as an errand boy for Grant Richards, ran into him again, years later, in the streets of London, and their final meeting left just as strong an impression as the first one had:

> [Shiel] passed me, panting, a stout elderly man in a velvet jacket, running along the edge of the pavement, in and out of the gutter, elbows well tucked in. "Wait!" he gasped. "Back in a minute. I turn at St Martin's Church." I waited for him and he came back. He had long given up his early belief in sour milk as an elixir of life, at least in English sour milk, but now made a point of running each day from his lodging to St Martin's Church, and strongly advised me to do the same. If a man were to run a mile or two every day, he was sure, there was nothing to prevent his living for ever.

Eventually, Shiel found that his taste for writing fiction had returned. He started publishing novels again, including 1927's *How the Old Woman Got Home*, whose American edition, published the following year, pushed Shiel further than ever before into the long-coveted U.S. literary scene. Back in England, Victor Gollancz reissued several of Shiel's earlier novels—and, alongside them, the revised version of "About Myself," in which the Redondan legend was first revealed to the British reading public. It had only been thirty years since the first publication of *Prince Zaleski*, but between the ripple effects of the Oscar Wilde trial, the global horrors of the Great War, and the silence created by Shiel's own criminal behaviour, the gulf between past and present felt much larger. Now he had an opportunity to start again and present his work to an entirely new generation of readers.

Shortly thereafter, he received a letter from one of them. It was July 1931, and Shiel, now sixty-six and divorced for the second time, was living alone in a cottage in Sussex. Though still a teenager, the letter-writer claimed to be one of Shiel's biggest fans and most devoted readers. Shiel had never heard the name John Gawsworth before, but he was taken by the enthusiasm of the young poet and wrote back right away, thereby beginning a friendship that would lead both men into some very unexpected places.

PROGRESSION *by* DIGRESSION 7

AFTER FINISHING *All Souls*, I left Redonda alone for a while. As it was, I was already staying up too late trying to get my fledgling career as a writer up and running; my evening hours were not in need of another weird hobby to occupy me after the kids were asleep. Plus, the whole thing still felt too much like a prank laundered through the internet. I never went to journalism school, so as a self-taught freelancer — not to mention a fundamentally trusting (some would say gullible) person at heart — I'd already learned the saying *If it sounds too good to be true, it probably is* the hard way.

I did, however, keep reading Javier Marías. For the next couple of years, he became a comforting, familiar presence on my bookshelves; whenever I found myself in a reading slump, I would use Marías's novels to pull me back out. I always kept at least one that I hadn't read yet on hand, just in case. When I happened to mention on Twitter how much I'd loved *All Souls*, a couple of friends and I decided to read its quasi-sequel together — a book that, we'd heard, would explain how Marías came to be named the new King of Redonda. All three of us were enamoured by Marías's novels and the way they blended fact and fiction, but we were also a little intimidated by them, and figured that if we put our brains together we might be able to better decode what, exactly, he was up to. This time I splurged on a new Vintage paperback, this one with a cover featuring a different silhouetted couple leaning against what looked like a railing or gate. A blurb at the bottom, from the late Roberto Bolaño, declared Marías "by far Spain's best writer today."

Negra espalda del tiempo was first published in Spain in 1998 and appeared in English three years later, translated by Esther Allen as *Dark Back of Time*. The book was, somehow, even trickier to categorize than its predecessor: part sequel to *All Souls*, part retroactive disclaimer about the things people had (mistakenly) believed were autobiographical about it, part publishing tell-all, and part philosophical treatise on identity, memory, time, and truth. Marías scholar Gareth Wood calls *Dark Back of Time* the author's most "Shandean" novel, intentionally contorting and looping back on itself like Laurence Sterne's eighteenth-century classic — which, I learned, Marías translated into Spanish back in the 1970s, and which he still claims is his favourite book. Marías himself described *Dark Back of Time* as a "false novel" that "proceeds by digression," which are as useful descriptors as any.

"I believe I've still never mistaken fiction for reality," the novel begins, "though I have mixed them together more than once, as everyone does, not only novelists or writers but everyone who has recounted anything since the time we know began, and no one in that known time has done anything but tell and tell, or prepare and ponder a tale, or plot one." In other words, our experiences change the moment we start writing or talking about them. Trying to accurately depict the past is a fool's errand, but one we all attempt anyway.

The trouble, Marías writes, began with the publication of

All Souls in Spanish. He admits there were obvious similarities between him and his unnamed narrator, beginning with the fact that both were male Spanish novelists who briefly taught at Oxford. But Marías claims he never intended for the novel to be interpreted as a *roman à clef*, where every character had a particular real-life counterpart. Yet that was exactly what happened, leading many Oxonians into a frenzy to acquire the book and then attempt to decode it. A group of enterprising students even came across the Spanish edition while on vacation and returned to campus with "wagonloads" of copies, which they sold at a mark-up. The married owners of a used bookstore in town, meanwhile, were convinced that they were the inspirations for a similar couple in the novel; when the English translation of *All Souls* was eventually published, the couple proudly displayed copies in the window of their shop. ("Dear God," Marías thinks in disbelief when he hears about it.) In an attempt to make sure nobody mistook fiction for reality in *All Souls*, Marías created his narrator as married with a young child at home — two descriptors that were easily proven false in the author's own life. But that, too, had little effect. Back at Madrid, teaching translation at the Universidad Complutense, Marías would routinely encounter students gathered outside of his office, asking him questions about a baby who did not exist.

Ironically, while Marías's readers were quick to assume that most of *All Souls* was lifted from reality, many were wrong twice over, writing off as fictional the one character who actually was a real person, appearing under his actual name: John Gawsworth. One of Marías's colleagues wrote him a letter praising the novel and its use of opposites, including "the fictional Gawsworth" and "the real Machen"; other readers were sure that Gawsworth was "pure Kiplingesque invention." Again, this ran exactly contrary to the author's intentions. Marías had included photographs in *All Souls* specifically to show that Gawsworth really existed, but the gesture only confused things further. Marías's UK publisher, Harvill Press, even convinced him to add an author's note to the beginning of the English edition, clarifying that the novel was a work of fiction — with one exception. "Any resemblance," the note reads, "between any character in the novel (including the narrator, but excluding 'John Gawsworth') and any other person living or dead (including the author, but excluding Terence Ian Fytton Armstrong) is purely coincidental."

Dark Back of Time is a follow-up of sorts to Marías's earlier novel. But it also provides fascinating behind-the-scenes details about how that book was written, published, and received by the public. With a decade's worth of hindsight, Marías describes how he was manipulated by his Spanish editor into accepting a lower advance for *All Souls* than he had for his previous novels, despite having a track record of modest but increasing profits for everyone involved. The editor, whom Marías calls "more of a shopkeeper than an intellectual," acquired *All Souls* begrudgingly, then enjoyed a windfall as the novel was translated into nine other languages and sold 140,000 copies by 1998. In between relitigating these personal disagreements, Marías writes at length about the slippery nature of memory and experience. This intentionally meandering structure suited his style, which by now my friends and I were well acquainted with. But it also pointed to a larger human inability to give a simple and accurate answer to the question "What happened?" *Dark Back of Time* promises to explain the real-life ripple effects created by Marías's Oxford novel, but instead pulls the reader in a series of unexpected, sometimes unwanted directions until we reach an uncomfortable truth: the answers we crave simply aren't available. At times even Marías's wandering curiosity fails him. Hundreds of pages into the novel, the following stray parenthetical appears: "(this book isn't that important, not even to me)."

Eventually, however, Marías does circle back to the Redondan news at hand. Since the publication of *All Souls*, he has learned even more about the real-life Gawsworth, and the two writers' lives have become even more entangled. "He lives in me to some extent," Marías writes, "and his ghost lives in my house" — in fact, Marías finds himself referring to the part of his home where he keeps the poet's books and pamphlets as "Gawsworth's room." He has even acquired copies of documents from Gawsworth's personal life, including his marriage and death certificates. At times, Marías suspects he is being pursued by Gawsworth himself:

> The feeling that books seek me out has stayed with me, and all that has emerged into real life from *All Souls'* fictional pages has finally materialized in that form, as well: in the form of a book, a document, a photo, a letter, a title. So much has sprung from that novel into my life that I no longer know how many volumes I'll need to tell it all, this book won't be enough and its planned sequel may not be either, because eight years have passed since I published the novel and all of it continues to invade my days, stealing into them, and my nights, too, now more than ever, when I have become what Shiel and Gawsworth once were, or so it appears, and it seems incredible that I wasn't afraid of this and accepted it [...] It's hard to resist the chance to perpetuate a legend, all the more so if you've contributed to extending it. And it would be mean-spirited to refuse to play along.

Finally, in the middle of another multi-page paragraph about the ways fiction and reality overlap, Marías admits the truth: "following the abdication of the third one in my favor, since July 6, 1997 I have been the fourth of those kings, King Xavier or still King X as I write this, and also the literary executor and legal heir of my predecessors Shiel and Gawsworth, or Felipe I and Juan I." This admission is the climax of the novel, with the remainder dedicated to reproductions of Redondan maps, photographs, and illustrations, including the kings' custom ex-libris bookplates, which include a red crown, the years of their respective reigns, and the phrase "REALM OF REDONDA" at the top. Still, a sense of uncertainty persists. Marías admits that he is embarrassed to bring up his new title among his friends, for fear that they will make fun of him. But he also knows that the story will get out soon enough on its own.

As with *All Souls*, one of the things that stood out to me about *Dark Back of Time* was how truly strange its structure is. Marías's refusal to write directly at his subject is one of his great strengths. But when it came to Redonda, Marías seemed to approach his subject with trepidation, even superstition. At one point he claims he has never been a man who actively pursues the things that interest him. "[I] limit myself to registering them, taking them in," he writes. "I keep still and wait as if I believed that only what comes to me anyway, without any effort on my part, will be worthwhile or deserved." With Redonda, Marías worries that the only reason he became entangled in the story is because of his lackadaisical attitude towards it; if that's true, then appearing too eager now might scare it away. Instead, *Dark Back of Time* ends with Marías making a series of negative affirmations: *not* to learn too much about his new kingdom, *not* to interview surviving friends and relations of previous kings, and—most import-antly—*not* to argue with other claimants to the throne, lest the legend become deprived of its mystery. Facts, he writes, are overrated. "If I did know everything I don't believe I would ever tell it, we're always selecting and discarding, knowing or not knowing often doesn't matter much," Marías writes. "Or sometimes true knowledge turns out to make no difference, and then invention can begin."

CLEARLY, this was not going to be as simple as I'd hoped.

For every question *Dark Back of Time* answered about *All Souls*, a new one emerged. Not only did I still not under-stand how Marías wound up being named Redonda's new king, but I also had no idea who had done the crowning. If Shiel and Gawsworth were the first two Redondan kings, and Marías, as he claimed, the fourth, then who was the third? Why was being a writer a prerequisite to the throne? And who were these other people who thought *they* were the real king, and why? *Dark Back of Time* hinted at a lengthy trail of Redondan documents and titles that Marías was now in charge of, but it also suggested a level of playfulness and ambiguity that the author was still trying to figure out how to navigate. And, of course, Marías's refusal to simply let the story exist as non-fiction—wrapping it again inside the category of fiction then confounding *those* expectations, too, by calling it a "false novel"—meant that he could eas-ily disavow the whole thing at any time. My friends and I had been entertained, but what had we really learned? At the same time, we were aware that we'd been trying to pry straightforward answers out of a man whose favourite book is *Tristram Shandy*—a novel that purported to be the life story of its main character, but which didn't even get around to his birth until volume three. It seemed foolish to have ever expected anything more.

Still, I could tell the itch was back, and this time it would not be soothed so easily. If you added up the clues in *All Souls* and *Dark Back of Time*, there was enough to start putting together a larger story about the kingdom. Everything Marías had written in those books was consistent. But it had also all appeared under the label of fiction. If I was going to get anywhere with this, I would need to consult a more reliable source.

The problem was that other books about Redonda were not particularly easy to find. Marías's narrator in *All Souls* had struggled to acquire titles by Gawsworth—and he lived in Oxford, a place teeming with books. Things were a lot sparser in my little corner of Canada. Plus, twenty-five years had passed since even that novel had been published, during which time Gawsworth's memory had faded further into the background. The internet should, in theory, have made my life a lot easier. But when I typed Gawsworth's name into the search bars of websites selling second-hand books, I realized the true extent of my problem. Gawsworth may have been out of vogue, but his works were uncommon enough that they still commanded a lot more than I could afford. Plus, there were *so many* of them, and I had no idea where to start— which ones contained useful Redondan intel, and which were simply collections of old-fashioned formal poetry. Many of the descriptions I read focused on the specs and condition of each title. Few mentioned his second life as King of Redonda, and those that did tossed this information in at the end, as though the dealer was obligated to mention such a strange biographical quirk but wanted to be clear they didn't personally give it any credence. It seemed that my interests were not shared by the average bookseller.

I repeated these searches for Redonda itself, with equally discouraging results. In addition to the many Spanish-language titles that inevitably clogged up search results — *round* being a common word, in book titles or otherwise — I was also greeted with a selection that appeared to be self-published. One even explicitly advertised itself as a print version of the Wikipedia page I'd already read. My feeling that the Kingdom of Redonda attracted more than its fair share of eccentrics was further confirmed with every click of the "Next Page" button. Then I did it all a third time for the works of M.P. Shiel, Gawsworth's Redondan predecessor — and that's when I learned that one of *his* titles was not just readily available second-hand, but actually still in print. In fact, it had recently been reissued under the august black umbrella of the Penguin Classics line, with jacket copy dubbing it "the first great science fiction novel of the twentieth century." I called my local bookshop and ordered a copy of *The Purple Cloud* that same day.

My first impression of Shiel's 1901 novel was that it contained enough material to fill at least three different books. As the tale begins, the richest man in the world has recently passed away, and his will stipulates that $175 million be awarded to the first person to reach the North Pole. Our narrator, Adam Jeffson, enlists onboard a ship called the *Boreal*, where any camaraderie between crew members is reluctant and temporary: as soon as the boat docks in the Arctic, it is understood that each man will be on his own. This is because the rich man's will specifically states that the fortune is to be given, in its entirety, to "the individual, whatever his station in the expedition, whose foot first reached the 90th degree of north latitude." In other words, no prizes for second place.

Big breath now: The *Boreal* sets off in mid-June and arrives at the edge of the ice sheet the following March, at which point Jeffson races out, along with two other crew members, on foot. Along the way they notice what appear to be diamonds strewn across the frozen landscape and assume them to be detritus from a meteor. Once the group is within ten miles of its destination, Jeffson wakes up early in the morning and takes off from the shared camp on his own. He arrives at the pole solo, where he discovers "a circular clean-cut lake" with a huge chunk of ice at the centre, inscribed with a series of names and dates he cannot read. He then passes out. Upon waking, Jeffson notices a strange purple vapour in the distance and is overwhelmed by the distinct smell of peaches, at which point he vomits and his sled dogs drop dead. His walk back to the *Boreal* brings him past scores of other dead animals, including polar bears, walruses, "kittiwakes, glaucus and ivory gulls, skuas, and every kind of Arctic fowl." Once he reaches the ship, Jeffson finds that all of the other crew members are also dead, covered in purple ash, and smelling sickly of peach blossoms. After managing to pilot the ship back towards Europe, he docks in a small Nordic port and discovers the horrible, mind-boggling truth: while he was off galivanting in search of fortune, some mysterious force has killed the entire population of Earth — except for him.

Which brought me all the way to the one-quarter mark of the novel.

I had a few different reactions to Shiel's book. First and foremost, it made me giggle. As I read on, in search of anything that might conceivably be a clue about Redonda, I kept having visions of Shiel at his desk, laughing as he burned through material at what would seem a foolish pace for most other writers. I kept pinching the remaining pages together and thinking, *How on Earth is he going to fill all of this?* Yet he did. In fact, Shiel made it look easy, as if generating new ideas was so effortless it was hardly worth acknowledging.

Once Jeffson's worst fears have been confirmed, the novel's driving question becomes, What would you do if you were the last person alive? Shiel gifts his narrator a powerful (and convenient) fictional fuel source called "liquid air," which allows Jeffson to commandeer ships and trains at will and zoom his way around the world. At first, Jeffson is driven by concern for the fate of human civilization. But before long his lizard brain comes up with a better plan: since everyone's dead anyway, he will burn the largest cities on the planet to the ground, beginning with London, and continuing on to Paris, San Francisco, and Constantinople. At one point, he decides to build himself a golden palace on the Turkish island of Imbros, and spends the next *seventeen years* doing just that. Meanwhile, in an old issue of the *Times*, Jeffson discovers the cause of the deadly cloud: a series of volcanoes, which suddenly emerged from the water and exploded near Krakatoa, releasing huge quantities of purple cyanide gas into the air.

It was a great book. Unfortunately, it didn't reference Redonda at all. But I could at least take solace in the fact that the kingdom's literary credentials were not in doubt. Plus, there was one particular image I couldn't shake—perhaps the single eeriest moment in the entire book. When Jeffson first arrives at the North Pole, he encounters an unusual iceberg engraved with inscrutable foreign writing. This iceberg, Shiel writes, is surrounded by water "wheeling with a shivering ecstasy, splashing and fluttering, round the pillar, always from west to east, in the direction of the spinning of the earth." This strange motion is never explained or returned to. Nor is where the (presumably human) writing came from. Yet it was this cryptic structure that attracted Jeffson's attention, thereby saving his life from the passing cloud. And when he first sets eyes on it, a parallel descriptor would no doubt have flashed through his mind: an island.

By this point, I could picture Jeffson's iceberg clearly in my mind. It was the same shape I'd been studying in photos online, as well as in the final section of *Dark Back of Time*: pill-like, with zig-zagging cliffs carved out of its sides and rising to a summit that few humans would ever set foot upon. But my version was brown, infested with rats, and ruled from afar by a bunch of writers. In *Close Encounters of the Third Kind*, Richard Dreyfuss's children started crying when he couldn't stop sculpting mashed potatoes into the shape of a mountain; my kids just rolled their eyes as more and more of our dinner conversation became occupied by factoids about Redonda.

I went back online and tried to contact anyone whose name had come up in the course of my research, in the hopes that they might be able to help explain even a small piece of the story. Most of these emails either bounced back or went unanswered. But I received replies, too: from fans of Shiel and/or Redonda, from amateur historians who'd written about the kingdom online, and even from people who'd at one point been claimants to the throne. The majority of responses were encouraging, and either included documents and images they'd collected about the kingdom or contact information for other potential sources. I was also warned, more than once, that I should be clearer up front that my interest in Redonda was strictly journalistic. The kingdom, these sources told me, attracted a lot of folks with an intermittent grasp on reality—not to mention those who were outright gunning for a royal title of their own.

So far I'd been able to convince myself that this was all just a lark, a couple of amusing emails dashed off during brief breaks from my work. But that changed once I made contact with one of Shiel's actual relatives. Richard Shiell (second L intact) lived in Australia and had been introduced to the works of his briefly famous family member by accident, while researching his family tree. It turned out that the two shared a distant relative back on Montserrat. "I am NOT an admirer of his literary style," Richard wrote of Shiel in his first email to me, "although I am constantly amazed at his vivid imagination and the speed at which one plot follows close on the heels of another." Shiell wasn't sure how much he knew about Redonda—the island or the kingdom—but he was happy to help if he could.

A FEW WEEKS LATER, a package arrived at my front door. Inside were four books. Two were copies of Shiell's family histories, each containing pictures, maps, timelines, and countless other carefully assembled details, including stories of M.P. Shiel's life both pre- and post-coronation. The other two were volumes of a difficult-to-find biography of Shiel, written by Harold Billings, a long-time library director at the University of Texas who had been instrumental in creating the archive of Shiel's work held at the Harry Ransom Center in Austin. Shiell explained that he had come across spare copies of first two volumes of the biography, which covered Shiel's life from birth up to 1923, in his basement.↓

Billings passed away in 2017 before he could complete the trilogy in full; however, a press in Romania gathered up some of his remaining research materials and published them as *An Ossuary for M.P. Shiel*, in a limited run of just eighty-five copies.

REALM of REDONDA

This Volume is from
the Bookshelves of

M. P. SHIEL, (1865-1947)

[H.M. King Felipe I, 1880-1947]

and

JOHN GAWSWORTH (1912-   )

[H.M. King Juan I, 1947-   ]

Realm of Redonda bookplate.

He'd decided to send them to me, along with his family history, figuring that I might be able to put them to use. One of the volumes had been previously signed by Billings; Shiell now inscribed all four of the books to me, wishing me luck with my research.

As I sat at my desk, studying Shiell's slanted handwriting, I felt everything I'd been doing come into focus. I wasn't sending all these strangers detailed questions late at night just for fun anymore. There was a bigger project here — and it started with books. Being a writer, it seemed, was the one prerequisite to becoming king of Redonda, and Shiel, Gawsworth, and Marías were all prolific authors in their own times and genres. In *All Souls*, Marías had also memorably described Gawsworth's lifelong hobby as "the morbid searching out and collecting of books." So maybe the best way for me to understand the Redonda story was to try to gather together all of the texts where it had been discussed, footnoted, and alluded to. The content would be important, of course, but so were things like the inscription connecting Shiel to Shiell, and then, in turn, to me. Even as objects, these books were pieces of a grander narrative about Redonda and the men who claimed to be its rulers. But first they needed to be placed in their proper context. Either way, it was clear to me that the books I'd gathered so far couldn't sit just scattered throughout my office. They called out for order.

I walked over to my bookshelves and cleared a foot of horizontal space. Then I placed upon it the Billings biographies, the pair of Shiell family histories, and my copies of *The Purple Cloud*, *All Souls*, and *Dark Back of Time* all in a row. It was the beginning of what I started calling my Redonda shelf, and no sooner did it have a name than it began to grow, eventually requiring a separate glassed-in cabinet to hold everything I'd acquired — including several books by the man who had previously haunted the bookshelves of Javier Marías. In all of the kingdom's history, nobody told the story of Redonda as well, or as loudly, as John Gawsworth, who inherited the mantle from Shiel upon his death and reinvented himself as King Juan I. Thanks to Gawsworth's tireless advocacy following World War II, the kingdom transformed from an inside joke to something more — at times a gang of talented drinking buddies, at others an "intellectual aristocracy" that tied far-flung writers and artists together, and always a fixture of the British tabloid scene. King Juan I is the reason anyone still knows about the Kingdom of Redonda today. He's also the reason it has broken into so many pieces that it may never again be fully reassembled.

MAGNETIC FINGERS 8

JOHN GAWSWORTH barged onto the London book scene when he was still a teenager. Born Terence Ian Fytton Armstrong on June 29, 1912, Gawsworth was a natural and compulsive collector: of stamps, coins, and, eventually, books. At the age of twelve, he found George Bernard Shaw's house and managed to get an autograph before the elderly playwright had a chance to get out of bed. Later, at the prestigious Merchant Taylors' School, visiting authors like Arthur Conan Doyle and Walter de la Mare would deliver lectures to the students, and afterwards Gawsworth would be there, wearing his school cap and short pants, holding out a copy of their latest novels to sign.

Gawsworth was a dedicated reader, and at a young age zeroed in on the forms and eras that would consume him for the rest of his life. He particularly loved the work of the Georgian poets, a loose collective whose work appeared in a series of anthologies throughout the 1910s, early in the reign of King George V. Gawsworth's taste for formal, elegant poetry matched his bloodlines, too—or at least the way he chose to trace them. His family was part Irish, part Scottish, and part French, and he claimed to be descended from top-drawer poetic stock, including both Ben Jonson and the third wife of John Milton. At age nineteen, when he decided to create a writerly alter ego for himself, he looked to another distant ancestor: Mary Fitton, long rumoured to be the "Dark Lady" from Shakespeare's sonnets, and who at one time lived in a country house in Cheshire named Gawsworth Old Hall. It is also possible that Gawsworth's choice of pen name contained an element of chaos, deliberately creating confusion with the novelist John Galsworthy, who, like Gawsworth, lived in London and who, unlike Gawsworth, won the Nobel Prize in Literature in 1932.

After dropping out of school at age sixteen, "the book boy," as Gawsworth was known, set off into the heart of London with his sights squarely set on a career in poetry. This independence was not entirely his own choice: Gawsworth's parents had divorced, and shortly thereafter his mother had gone overseas to go live with family in Montreal. Gawsworth's father, meanwhile, preferred the comforts of his local pub, where his drinking buddies gave him the nickname "the Duke." Young Gawsworth was witty and exuberant, and also had a striking appearance. He was short and thin, with an outsized nose that had been knocked crooked during a boxing match at Merchant Taylors'. His reddish goatee, meanwhile, reminded more than one person of the Decadent poet Algernon Charles Swinburne.

One of Gawsworth's earliest jobs in London was at Andrew Block's bookshop, which was famed for its towering piles of literary ephemera. He also worked for a time at the publisher Ernest Benn. No matter where he was, Gawsworth soaked up as much information as he could about the authors of the day, their lives, and especially their bibliographies. Whenever a writer would visit Block's shop, Gawsworth nearly fell off his stool trying to ingratiate himself with them and to pitch them his own publishing ideas, of which he had almost too many to count. Starting in 1931, when he was still a teenager, Gawsworth's own writing also saw its way into print. His first book was a pamphlet of verses entitled *Confession*, which he published himself in multiple small batches: six copies of the first issue, twelve copies of a second issue on larger paper, and 250 copies that were put up for sale to the public.

Gawsworth made a few key connections in these early years that would have a profound effect on the rest of his career. One was Arthur Machen, whose work Gawsworth idolized — his fledgling small press, Twyn Barlwm, took its name from the Welsh hill near where Machen grew up — and whose son attended Merchant Taylors' at the same time Gawsworth was there. Another was Count Potocki, a theatrical and flamboyantly dressed poet who walked around claiming to be the exiled king of Poland. The third, and ultimately most important, was M.P. Shiel.

IT WAS FITTING that Gawsworth and Shiel's first encounter came via the written word. As Gawsworth remembered it: "In July 1931 a nineteen-year-old publisher's clerk, imbued with fanatic literary enthusiasm, wrote a letter of appreciation to an entire stranger, a novelist entering his sixty-seventh year, living alone in a bungalow hermitage off a Sussex highroad, and received an immediate reply." Shiel was one of the older writers whose work Gawsworth obsessed over, and the young poet was delighted by Shiel's response to his letter. He was also surprised at how easily Shiel treated him as an equal, despite the sizeable gap between them in terms of age, output, and aesthetics. "The novelist preached Science and professed pure Socialist principles," Gawsworth wrote, whereas he focused on classical poetry and was "frenetically furious for 'Form in Art.'"

Shiel's willingness to befriend Gawsworth was partly informed by a lack of companionship, as he and Lydia had quietly separated a few years earlier. But for all their differences, the two men also had a surprising amount in common. Both, for instance, had a penchant for fanciful connections in their family trees. They also shared a healthy sense of self-worth and an all-consuming belief in the power of literature.

One of the things Gawsworth wanted from Shiel was guidance, even though his literary career didn't seem to need the help. Encouraged by the response to his first publications, Gawsworth continued writing poetry at a rapid clip, and just as often gathered up older pieces and resold them as collections to more established presses. He stayed just as busy as a publisher, using his Twyn Barlwm Press to print limited runs of poems by his fellow neo-Georgians, as well as figures like Edmund Blunden and Edith Sitwell. In 1932 Gawsworth also managed to edit a pair of books for other publishers. *Known Signatures* was an anthology assembled as a pointed response to an earlier one called *New Signatures* that, Gawsworth felt, was moving poetry in the wrong direction. "The course of English Poetry has deviated far enough now from the channels of tradition in many cases hardly to be called poetry," he wrote in his introduction. "It is sinking underground into the marish morass of incoherence, led there through the cloaca of experiment." Modernism was knocking at the door, and Gawsworth wanted no part of it. The second book, *Ten Contemporaries*, was a bibliography for collectors, focusing on writers whom Gawsworth felt were falling unfairly out of fashion — including Shiel, who wrote an essay called "The Inconsistency of a Novelist" to accompany his entry.[†]

Gawsworth had another important point in common with Shiel: both were all too aware of the rate of churn in the industry, and how quickly one's fortunes could change. By the time he was twenty-two years old, Gawsworth had published five different titles in hardcover. Yet in his introduction to the fifth one, Gawsworth noted that several of the others were already out of print. The difference between the two men's approaches was largely one of business acumen. Whereas Shiel was content to fire off prose to whichever publishers or periodicals would have him, Gawsworth took a more active hand in shaping his career. He figured out early on that by publishing and anthologizing the work of his peers, he could stave off, or at least slow down, the modernists at the gates. And by keeping the names of his fellow neo-Georgians in the public eye, Gawsworth's own work would seem less of an outlier.

As for the work itself, it was published and read, but admired with some reservation. Gawsworth's strictly metered and rhymed poems required technical chops. But some felt that he was affecting a persona that outlapped his actual experience, others that he wore his influences a little too strongly. When reviewers pointed out that certain phrases in his collection *Lyrics to Kingcup* were uncomfortably close to those of Ernest Dowson, a Decadent writer who coined the phrases "gone with the wind" and "the days of wine and roses,"

"It is not very consistent of me to have written books," Shiel's contrarian piece begins, "since I can see that people read much too much, through a certain laziness of mentation." He then admits to not reading many novels himself, because "in those that I have got through I saw nothing novel."

Gawsworth ended up revising them in future printings or, in some cases, removing them altogether.

More seriously for his commercial prospects, there wasn't a lot of continuity between the original Georgian movement and the select few youngsters like Gawsworth who remained committed to the cause decades later. For one thing, World War I had gotten in the way. But so had the arrival of poems like T.S. Eliot's "The Waste Land," which signalled a significant shift for the entire medium. Both of these things made Georgianism appear fatally quaint and out of touch with the modern world. Even at its height, the movement had been mocked as a bunch of "fake pastoralists, based in the city"; its chances of surviving in a world still grappling with the horrors of global war appeared to be basically nil. Dylan Thomas, whose social circle overlapped with Gawsworth's for many years, referred to him and his peers as "not poets at all but just bearded boils in the dead armpit of the nineties."

Still, Gawsworth did have admirers. The *Times Literary Supplement* called him "an accomplished craftsman," and Hugh MacDiarmid, a friend of Gawsworth's who would later dedicate poems to him, believed he was underrated, but wouldn't stay that way for long: "I think [Gawsworth] will soon emerge from the press of his competitors and win for himself a definite niche within the tradition of English poetry." And even if the book sales weren't there, Gawsworth saw immediate returns in his other life as a collector and informal literary archivist. His ability to find sleepers in the stacks of used bookshops, a quality he described as possessing "magnetic fingers," was evident as a teenager and only improved with time. Gawsworth's obsession with the older Georgian poets, for instance, dovetailed usefully with a lack of public interest in their work, which allowed him to scoop up literally hundreds of books at bargain-basement prices. Over the years he rescued and reassembled entire collected works that might otherwise have been not just forgotten but discarded outright; one friend remembered Gawsworth labelling a map of England with the approximate address of every living pre-modernist writer and then visiting each in turn to pay homage and request signatures. Whenever he needed cash, Gawsworth would simply wander down Charing Cross Road, pluck out a couple of rarities hiding in plain sight in the shops' clearance boxes, then walk up the road to flip them to the rare book department at Foyles. "His memory for bibliography was simply amazing," wrote the novelist Lawrence Durrell, "and had he cared to be a bookseller he would now be the greatest one in England."

Gawsworth and Durrell first met in the mid-1930s, at a café in Bloomsbury. At the time Durrell was newly arrived in London, and one night he loitered excitedly near Gawsworth as the latter corrected a set of page proofs while guzzling black coffee at 3 a.m. "I was in the presence of a Real Writer," Durrell wrote later, "someone who could tell me something about literary life in the capital." The two struck up a conversation, and by evening's end Gawsworth was leading Durrell and his wife, Nancy, back to his cramped attic apartment to show off his collection of manuscripts, letters, and other literary oddities, including a pen owned by Thackeray and one of Dickens's old skull caps.

Gawsworth was also keen to put up peers his own age, like MacDiarmid and Patrick Kavanagh, when they needed a place to stay. During one such visit to London, Kavanagh was in the middle of writing his autobiographical novel, *The Green Fool*, and as a show of thanks, the Irish author gave Gawsworth a cameo at the end of the book, in which he lends

Gawsworth at home.

the young poet-narrator five shillings. Kavanagh would later write that Gawsworth was his "only literary mate" at the time.

Yet for all his gregariousness, Gawsworth often found himself isolated, yearning to ingratiate himself with his elders while living in bohemian squalor. Those around him noticed, for instance, that while Gawsworth inevitably knew everyone in any bookshop he walked into, he tended to arrive and leave on his own. Durrell also pointed out that Gawsworth's elderly "literary admirers and acquaintances" — he seems to make a point of not using the word *friends* — didn't have the stomach for the younger man's diet of beer and potato chips.

In addition to his knack for retaining bibliographic details, Gawsworth memorized literary trivia more broadly, and he walked the streets of London pointing out which bars on Fleet Street Arthur Machen used to frequent, or which days of the year required a toast to Dr Johnson, and why. More than anything, Gawsworth loved the idea of London as a massive, constantly evolving cultural organism. This was an alternative framework to the brutal and unforgiving English class system, which so often made life difficult for those stuck on its lower rungs, and its bar to entry was immune to such snobbishness; the only thing that mattered in Gawsworth's London was literary ability. As he wandered through the city on foot, he imagined himself a successor to earlier luminaries like William Hazlitt, Leigh Hunt, and Charles Lamb. "Indeed," Durrell wrote, "he never tired of talking about them and their London, and comparing it to the rushing and grubby city in whose rainswept streets he walked, determined to carry on the great tradition they had left us."

Gawsworth had always been eager to create a legacy for himself. Writing books was one way to accomplish this. Building and maintaining collections of other writers' work was another. But in thinking about the city's literary past, Gawsworth saw a larger tradition that he could tether himself to, and maybe even enhance in his own small way, with no permission needed from anybody else. No matter how out of step his poetic sensibilities might have been with the general public, he was still a citizen of literary London, just like any other. After spending years lionizing poets of the previous generation, it was perhaps natural that Gawsworth went one step further and fell in love with ghosts.

SHIEL WASN'T A GHOST. But he did occupy an unusual place in Gawsworth's already-atypical social circle. One of the things Gawsworth admired about Shiel was that, unlike many elderly writers, he showed no signs of slowing down or softening in his old age. The same fiery spirit that led Shiel to bristle at being compared to Arthur Conan Doyle in the 1890s was still present well into his senior citizenship. In 1938, Shiel was asked to contribute to a volume of "literary confessions." His answers were breathtakingly confident. After taking shots at Pope, Kipling, Shaw, and Wilde, and listing the Biblical Job as the "greatest genius among writers who ever lived," Shiel named Gawsworth his favourite living English poet, and *himself* the best living writer of prose. Gawsworth, no stranger to contrarianism himself, also wasn't immune to flattery.

As Gawsworth and Shiel's friendship strengthened, they started collaborating on a series of jointly authored short stories. This partnership was made possible by Gawsworth's exhaustive memory of which documents found among Shiel's cluttered archive had already been published, and which hadn't. "A live wire, he, young! and live!" is how Shiel described his protégé, "who fumbles like the bee among my written things, and knowing wondrously all that I have published, if he comes upon aught unpublished, utters sound of discovery." Thanks to Gawsworth, entire pieces — even entire genres — were being unearthed and assembled for print. "I never dreamt that I had written poems," Shiel marvelled, "but he has contrived to discover a surprising number."[↓]

> Their friendship extended beyond literature. When Gawsworth realized that Shiel insisted on taking his nightly jogs along unlit roads in the Sussex countryside, he gave Shiel a special belt with a light on the back so that the elder writer wouldn't get struck by passing cars.

Once these pieces were polished, Gawsworth used his growing number of connections to sneak them into print. In 1933, he had married Barbara Kentish, who worked on the *Daily Mail*'s society page, and she helped Gawsworth land a job compiling a series of pulp anthologies with interchangeable titles like *Thrills, Crimes, and Mysteries* (1935), *Thrills* (1936), and *Crimes, Creeps, and Thrills* (1936), which were produced by newspaper companies by the tens of thousands and given out to their subscribers as gifts at Christmastime. Gawsworth's name wasn't always included on the title pages of these anthologies, but his presence was hard to miss in the tables of contents. *Crimes, Creeps, and Thrills*, for instance, contained two stories credited to Gawsworth as a co-writer, and two to Shiel and "Fytton Armstrong" — Gawsworth's little-known birth name, which in this context became the real alias. ("Fytton Armstrong" was even given a separate biographical note in the anthology's list of contributors.) These pieces were billed as collaborations, but in reality Gawsworth was lifting unfinished scraps from Shiel's desk and filling in the gaps himself with the novelist's blessing. "He would recruit unpublished tales from his literary friends," his cousin R.F.A. Jackson remembered, "paying £15 to £20 each, making up the rest with his own effusions under various pseudonyms, [and] pocketing the difference."

It's not known when Gawsworth first learned about Redonda, though the story would have been in the public record by the time he started working for Andrew Block. But his conception of royalty in exile was equally informed by one of the regulars he saw around Soho: a pagan poet who walked around the neighbourhood carrying a book of parchment deeds that proved, supposedly, that he was the one true King of Poland.

Geoffrey Wladislas Vaile de Montalk was born in New Zealand and arrived in London (leaving behind a wife and young child) to fulfill his dream of becoming a poet. But those plans were thwarted when a copy of his manuscript of lewd verse, including a poem called "Here Lies John Penis," was shown to police. Montalk was convicted of libel and sentenced to six months in prison. The trial was another tabloid sensation, as Montalk took delight in mocking the legal process, wearing sandals to court, swearing his allegiance to Apollo rather than the Bible, and performing a Roman salute in the courtroom. The trial's implications for freedom of expression, meanwhile, were serious enough to draw defenders including Virginia and Leonard Woolf, who organized meetings at their home to establish a fund for appealing the conviction. Upon his release in 1932, Montalk—or "Count Potocki," as he now insisted on calling himself—dedicated himself to publicly and defiantly rejecting the English society that had wronged him. He now dressed in long medieval-style silk gowns and bestowed impressive-sounding jobs in his future Polish government upon those in his extended social circle.

Gawsworth had first met Count Potocki in simpler times: before the latter's imprisonment, and before the former had changed his name to mark the dawn of his new life as a poet. But when Gawsworth witnessed Potocki's new faux-royal persona for the first time, he was completely transfixed. Friends say he talked about nothing else for days.

KINGDOM COME 9

SEVERAL AREAS of Gawsworth's life were starting to converge. His ambitions as a writer and publisher, his longing to be part of a literary group, and his hunger for validation without compromise: all of these were blending together in his mind into one big puzzle. In Count Potocki, however, Gawsworth saw a potential solution. By reinventing himself as the exiled King of Poland, Potocki had inverted his outsider status, reframing it not as a mark of rejection but rather a defiant flourish of independence — *You can't fire me, I quit.* Plus, through his haphazard appointment system, Potocki got to pick and choose who was admitted into his royal court, and who was forced to wait outside. Gawsworth liked this arrangement. And it just so happened that one of his friends had a kingdom of his own that he wasn't doing much with.

We don't know whether Shiel's father ever gave his son any instructions in the way of succession planning. If the Kingdom of Redonda was meant to be handed down via typical methods, then Shiel's children would have been first in line. But he wasn't in regular contact with any of his three kids, including Kenneth, his only son. More importantly, Redonda wasn't a topic of any interest in Shiel's life to that point. When Gawsworth first told Shiel that he was interested in taking over the kingdom, the story of Redonda was still more holes than fabric—which was just how Gawsworth, who already knew how to take Shiel's discarded notes and turn them into a compelling story, preferred it.

In the annals of Redondan lore, there are few dates more significant than October 1, 1936. That was the day Gawsworth and Shiel met at the novelist's home in Sussex, which he had nicknamed L'Abri, or *the shelter*. L'Abri was a two-storey cottage in a tucked-away corner of Horsham, a market town about forty miles south of London. The visit started as a routine social call, for which the novelist Edgar Jepson was also present. But when their conversation turned towards Redonda, the seventy-one-year-old Shiel informed Gawsworth, twenty-four, that he agreed to his request. Gawsworth was now next in line for the Redondan throne. For such a momentous occasion, however, Shiel's word alone wasn't enough. This required ceremony. A pen knife was thus produced, at which point both men cut open their right wrists and pressed them together, commingling their blood and officially sealing the deal. Shiel then pulled out a sheet of special notepaper and wrote out a contract:

> We hereby proclaim that our most noble puissant
> Terence Ian Fytton Armstrong, "John Gawsworth"
> Prince of Our Blood, Poet Laureate of our Kingdom,
> succeeds us as Monarch of our Island Kingdom of
> Rodundo. Our sovereignty, upon our death, is his
> possession to be conferred by him on his death
> unto such of his blood as he appoints.

The contract was signed by both parties and witnessed by Jepson, who had recently — perhaps that very evening — joined the Redondan ranks himself. At Gawsworth's request, Shiel had dubbed Jepson the Duke of Wedrigo, a reference to Shiel's childhood in Montserrat. The wedrigo was both a large, real-life animal (nicknamed "the devil bird") found in the area, as well as a legendary beast whose cries were said to announce which person was next to die. Shiel had previously mentioned the wedrigo in his novel *Children of the Wind*, but this is the first known instance of him bestowing a Redondan title onto one of his peers.

With the written agreement and blood pact in place, the Kingdom of Redonda now had its first real succession plan. For Shiel, this had benefits that went beyond the amusements of an idle afternoon. He understood that there was value in aligning himself, in a binding yet still playful capacity, with such an energetic young advocate. And for Gawsworth, Redonda was a way of forging a stronger personal connection with one of his heroes. But the mysterious, distant island also held its own appeal. Gawsworth's love of London may have been well documented, but he was far from enamoured with England as a country, alternately pledging his allegiance to the Jacobites, Sinn Féin, Indian nationalists, and French republicans. *English*, noted his friend Ian Fletcher, was "his prime word of contempt." His poetic sensibility was clearly out of step with many of the country's readers. Plus, he had a strong interest in titles and the aura of legitimacy they projected.[↓]

> Later in life, Gawsworth spent years petitioning a friend who taught at an American university to give him a degree and took the friend's gentle refusal as an act of personal betrayal.

Redonda offered Gawsworth a chance to shed his unglamorous past and start anew, in an alternate reality in which he was no longer the misfit. Instead, his kingdom could be a place populated exclusively by his friends and inspirations, where neglected forms of culture could flourish and, most importantly, where he alone made the rules. Like Count Potocki before him, Gawsworth realized that by becoming fantasy royalty, he could give his actual life new purpose.

BUT FIRST, Gawsworth had business to attend to in England. One unexpected by-product of idolizing an older generation of writers was that Gawsworth grew uncomfortably aware of the dire straits many of them were in financially. A young man, full of energy, might be able to simply write his way out of debt; for an author in his sixties or seventies, whose best-known work was decades behind him and no longer in print, this was far more difficult. Gawsworth felt compelled to help however he could.

His preferred method was simply to republish the elder writers' work, either via the anthologies he edited for the newspaper companies or through his own Twyn Barlwm Press. "Most writers are too busy to spare time giving aid to others," one acquaintance recalled later. But not Gawsworth, who "put everybody into print who deserved it." He also petitioned the British government on these writers' behalf for pensions from the Civil List, which were given out to artists and scientists around the country in recognition of their service. Eventually, Gawsworth was able to secure pensions for both Machen and Shiel; the latter, from 1935, included as support a signature from Virginia Woolf.

"The faintest whisper that told of a writer in straits alerted him like a foxhound," Lawrence Durrell wrote of Gawsworth.

"A mixture of ferocity and brute determination irradiated his features. He would drop everything and work night and day until he found some help for the writer in question." In his travels around London, Gawsworth was constantly checking in on older authors, asking whether they needed any help and then taking their cases to groups like the Royal Society of Literature directly. One weekend he impulsively took a train out to Buckinghamshire, just because he had a hunch that Arthur Machen was low on money. (He was correct.) Gawsworth also started gathering material for a full-fledged biography of Machen, which he hoped would help rejuvenate interest in the aging writer's works.

He didn't just advocate for his friends, either. Once, as a joke, Durrell suggested that the well-known poets W.H. Auden and Stephen Spender were living in poverty and quietly starving. Gawsworth despised both men's work, but his eyes widened when he heard of their misfortunes, and he'd nearly taken off down the street before Durrell could admit he was kidding. He may have scorned compromise when it came to aesthetics, but in his pursuit of financial justice Gawsworth was surprisingly democratic.

One reason he was so successful in these efforts was that Gawsworth had already built up a certain amount of institutional reputation. His work as an editor and anthologist, plus his numerous volumes of poetry, led to him being the youngest fellow ever elected to the Royal Society of Literature. This was no small feat: as Durrell mused, "In those days one had to be a hundred before achieving such an apotheosis." Gawsworth's ability to get the attention of the media, meanwhile, was also already apparent. He bragged to the *New York Times* that he had read 26,000 poems in order to assemble *Fifty Years of Modern Verse*; in reality, the anthology was merely an expanded and slightly repurposed reprint of *Known Signatures*, minus the fiery introduction.

Towards the end of the decade, with a second global war looming and then suddenly in full force around him, Gawsworth's own poetry turned darker. He was starting to shake free of his influences—"the counterfeit nineties diction was now gone," noted the critic Steve Eng, "along with most of the Georgian staleness"—but along with a more mature voice came a new streak of cruelty. In the early 1930s, Gawsworth was producing starry-eyed poems like "Carpe Diem," in which the narrator asks, "Do you not know that all narrated bliss / Is but a fingersnap to your next kiss?" By the end of the decade, however, he felt more at home in darkness. A poem like "Advice of Juan" found Gawsworth decidedly in goth mode, destroying what he loves in the name of art:

> I am a vampire of love
> And gorge upon it.
> I fret a fury
> And erupt a sonnet.
>
> In selfish arrogance
> I crush the mood
> Between black wings
> And spill what is my food.

This brooding Juan character appeared in Gawsworth's poems beginning with his 1940 collection *The Mind of Man*. In "Reformation of Juan," Gawsworth writes, "I have of late the rags of virtue donned / And they become my fashion not at all." These poems were, perhaps, an early trial run for his royal persona, King Juan I, which Gawsworth would adopt upon his ascension to the Redondan throne a few years later. But with England under near-daily siege from German bombs during the Blitz, this version of Juan was darker, more pessimistic, and altogether less certain about what the future had in store.

EVENTUALLY, Gawsworth decided to put his writing career on hold and enlist in the military. The army rejected him on medical grounds, but in 1941 he was able to enrol, under his birth name, in the Royal Air Force. Before leaving, Gawsworth took care to pre-emptively bolster his literary reputation just in case he was killed in action. The introduction to his collection *Legacy to Love* more than hinted that it could be Gawsworth's final book, with the final lines of the last poem doubling as a potential epitaph:

> So I must be considered one
> Who fought to save his farm and field
> And left his shy place in the sun
> To prove not even poets yield[↓]

Gawsworth was sent to North Africa, where he quickly distinguished himself and was promoted to flying officer. But, as ever, his interests lay more in literature than anything he found on the battlefield. While in Algiers, Gawsworth discovered the world of North African poetry and spent hours rooting around for it in whatever shops or abandoned houses he wandered past. He visited local writers in the hospital, and—in one instance—a French airman and poetry fan

---

Of course, as Steve Eng has pointed out, Gawsworth was a proud urbanite who had exactly zero experience with either field or farm.

Gawsworth in uniform.

flew all the way across the desert just to meet *him*. In Tunisia, meanwhile, Gawsworth's literary reputation extended far enough that he was welcomed into the capital by a royal escort of lancers, courtesy of the bey himself. Gawsworth was then transferred to Cairo, where he came across a cluster of British soldier-poets who continued writing and publishing even while on active duty. One of them was Gawsworth's old friend Lawrence Durrell, who was now working as a press attaché for the British embassy. The men called themselves the Salamanders and published an occasional magazine under the same name. Gawsworth was introduced to the group in 1942, and it wasn't long before he'd whipped them into shape as a formal club. "John, in fact, had a great fondness for institutions of all kinds," wrote G.S. Fraser, a Scottish poet and Salamander. Fraser noted that Gawsworth was inordinately proud of his wartime titles and accolades, and called him "good but dangerous company." The first time the two met, in a pub, Fraser correctly identified Gawsworth's odd habit of passing his beer over a glass of water as an eighteenth-century Jacobite ritual paying tribute to King James III and VIII. "But hist!" Gawsworth replied approvingly, tapping his crooked nose. "We are observed."

From there, the pair logged long sessions at the bar dashing off poems together, with Gawsworth chattering all the while. As Fraser remembered it:

He talked, while he wrote, but not about his poetry.
"Here I am," he would say humorously, "a pore
scruffy sergeant, a pore gorblimey, and me wife,
God bless 'er, is an orficer of field rank in the ATS"
(When John was in a good mood, he tended to
talk in this way, in stage Cockney.) "Stow it away,
George, stow it away. I got millions of 'em. Millions
of poems at home. Write 'em on little scraps of piper
and stow 'em in an old tin trunk." Another sip of
brandy and more concentrated scribbling. "What
rhymes with 'diaphanous,' George?" I would pause
and think. "'Cacophonous,'" I would say, "nearly."
"Nearly ain't good enough for the old traditional
school. Cacophonous, eh? And what rhymes with
'dastard,' you old unutterable, you!"

At other times, however, Gawsworth was more difficult to
deal with. His moods were subject to sudden change, and
his dependence on alcohol sometimes left him unsure as to
the current state of his many shifting loyalties. Once, during
a shared cab ride, Gawsworth fell asleep for fifteen minutes
and woke up in a particularly irritable mood. When one of
his companions happened to say something complimentary
towards England, Gawsworth, now in full Irish Republican
mode, was so offended that he flung his door open and rolled
out of the moving vehicle. By the time the cab circled back,
Gawsworth had already limped away, defiant, and wound up
spending the night in a rough part of Cairo with his hotel-
room furniture pressed up against the door for safety.

From Egypt, Gawsworth was reassigned to Italy and then
to India. His bibliographic streak was undiminished in the
face of so much travel; if anything, he seemed energized by

the new traditions and poetic cultures he witnessed. From 1943 to 1945, he published several new booklets of poetry while on active duty and continued charming the locals wherever he went. While in Italy, Gawsworth wrote poems in the same room where Keats died and visited the philosopher-turned-politician Benedetto Croce; in Calcutta he met the publishers who would bring out a six-volume collected works as well as another anthology, *Fifty Modern Poems by Forty Famous Poets*. "Gawsworth always seemed hovering on the verge of some romantic disaster," Fraser remembered later. "But all the news was good." To most of his friends, Gawsworth appeared so self-confident that by the time they all met up again in London in peacetime, Fraser believed him to be "less changed than any of us." Others, like Gawsworth's half-brother Mark Holloway, believed the war had left a deeper mark on him than he let on.

FOLLOWING THE END of World War II, Gawsworth was eager to rejoin his old literary scene, and upon his return to London he fell in with a group of writers gallivanting around a series of pubs near Soho: the booze- and story-soaked district known as Fitzrovia.

Named after the Fitzroy Tavern, a nineteenth-century pub on the corner of Charlotte and Windmill Streets, the Fitzrovians were a loose assortment of creative types whose individual members came and went over the years. The group's origins dated back decades earlier, but it didn't acquire its name until after World War II, at which point its regulars included Dylan Thomas, Nina Hamnett, Augustus John, and Julian Maclaren-Ross; visiting celebrities like Pablo Picasso were also said to drop by whenever they passed through town. The first reporter to mention Fitzrovia in print described it as "a world of outsiders, down-and-outs, drunks, sensualists, homosexuals and eccentrics." Gawsworth fit right in.

It wasn't hard to see what drew Gawsworth to the Fitzrovians. They may not have shared his taste in literature, but they were bold, brash, and always up for another pint. They were also suckers for self-mythology and took delight in making their gatherings sound grander than they really were. Historian Hugh David described Fitzrovia as fundamentally a "district of the mind" and a "dream-kingdom," and if that sounded simpatico with Redonda, there was an even more direct connection. When the idea of Fitzrovia was first conceived, in the early twentieth century, it was meant to be a place to reimagine bohemianism in the wake of the Oscar Wilde trial—the same trial that had sent M.P. Shiel onto a new career path.

Not everyone in Fitzrovia was enamoured with Gawsworth, however. The best-known writer to emerge from the post-war cohort was Thomas, whose private letters contain no positive words about Gawsworth and several negative ones. "Gawsworth would be a standing joke if he weren't completely supine," the Welsh poet wrote before the war; later on he called Gawsworth a "leftover, yellow towelbrain of the nineties soaked in stale periods."[↓] Others felt that it was Gawsworth's personality, not his poetics, that was the real problem—and drinking only made it worse. The biographer and essayist Derek Stanford described Gawsworth as "a violent man, fantasist, and alcoholic" who belittled fellow writers in public and harassed women in private. "There was also some faint suggestion of Hitler about him,"

The feeling ran both ways: in his own diary, Gawsworth called Thomas "anaemic diarrhoea" and "a Welsh slag-heap."

added Stanford in his memoir, *Inside the Forties*. "Was it in his eyes, I wonder?"

As Gawsworth settled back into his familiar roles, he became increasingly sensitive about anyone who he felt was disrespecting him. His temper, already apt to blow from minor provocations, grew even shorter. Again, alcohol was a consistent factor. There are stories from these years of Gawsworth taking off his scarf and trying to choke out a fellow committee member over a small miscommunication at a poetry meeting. Another time Gawsworth thought he saw the painter Lucian Freud laughing at his outfit—Gawsworth had taken to wearing the uniform of a French admiral around town—so he pulled out the sword he happened to be carrying and chopped a branch off of the artist's magnolia plant as payback.

MEANWHILE, up in L'Abri, Shiel's health was failing at last. After signing Redonda over to Gawsworth in 1936, word of his peculiar kingdom had reached the British press, who were eager to write about it. "I sat next to a king at the Poets' Club dinner—grey-haired, distinguished-looking King Philip I of Redonda," began a piece in the *Daily Sketch*. "In private life he is Mathew Phipps Shiel, novelist. His—I think he said 50th—novel, 'The Young Men Are Coming,' has just been published." Other stories soon followed, under headlines like "Author Is King of Isle His Father Seized with Own Navy" and "Island King Now Lives in a Cottage." Shiel was willing to indulge these journalists, even making jokes about misplacing his crown behind a pile of books, because he figured any press would also raise interest in his writing. Ironically, in the *Daily Sketch* story containing improbable-sounding details about a distant Caribbean kingdom, King Felipe's tallest tale was how many books he'd written.

During the war years, Shiel lived alone in his candle-lit cottage, tinkering on manuscripts but not publishing anything new. When it came to money and supplies, he relied almost entirely on his government pension, as well as the occasional care packages he received from a couple of devoted overseas fans. His beloved running regimen, meanwhile, had shrunk to just a mile per day, if he was lucky, and he had pulleys installed on the ceiling of his bedroom to help hoist him out of bed each morning. Shiel's reputation in the literary world had once again faded, and this time he lacked proof of his own heyday. When his second bibliographer, A. Reynolds Morse, asked for details about particular titles, Shiel replied that he didn't know and couldn't check. "What a formidable list of my books you send," he wrote, "which I seem to have written at one time or another, but I have a copy of hardly any of them."

Even in his old age, however, Shiel was determined to finish the book that he believed would be his masterwork: a novel called *Jesus* that audaciously reimagined the Gospel of Luke. Shiel had already spent a full decade working on it, re-translating the gospel from its original Greek in an effort to restore facts that he believed had been ignored—among them, that Lazarus and Paul the Apostle were the same person. H.G. Wells, who had once been one of Shiel's harshest critics, read an early draft of the first chapter and found it "very interesting." By then, the manuscript had already ballooned to 145,000 words, and no publisher would take it on. Shiel continued tinkering, and in late 1946 considered the manuscript finished once again—only to then lose the twenty-one notebooks that comprised its first half. Not long afterwards, Shiel fell seriously ill and was taken to St. Richard's Hospital in

Chichester. He passed away on February 17, 1947, at the age of eighty-one.

News of Shiel's death took Gawsworth completely by surprise. During their last visit together at L'Abri, just a few months earlier, Shiel had handed Gawsworth the final text for a new essay collection entitled *Science, Life and Literature*, and the pair had made plans to get together again soon to polish and republish more of Shiel's old manuscripts. Now Gawsworth's friend, collaborator, and mentor was dead. The younger writer was devastated.

A few days later, the *Times* printed an obituary for Shiel that was written by Gawsworth and published anonymously. Shiel, Gawsworth wrote, was "a master of fantasy less widely known than he deserved," who wrote in a bizarre yet original style, and who "tossed the world about in his dreams, not with a juggler's detachment, but with a sense now bitter, now exultant of the tragedy and splendour that enwrap the *mysterium tremendum* of existence." The published version of Gawsworth's piece didn't mention Redonda, but the story of the kingdom had already grown large enough to cross the Atlantic. Shiel's obituary in the *New York Times* actually led with an anecdote about Redonda before going on to describe Shiel as a man "noted for ingenuity of plot and weirdness of character."

Shiel's funeral was held the following week at Golders Green but was a sparse affair, with just thirteen people in attendance. The eulogy was delivered by the poet Edward Shanks, who praised *The Purple Cloud* and compared Shiel to Herman Melville, another "'one-book' man" whose true catalogue ran far deeper. Shanks admitted that Shiel's reputation was then at a low point. But he had faith that *The Purple Cloud*, at least, would resurface someday:

For a number of years his best-known book was out of print, like most if not all of the others. Yet when it was at last revived it was met with sincere enthusiasm. Whether it is now obtainable or not I do not know. I dare say it is not. But it will be revived again and it will again strike those who have not known it with the peculiarly wild yet disciplined force of its imaginations. There will be more tributes than this.

One immediate tribute was stranger than anything Shanks likely had in mind. Following the funeral, Shiel's remains were cremated and intended to be scattered. Instead, Gawsworth took the ashes for himself. After decades spent acquiring his mentor's books, Gawsworth was now, in Steve Eng's words, "literally a Shiel collector." On his way home from the funeral, Gawsworth stopped in at a pub with his wife, Barbara, for a drink. Gawsworth asked the bartender to put Shiel's ashes up on a shelf for safekeeping, but later looked up and saw, with horror, that the cardboard box containing them had gotten wet, and some of the contents were spilling out—directly into a salmon sandwich that was being prepared for a different customer. This happened to be a well-known theatre critic who hated Gawsworth, so the couple decided to say nothing until they left, at which point they triumphantly told the critic what—and who—was garnishing his lunch. Back at home, Gawsworth moved Shiel's ashes into a tin and placed it on his mantlepiece. For years afterwards, whenever a noteworthy guest would drop by his home for dinner, Gawsworth would bring the container of ashes to the table and sometimes even decorate their meals with a pinch of Shiel. His guests went along with this macabre ritual largely out of politeness to their eccentric host.

Gawsworth with Shiel's ashes.

In his will, Shiel named Gawsworth his official literary executor, which meant that he now controlled the fate of all of his late mentor's works. It was a job that Gawsworth had already been performing, in an unofficial capacity, for years. What the will *didn't* mention, however, was the kingdom. Perhaps Shiel didn't think Redonda important enough to merit mentioning in a legally binding document; perhaps he considered the blood pact and signed proclamation proof enough that the kingdom and the executorship were in steady and uncontested hands.

Either way, the day Gawsworth had dreamed about for more than a decade had finally come to pass. While Shiel had ascended to the Redondan throne at the insistence of his enterprising father and the local bishop, Gawsworth simply crowned himself. The man born Terence Ian Fytton Armstrong also took this opportunity to give himself yet another new name: King Juan I. From that day forward, Gawsworth would take the story that Shiel had begun and carry it to greater heights than his mentor had ever dreamed of.

A MOTLEY LOT 10

GAWSWORTH WASTED little time putting his stamp on the kingdom he'd inherited. A few months after Shiel's funeral, King Juan I celebrated his thirty-fifth birthday by issuing the Kingdom of Redonda's first ever royal proclamation.

This document, which has become known as State Paper I, put the scope of the Redondan project into focus for the first time.⌄ Printed on a sheaf of eighteenth-century paper and distributed privately among friends from his "Court-in-Exile" in Kensington, State Paper I presented the first iteration of what Gawsworth called his "intellectual aristocracy." The names on the list covered many of Shiel's friends and colleagues, but also included several people who were strictly Gawsworth's peers. The highest position in the Redondan realm was arch-duchy, and this was bestowed upon Arthur Machen, who was well acquainted with both kings and who himself would pass away a few months later. Next in the hierarchy was the title of grand duchy, all six recipients of which had ties to Shiel: Kate Gocher (his neighbour at L'Abri),

All three of Gawsworth's state papers are reproduced in their entirety in Appendix 1.

Victor Gollancz (one of his publishers), Annamarie V. Miller (an overseas pen pal), A. Reynolds Morse (his bibliographer), Edward Shanks (who delivered the eulogy at his funeral), and Carl Van Vechten (his American advocate). Then came thirty "Duchies of the Realm," and it was here that the logic became more difficult to decipher. Some of the names had ties to Shiel, such as Arthur Ransome and Grant Richards, while others were known only to Gawsworth—his fellow Salamander John Waller received a duchy, but so, curiously, did his Fitzrovian rival Dylan Thomas. Even in these initial appointments, Gawsworth was intentionally blurring the line between fantasy and reality. Ellery Queen was a pseudonym for a pair of American crime writers, as well as their fictional character of the same name. It's unclear which of these personas was meant to receive the Redondan duchy named in State Paper I—the Queen name appears in quotation marks—though Shiel did once sell a story in the 1940s to the real-life pair for their magazine, which was also named after the character. Finally, King Juan confirmed a series of eight duchies he had previously assigned on Shiel's behalf while Shiel was still alive. These included the antiquarian bookseller Bertram Rota, Edgar Jepson (who had witnessed the blood pact at L'Abri, but had since passed away), and Lawrence Durrell.

State Paper I marked the first real effort to establish a conception of Redonda that extended beyond a lonely king-in-exile, and it's worth pausing here to consider Gawsworth's motivation in issuing it. Why did the proclamation take this particular format? And why this stuffy tone? If you knew nothing else about Redonda, you might come away from the document believing that Gawsworth took this whole kingdom thing deadly serious—an impression that would not reflect well on Gawsworth's overall grasp on reality. And yet nothing could be further from the truth. On a fundamental level, Gawsworth knew he was putting something ridiculous into the world. But he had also decided that Redonda only worked if you never broke character. No more of Shiel's self-deprecating stance towards the kingdom; Redonda under King Juan would be defined by a total, straight-faced commitment to the bit. Beginning with State Paper I, every document, every public statement, and every ounce of Redondan public spectacle was to be delivered in strict kayfabe.

Even better, once this excessively formal tone of voice was established, Gawsworth discovered that he was then free to be as silly as he liked with the particulars. He could convincingly hand out absurd titles like "The Duke of Guano" (to novelist Philip Lindsay) because *he* appeared to be taking it seriously — and because they appeared after an entire paragraph of floral, official-sounding preamble: "His Majesty is Graciously pleased to Confirm the following Appointments, Admitted under His Patents as Regent in the Reign of His Royal Predecessor . . ." The interstitial text was so boring that it automatically passed muster as legitimate royal-speak.

But that didn't mean that Gawsworth wasn't in on the joke. He was the one telling it. And because he never broke character, the new inductees to the Redondan court tended to want to play along with him. The correct response was not to laugh — which would dispel the effect — but rather to quietly nod and keep the story going. G.S. Fraser had intuited this tendency when he first met Gawsworth in that bar in wartime Cairo. Now his signature adorned the bottom of every copy of State Paper I as Redonda's official chamberlain.

Gawsworth leaned into his new persona off the page as well. Whenever he encountered his old friend Count Potocki on the street, the two would now greet one another as peers: "Good morning, Poland!" "Good morning, Redonda!" Gawsworth's ascension to his mock throne dovetailed with a personality trait that, in the past, had confused some of his friends. For someone who voiced such vehement disdain for the British monarchy, Gawsworth had a strangely persistent royal streak. Steve Eng points out that in the various magazines he edited, Gawsworth published articles about "a lady novelist who briefly became 'king' (not queen) of an island, about a crackpot's attempt to become the king of New Zealand, and about the pleasures of owning your own island" — a trio of stories that look an awful lot like a Redonda starter kit. Years earlier, Gawsworth had edited an anthology of poems written by English kings and queens called *The Muse of Monarchy*, leading some in his social circle to believe that he was angling for the job of poet laureate. Gawsworth kept up this behaviour even when it appeared nobody was watching. On the anniversary of the execution of King Charles I, he would get up at dawn and walk down to Charing Cross to place a white rose on the statue of Charles on horseback.

It is a testament to the eccentricity of Gawsworth's character that his Redondan titles were received with the same good cheer with which they had been assigned. Durrell was flattered at his new designation of Duke of Cervantes Pequeña (or "Little Cervantes," perhaps as a mock-diminutive foil to Bertram Rota's Duke of Sancho), but joked that his official documentation never arrived, on account of King Juan being once again short on cash. "To this day I am still lacking armorial bearings, and do not know what the devices on my shield should be," Durrell wrote years later. "We are a motley lot, we dukes of Redonda." Gawsworth's scattershot organizational skills meant that some received less than that, not even learning of their appointment to the court until years after the fact. Everett Bleiler was a science-fiction bibliographer who had never met Shiel or Gawsworth—but who one day walked into Andrew Block's bookshop in the early 1950s and was surprised to see his own name listed in a framed copy of State Paper II, where Block's name also appeared. For Gawsworth, handing out titles was serious business. But behind the theatrical stiff upper lip, it was also an awful lot of fun. Under his entry in *Who's Who*, the British reference book, Gawsworth listed his hobby as "creating nobility."

AT THE SAME TIME that the kingdom began to occupy more of Gawsworth's attention, his literary career was reaching its apex. In the years following World War II, Gawsworth edited three different poetry magazines, often at the same time. Most noteworthy among them was the *Poetry Review*, which Gawsworth took over as editor in 1948, succeeding novelist Muriel Spark when the magazine's board decided that her approach was too radical. The board installed Gawsworth to help re-right the ship, and the proud conservative went on to edit the *Review*'s next twenty issues. He also achieved the poet's equivalent of the brass ring when Sidgwick & Jackson published his *Collected Poems* in late 1947—an honour all the more impressive considering Gawsworth was still in his mid-thirties at the time. The collection was released to positive reviews, but unfortunately, the achievement remained largely symbolic, as much of the book's print run suffered water damage while in storage and had to be destroyed by the publisher.

Gawsworth's prowess as a book collector, meanwhile, led to him managing the literary estates of several other deceased writers in addition to Shiel. As in other areas of life, his reputation preceded him, and a joke started to make its way around Fleet Street: if you saw Gawsworth more than twice in one day, you would be dead within the year, and he would become *your* literary executor, too.

In the 1950s, however, signs began to appear that the consequences of Gawsworth's reckless behaviour were catching up to him. He edited new editions of Lord Tennyson and John Milton but was also fired from his job as editor of the *Poetry Review*—allegedly to save money, but in fact because his dependence on alcohol had become too pronounced to ignore. Mark Holloway, his half-brother, remembered Gawsworth drunkenly emerging from the pub one afternoon only to realize he'd forgotten what day it was and speeding off in a taxi to rush the next issue of a magazine off to the printer. Meanwhile, Gawsworth had gotten divorced and then remarried, this time to a French furniture designer named Estelle Hayward, and she often became the target of his drunken wrath. He regularly castigated Hayward in front of others as a "bloody French whore" and a "foul treacherous bitch" if she forgot to remind Gawsworth of a pending appointment or dared to suggest that the table might not need another bottle of wine.

With fewer prospects in front of him, Gawsworth began clinging to past accomplishments instead. When he was fired from a second magazine job, his successor walked into the office to find a depressed Gawsworth trying to cheer himself up by reading his own entry in *Who's Who*, which was already rapidly becoming out of date.

AS GAWSWORTH'S LITERARY CAREER sputtered, he turned to one of the few promotional tools still available to him: the Kingdom of Redonda. If he couldn't keep his name alive on the shelves of London's bookshops, he could at least do so via the press.

Gawsworth understood that, to a certain type of reporter—and in turn to a certain type of reader—Redonda was catnip. In a fiercely competitive news market, the story of a semi-fictitious kingdom, located in an exotic, faraway land but administrated by a group of writers and intellectuals scattered across London, was guaranteed to attract eyeballs. It was simply too good, and too strange, of a tale to pass up. In Shiel's later years, Gawsworth had watched his royal predecessor appear in the pages of multiple newspapers, the stories deemed newsworthy by the mere fact of the island kingdom's existence. Shiel went along with the media attention because it guaranteed at least a passing mention of his latest novel. Gawsworth, however, had nothing to promote but the kingdom itself.

One evening in June 1949, Gawsworth called his friend, the writer and publisher Jon Wynne-Tyson, complaining that he'd been arguing with his wife and they were low on groceries. Later that evening the obliging Wynne-Tyson showed up in a taxi, bearing, as he later put it, "milk, bread, bicarbonate of soda, liver salts, and youthful susceptibility." Once there, however, Wynne-Tyson discovered that Gawsworth intended to thank him by awarding him the title of Knight Commander with the Order of the Star of Redonda—and that he'd *also* invited a slew of reporters and photographers to document the event. Gawsworth opened the door clad in an old velvet smoking jacket that had once belonged to Shiel, and the ensuing ceremony took place in front of the container of Shiel's ashes while cameras from the *Evening News*, among others, snapped away. (Estelle, still fuming and now sporting a fresh black eye, stayed behind in the kitchen.) That same year, Leigh Vaughan-Henry, a composer who was also Gawsworth's one-time landlord, wrote a Redondan national anthem entitled "O God Who Gave Our Island Soil."[↓] And Colwyn Jestyn John Philipps, a peer twice over as the Viscount St. Davids in the UK and as a second Redondan Duke of Guano, designed the first Redondan flag—white, with a green ring around a yellow circle at the centre—thereby adding yet another item to its growing list of nation-building paraphernalia.

Each successive piece of Redondan regalia was a new tag on Gawsworth's ever-expanding communal joke, and it is easy to imagine King Juan roaring with approval when he was presented with the sketches or the sheet music for the first time. But these items also helped nudge the kingdom, whether intentionally or not, towards legitimization. Despite their comic intent, each of these markers was a small provocation towards the very idea of nationhood. Is Redonda a real country now? What about now? OK, how about *now?*

The media circus wasn't strictly for Gawsworth's sake, either. If a rising tide floats all boats, then the more publicity the Kingdom of Redonda received, the more Shiel's reputation was buoyed as well. Shiel had already suffered

During his lifetime, Vaughan-Henry was an acclaimed musician and critic who regularly appeared on the BBC. It wasn't until 2018 that author Tim Tate revealed that Vaughan-Henry was also "a diehard fascist and violent anti-Semite" who was a leading member in Hitler's British Fifth Column—a clandestine effort to overthrow the British government during World War II and then offer the country up to the Third Reich. In the years before the war, Vaughan-Henry travelled to Berlin to meet with Goebbels and Goering and signed an interview request with "Heil Hitler." While Gawsworth was serving overseas in the RAF, Vaughan-Henry was incarcerated at an MI5 facility on the Isle of Man. It's not known what, if anything, King Juan knew about this shocking chapter in his royal composer's life.

what A. Reynolds Morse called "an unaccountable mantle of obscurity" not once but twice during his lifetime: the decade of silence beginning in 1914, which included his stint in jail, and a more voluntary withdrawal beginning in 1937, when he was holed up in L'Abri working on *Jesus*. Now that Shiel was dead, it fell to others to keep his memory alive. Morse, in addition to being a wealthy American entrepreneur who collected paintings by Salvador Dalí, was also one of Shiel's biggest fans. Not long after Shiel's death, he

Gawsworth and Wynne-Tyson.
(Evening News, 1949.)

published *The Works of M.P. Shiel*, a comprehensive bibliography that itemized and annotated Shiel's "honeyed, frenzied madness." The majority of his novels had already become difficult to find in any edition. Without posthumous intervention, Morse worried that Shiel's "royal heritage may soon become dispersed beyond recovery."

In that sense, Gawsworth's Redondan gambit paid off immediately, as two new collections of his mentor's work appeared in print early in the reign of King Juan I. *The Best Short Stories of M.P. Shiel* was published by Victor Gollancz in 1948, followed two years later by *Science, Life and Literature*. Both titles were edited by Gawsworth himself, and the latter was a wide-ranging essay collection that led off with a reworked version of "About Myself": the first time the story of Shiel's coronation had appeared between boards.

Meanwhile, King Juan's court was still growing. Two additional state papers, issued on Gawsworth's birthday in 1949 and 1951, respectively, added dozens of new members, most of whom were more connected to Gawsworth than Shiel. The vast majority did, however, have some sort of connection to the world of arts and culture: publishers Alfred A. Knopf and Martin Secker were recognized, as were writers like Dorothy L. Sayers, J.B. Priestley, and Julian Maclaren-Ross. Other titles Gawsworth simply handed out in exchange for a favour, such as the recipient sending him copies of letters from Shiel for a biography that Gawsworth was then thinking of writing. In 1951, to celebrate his thirty-ninth birthday and the issue of State Paper III, Gawsworth held an investiture at a bar in Ewell, an hour outside of London. He invited all of the new members of the Redondan court to join him for an in-person ceremony, and showed up wearing the same velvet smoking jacket and carrying the container of Shiel's ashes. However, this time few members showed up — an indication that the joke, or perhaps just the teller, was starting to get tired. One of those who did attend the party in Ewell was Robert Fabian, former superintendent of Scotland Yard, who was confused as to why he had been invited. "All I ever did was to buy the king a drink when he was broke," he told a reporter from the *Daily Mail*. Gawsworth's response: "No finer service could there be."

Once members accepted their positions in the Redondan court, King Juan decreed that those with a talent for poetry should then produce new works celebrating the kingdom. Many of these poems were written off the cuff, and an equal number seemed to be aided in their production by booze. John Heath-Stubbs, for instance, was offered a dukedom around 1950, but only on the condition that he compose a poem to Shiel's memory — and when said poem didn't appear promptly enough, Gawsworth called him in the middle of a house party to remind him of his promise. Heath-Stubbs went off to the bathroom, wrote a quick ode, and dictated it to Gawsworth over the phone. Dylan Thomas's surprising new role as the Duke of Gweno also came with a poetic obligation, and he, too, eventually came through.[†] Thomas dashed off a pair of short poems for Gawsworth one night in January 1953 at the Caves de France, a pub on Dean Street.

Gawsworth gave Thomas his title as a show of thanks for a complimentary story the latter had written about Shiel while still a teenaged reporter for the *South Wales Evening Post*. The two men hung around in similar circles for years, and Thomas even slept on Gawsworth's couch on occasion, but their feelings for one another never softened. As Gawsworth remembered in 1967, "Where have I not drunk with Dylan—still loathing each other's guts?"

One of them riffed on the confusion between Gawsworth's last name and Galsworthy's. The other was "Two Epigrams of Fealty," which includes the following Redondan tribute:

> KING JUAN ADVOCATES KING FELIPE
> She'll do this, she'll do that:
> People sigh in the local vat;
> But Shiel *is* this, and Shiel *is* that
> Cries the vocal King with his golden hat.

Pleased, Gawsworth had thirty copies of Thomas's poems printed and privately distributed them to other members of his court. For decades these poems were so little-known that they weren't listed in even the most thorough of Thomas's bibliographies.

AS THE LEGEND OF Redonda grew, Gawsworth's reputation began to shift, as people became more interested in him as a king than they ever had been in him as a poet. This appeal was in part due to his penchant for theatricality and spectacle, but again was exacerbated by alcohol. "The legend was tailor-made for the tap room," noted Jon Wynne-Tyson, "and there were easy pickings to be had from journalists and hangers-on who found themselves in the company of a writer-monarch with Caribbean connections." All around Soho, interested parties would wander from pub to pub in search of the drunken king. More often than not, they would find him.

In these situations, you never really knew which Gawsworth you were getting. One night he might be the volatile man who routinely threatened his wife, and the next he was the gregarious King Juan. At other times, he was merely drunk enough to be exploited. Reporters looking for an easy story knew they could buy Gawsworth drinks until he said something suitably sensational. Eventually, even regular citizens started hanging around Gawsworth in the hopes of catching the king's favour and having a Redondan title drunkenly bestowed upon them. "If one kept John's glass filled for the evening," according to one friend, "ennoblement followed — complete with scroll." Some who knew him chalked up his behaviour to an underlying yearning for human contact. "He didn't want to drink so much as he wanted to have friends," another friend remembered, noting that Gawsworth's shabby one-room apartment was too small to entertain in. Pubs were a lot roomier, and also had better menus.

By this point, Gawsworth's alcoholism could not be ignored. One day, after spending hours drinking with a friend, Gawsworth decided they should drop in on a private club where he was a member. This meant, among other things, signing both of their names into a guestbook located in the front hallway. But as soon as Gawsworth picked up the pen, swaying slightly, he faltered.

"Oh, come on, John, get on with it!" the friend said. "You know me — I'm Kenneth Hare!"

"Of course I know you're Kenneth Hare," Gawsworth replied irritably, "but who the hell am I?"

ON SATURDAY, JUNE 21, 1958, an unusual advertisement appeared on the front page of the *Times*. It ran within a group of classifieds ads, sandwiched between a woman looking for passengers for an upcoming car trip to Austria and a husband publicly distancing himself from his spendthrift wife ("she has no authority to pledge my credit"). This ad's message, by contrast, was short, cryptic, and instantly intriguing.

"CARIBBEAN KINGSHIP," it read, "with Royal pre-rogatives." Inquiries were to be sent to a P.O. box care of the newspaper. The asking price was one thousand guineas.

No further information was provided. The ad made no mention, for instance, of the exact territory in question, the current ruler, or the reason for the change. But these were revealed soon enough. In an effort to stay afloat financially, King Juan I had put Redonda up for sale.

GAWSWORTH'S CLASSIFIED AD was not the *Times*'s typical fare, but it had the intended effect. Interested parties ranged from average citizens all the way to Sweden's Prince Bertil Bernadotte, whose note of inquiry came along with a £50 deposit. There was so much interest, in fact, that Gawsworth found himself overwhelmed, with a difficult decision to make. Was he really going to do this? If so, who was the right person to succeed him as the third king of Redonda?

Gawsworth had made the decision to sell the kingdom a couple of weeks earlier, as he sat on his royal houseboat (complete with flag and crown) in Little Venice, a canal in London. Also present were John Waller, ex-Salamander and current Redondan home secretary, and Noel Whitcomb, the Duke of Bonafides. Not in attendance, however, was a single woman — a fact that had thrown Gawsworth, clad in Shiel's velvet jacket and a pair of blue straw sandals, into despair. "My dear fellow, we feel that our kingdom is slowly sinking," Gawsworth told Whitcomb in the royal third person. "The entire absence of women at our court bodes ill for our monarchy. In other words, good Bonafides, we are sunk."

If Redonda was, indeed, doomed to fall apart, the only solution was for Gawsworth to sell high, while the kingdom still had cachet with certain segments of the British public. As king, he believed this was well within his rights. Gawsworth needed the money, but he also claimed he needed the time: once freed from his Redondan duties, Gawsworth now planned to write a book documenting the entire history of the kingdom, from Shiel to the present day. "I will become plain John Gawsworth again and some good administrator can buy the monarchy," he said, "which will provide me with enough money to sit back and write the book." The trio marched down to the *Times* offices that afternoon to compose the ad, though it was delayed appearing in print because the newspaper first had to verify with the British Foreign Office that such a transaction was legally Gawsworth's to make. When another newspaper inquired, two years later, to verify the claim, the government responded: "Perhaps Mr. Armstrong *is* entitled to call himself king; we're not sure. In any case, if it makes him happy, why not? We're not really interested unless something big happens, such as the pigeons revolting . . ."

Once the ad appeared in print, it was picked up as newsworthy in its own right and was reported on in newspapers as far away as the United States, which only increased the number of potential buyers. As the inquiries continued pouring in, Gawsworth had more to consider than simply who was most qualified to run the kingdom in his absence. Redonda was, by his own design, supposed to be a place of culture and intellect — could he really just sell it to the highest bidder? Perhaps Gawsworth saw a glimmer of artistic potential in Prince Bertil of Sweden — the duo ended up having dinner together three separate times at London's Royal Automobile

Club to discuss the details of the purchase. Or perhaps he just wanted an excuse to cash the prince's deposit.

There was, however, one respondent to the ad who was less than pleased. William Reginald Hipwell was another former landlord of Gawsworth's who claimed that he couldn't sell the kingdom, because Gawsworth had already signed it over to *him*, four years earlier, in lieu of hundreds of pounds of late rent. Hipwell claimed the two had even made a blood pact to seal the deal, similar to the one Gawsworth and Shiel had made back in the 1930s, and had signed a contract that was to go into effect upon Gawsworth's death. Thus, by "irrevocable covenant," Redonda was already sold.

When he saw the notice in the *Times*, Hipwell sent his lawyer after Gawsworth. He wasn't interested in Redonda as a bastion of culture so much as the kingdom's ability, thus far untapped, to generate revenue: he wrote through his attorney that "there is considerable money in it, especially if I can do anything about the stamp concession." Faced with the threat of legal action, Gawsworth suspended his talks with the Swedish prince and withdrew his offer to sell the kingdom—but not before turning the controversy into yet another round of press coverage. "I was vulgarizing a noble kingdom," Gawsworth said to one reporter, by way of spin. "Now I would not sell it for the moon."

When he wasn't trying to sell the kingdom outright, Gawsworth did at times remember his duty to maintain and expand the Redondan court. When he met Lawrence Durrell's younger brother Gerald in a pub in Soho, Gawsworth immediately dubbed the writer and zookeeper Duke Angwantibo of Redonda—using a pencil, because he'd forgotten his sword at home. In 1959, Gawsworth watched a performance of *Let Them Eat Cake* at the Cambridge Theatre and was so

Gawsworth in middle age.

moved by the lead actors, the real-life couple Michael Denison and Dulcie Gray, that he decided to bestow titles upon each of them. The next day Gray received a call from a man who identified himself as the home secretary to King Juan I↓ and proposed an official ceremony onstage at the theatre that afternoon, following the matinee. As usual, Gawsworth had secretly alerted the press of his plans ahead of time, and a story about the newly christened Duke and Duchess of Essexa y Stebbingo duly appeared in the *Daily Telegraph* the next morning. Once again, Gawsworth's sword was absent. "It happens to be in pawn at the moment," he admitted.

IN 1962, John Gawsworth turned fifty years old. By this point, time had caught up to the mercurial poet, with the help of his more destructive habits. Gawsworth still maintained a youthful twinkle in his eye, but his thin frame had become bloated; his facial hair, too, had expanded, from the neat moustache of his youth to a full shaggy beard. He also suffered from a hernia and would soon resort to using a cane to stay upright. Gawsworth still hadn't published a new book since his *Collected Poems*, though he never stopped filling notebooks with material; to earn money, he flitted between

In case there was any doubt, this was almost assuredly Gawsworth himself on the line.

a series of unrelated jobs, including dishwasher, bartender, and archivist at an insurance company. To mark the occasion of his fiftieth birthday, however, Gawsworth's name was at last attached to a new anthology. This was the kind of project he had overseen countless times in the past, but this time he would have a different role: not as the book's editor, but rather its subject.

The idea was conceived by the poet and magazine editor Charles Wrey Gardiner, who sent out dozens of requests, to people all around the literary world, for short essays and remembrances about Gawsworth. In reply, Gardiner received a few dozen submissions, from loyal friends like Lawrence Durrell and Hugh MacDiarmid, as well as looser acquaintances who were happy to have their memories of King Juan recorded for posterity nonetheless. Some who were unable to write something official still sent admiring notes, like novelist Sylvia Townsend Warner, who fondly recalled Gawsworth's efforts to help struggling writers like Arthur Machen. Unfortunately, the full anthology was never published or even distributed privately. Gawsworth himself tried repackaging the material as a book tentatively entitled *Gawsworth — Poet: King*, but the literary agent he worked with reported back that its commercial prospects were nil.

A few years later, the fate of Redonda was thrown into flux again when Gawsworth's would-be successor, Reginald Hipwell, passed away in 1966. This returned the kingdom to Gawsworth's sole possession — or, as he interpreted it, made it his to sell once more. He had already been loudly threatening abdication, but a group of Redondan peers took him down to the pub and talked him out of it. Or at least they thought they had. In reality, Gawsworth immediately entered into a new blood pact, this time with Arthur John

Roberts, manager of the Alma, which was Gawsworth's preferred drinking establishment in his later years. ("He was in constant demand with visitors and reporters," Roberts later said of King Juan. "The Alma was his forum.") Their contract was signed on October 20, 1966, and was set to take effect the following February: exactly twenty years after Shiel's death. Gawsworth undoubtedly needed the money from the sale, which amounted to £1,000, paid in cash. One bookseller remembered Gawsworth at around this time, dashing out of a taxi with an armful of manuscripts, needing cash most pressingly to pay the meter that was still running. But the new contract was also a sign that Gawsworth knew he wouldn't be able to look after the kingdom for much longer.

THE END began with another eviction. In 1968, Gawsworth's landlord at 35 Sutherland Place—Gardiner, the same man who'd organized the fiftieth-birthday anthology—sold the apartment building to a new owner, who had considerably less patience for flaky tenants. The new landlord offered Gawsworth £100 to leave on the spot. Gawsworth was so desperate for money that he agreed, a decision that his neighbour John Heath-Stubbs felt was "disastrous."

On the day of Gawsworth's departure, his friend Jon Wynne-Tyson arrived with a six-foot trailer to help him gather his things. But it turned out there was little in the apartment worth packing up, save for a bunch of beat-up cardboard boxes containing what Wynne-Tyson "euphemistically" called Gawsworth's "remaining archive": notebooks, letters, press clippings, and assorted scraps covered in handwritten notes. Gawsworth still had the container of Shiel's ashes, as well as his old velvet smoking jacket, "from which," Wynne-Tyson noted, "a flurry of moths ascended as I shook it gingerly in the street." Despite his meagre possessions, Gawsworth insisted on taking his leave defiantly, and he clambered on top of the boxes in Wynne-Tyson's trailer, where he remained perched for the duration of the trip—which, it turned out, was just a few blocks to the front door of the Alma. Inside, Gawsworth held court as if nothing had changed, ordering a bottle of champagne for a table of friends who'd joined them and then insisting on singing the entire French national anthem before allowing it to be opened. At one point in the day Gawsworth asked an acquaintance to make some tea, then headed off to the bathroom. The man, however, mistook the container of Shiel's ashes sitting on the table for a tea caddy—"unsurprisingly," wrote Redondan historian Roger Dobson, "since it *was* a tea caddy, though a most elegant one"— and ended up preparing the group a pot of King Felipe himself.

From there, Gawsworth's situation only grew more dire. Without a permanent address, he didn't qualify for social security, or for the same Civil List pension for which he had previously lobbied for other writers over the years. He appealed to the friends he had left, particularly Eleanor Brill, his last significant romantic partner, whom he referred to as "Queen SJ," or *sub judice*, since they weren't married, for a temporary place to stay. When he couldn't find one, he resorted to sleeping in Hyde Park. On one of the last times Lawrence Durrell saw him, Gawsworth was pushing a baby carriage down Shaftesbury Avenue. Durrell was cheered to think that his old friend had finally settled down and had children. As he got closer, however, Durrell realized the carriage was full of empty beer bottles that Gawsworth was on his way to cash in.

Meanwhile, there were still questions of succession to resolve. Gawsworth had already sold Redonda to Arthur John Roberts of the Alma, but he was anxious about who would look after his literary estate—and, by extension, Shiel's—upon his death. Wynne-Tyson had agreed to look after the battered archive from his last apartment, which he duly transported to the attic of his home in Sussex. Some of Gawsworth's other pieces of Redondiana, however, were unsalvageable. Shiel's smoking jacket had been worn until it was threadbare, and decades of misadventures with the ashes had led to a similarly depleted end: when Wynne-Tyson's daughter asked to look inside the repurposed tea caddy, they discovered only a small pile of "mongrel ash," carelessly mixed with a set of Gawsworth's false teeth and a copy of a poem written by Heath-Stubbs for Shiel's centenary a few years earlier. "Friends are seriously concerned at the plight of John Gawsworth," began a piece in the *Times* in late 1969, noting that the poet had been seen wandering the streets of London "physically broken, sick and quite unfit for work." The story outlined the Redondan legend, including Gawsworth's now-abandoned tradition of awarding "imaginary titles" onto his court members on his birthday; it also mentioned a recent fundraising drive organized on Gawsworth's behalf by Ian Fletcher.

Fletcher was a poet and former Salamander, as well as the recipient of one of King Juan's original Redondan duchies (later upgraded to Duke of Urgel in State Paper III). In the years since, he had settled into a career teaching at the University of Reading. While Fletcher's fundraising efforts continued, Gawsworth moved in with the professor and his family, off and on, for the next year and a half. "He slept in our large living room," Fletcher wrote later, "and his constant accompaniment was a large bucket of several roles: comfort station, vomitorium and vessel of blood." As soon as the fund had raised enough to pay rent on a basic apartment,

Gawsworth was shown several options. But when he realized he wasn't being given full control over how the money was to be spent, he grew incensed and refused them all out of spite. In early 1970, Gawsworth received an unexpected letter from a well-wisher in Italy, who had read the story in the *Times* and wanted to help. Soon thereafter, Gawsworth arrived, unannounced, at the man's home outside of Florence, thanks to some funds only reluctantly handed over by Fletcher. "It is a real problem," Fletcher told the *Times* in a follow-up piece. "The money at present being held for him in England was really intended to provide him with a fixed address here." To Fletcher, Gawsworth needed stable housing and medical attention, not a vacation. But he conceded that Mediterranean sunshine — and a return to a country Gawsworth had fond memories of during the war — could have a restorative effect.

Two days later, however, Gawsworth collapsed and was taken to an Italian hospital, where he was treated for internal bleeding. "Tho' utterly broke," he wrote cheerfully to Wynne-Tyson from his hospital bed, "am determined to stay here indefinitely, as the way of life has already set me on the mend and I feel ten years younger." While laid up, Gawsworth continued writing poetry and began taking notes for an autobiography. Gawsworth also informed Wynne-Tyson that he and Fletcher were to be his joint literary executors, a complicated and likely prolonged duty from which Wynne-Tyson did his best to demur.

Yet just as Gawsworth's health was taking what appeared to be a final turn for the worse, he found himself back in the public eye one last time. In July 1970, the BBC aired a half-hour documentary about Gawsworth on its program *Late Night Line-Up*. The episode, which had been filmed the previous winter, used a fly-on-the-wall technique to follow

Gawsworth to several of his old haunts, including the offices of publisher Ernest Benn and the homes of old friends like the Irish novelist Kate O'Brien, who described him as "an often-exhausting dynamo." In between, Gawsworth marched down the streets of Soho and Bloomsbury, rifling through book bins and leaning on a cane. He also grew steadily drunker, at one point struggling onscreen for several seconds to uncork a bottle of sparkling wine. Perhaps loosened up by the alcohol, Gawsworth spoke frankly about his homelessness. "Now, I haven't an address, you see," he said. "Until I have an address I can't collect my books, papers, or anything." Despite this, Gawsworth did his best to dress up for the cameras, wearing a double-breasted suit and conspicuously polished shoes. The kingdom made a subtle appearance, too. In one scene, Gawsworth met up with Lawrence Durrell at a pub called the Elephant and Castle. Durrell greeted his old friend with what may well have been their traditional Redondan refrain: "Hail, O king! Hail, O king!" Gawsworth beamed drunkenly in response.

Two months after the documentary aired, Gawsworth was back in England and an inpatient at the Princess Beatrice Hospital in Kensington, the same neighbourhood where he'd grown up, this time to treat a series of hemorrhaging ulcers. The ensuing operation appeared to be successful, and Wynne-Tyson felt comfortable enough to leave the country on business. That same day, Fletcher phoned the hospital for an update and was told to call back twenty-four hours later. But by then it was too late. King Juan I died in his sleep on September 23, 1970. Found among his possessions in the hospital were hundreds of new poems, including a fifty-verse sequence called *Preoperation*, completed just before Gawsworth went under for his final surgery.

FOR THE ENTIRETY of his career, Gawsworth was a man out of time. He grew up idolizing an era of poetry that was already hopelessly out of fashion by the time he was old enough to contribute to it. When he returned home from the war, he found himself even further out of touch with most of the people around him. "I feel 999 years old," he wrote to a friend. "Everyone now—except your princely self—has died in my absence [...] and where the survivors will have got themselves evacuated to, will tax me to discover." Yet for a surprising number of years, Gawsworth was able to almost single-handedly keep the neo-Georgian tradition alive, thanks to his own abundant output, the numerous anthologies he edited, the collections of other people's poems he put out through Twyn Barlwm, and the borderline-fanatical way he gathered up discarded bits and pieces from writers he admired, assembling a collection that helped preserve their works for decades to come.

That sense of being born into the wrong generation extended to the way Gawsworth conducted himself as King Juan. When he assumed the title upon Shiel's death in 1947, the western world was still raw from the end of the Second World War. As models of government went, monarchies like the United Kingdom's seemed increasingly irrelevant: the British Empire was not only left bankrupt at the end of WWII (bailed out by a massive loan courtesy of the new world superpower, the United States), but it also faced growing anti-colonial backlash from occupied territories ready to demand their independence. Amidst a wave of international democratic cooperation spreading across North America and parts of Europe, Gawsworth the contrarian turned the other way, conjuring for himself an insular, fantasy version of an already old-fashioned concept.

And yet, perhaps the timing of Gawsworth's birth ultimately worked out in his favour. After all, how do we know that he would have thrived in the 1890s he so admired? On the contrary, one of his closest readers, Steve Eng, believed that Gawsworth's firehose energy was directly attributable to his status as an outsider. "As a professional anachronism," he wrote, Gawsworth's "traditional tastes gave him a strange strength by way of novelty [...] His verse is all the tougher for having been written in the age of Eliot, and later of Dylan Thomas." Had he actually come of age during the Georgian era, perhaps Gawsworth would have been content to remain a reader and a collector. If the books he wanted to read were already being published, perhaps Gawsworth wouldn't have felt the need to write them himself.

NEWS OF GAWSWORTH'S DEATH was reported across the English-speaking world, and each time the reports touched on both his literary achievements and the larger-than-life personality behind them — including the odd little kingdom he presided over. This was the final confirmation, if one were needed, that Gawsworth had taken an inside joke and successfully transformed it into a legitimate, if fanciful, part of his biography. At the same time, the press's reporting on Redonda was unusually rife with errors — a fitting twist for a story that itself approached the truth with room to negotiate. The *New York Times* obituary referred to Gawsworth's predecessor as "the late Irish poet Michael Shiel" (not Matthew), got the date of the royal transference wrong (it was reported as 1974, not '47), and at one point reported the name of Gawsworth's kingdom as "Radonda." That December, the *Times* of London used him as a trivia question for the newspaper's year in review: "Who was the

King of Redonda?" The answer, again garbled: "The poet, John Gainsworth."

Gawsworth had clearly been a difficult man to deal with. But once he died, stories began to appear in print from those who had known him, in a group effort to sift through a complicated life and assess its true legacy. His fellow Salamander G.S. Fraser remembered being instantly taken by Gawsworth's theatrical streak during their time in the war. "We found ourselves playing up to him," Fraser wrote. "Was he living in a world of fantasy? Well, what sort of a world were we, of Groppi's Light Infantry, living in?" Jon Wynne-Tyson believed that he would ultimately be remembered "as an excellent bibliographer, as a minor poet of occasional distinction, and no doubt as Redonda's second king," describing the legend as "a small grace-note in the history of literature." He added, "If posterity relegates all else about him to a footnote, they will have got the balance about right." Even those who seemed to exclusively butt heads with Gawsworth, like Derek Stanford, allowed that there must have been more to him than what they had witnessed. Ian Fletcher, who had spent more time with Gawsworth at his lowest than almost anyone, wrote that life since his friend's death "has seemed smaller and more drab."

The most fitting tribute, however, was the publication, at long last, of a new Gawsworth book. Oliver Cox, a poet and Redondan grand duke, issued a slim collection in 1971 entitled *Some Poems*. The booklet's cover featured a striking black-and-white photograph of the poet's death mask, and inside collected the poems by Gawsworth that Cox had read aloud at his memorial, as well as other tributes and unpublished verses composed at the Alma. After a painfully long silence, Gawsworth's bibliography finally gained one last entry.

STACKS 12

IT'S HARD to pinpoint exactly when my interest in Redonda tipped into a full-on obsession, but if I had to guess, it would be around the same time I started having dreams about it. Nothing much happened in these dreams, but it was their very stillness that became off-putting once I woke up. It felt like I'd been watching a stranger's old home movie: grainy handheld footage of the island from a distance — at sea? from back on Montserrat? — with the audio cut. I almost never remember my dreams, so it seemed obvious my mind was holding on to these for a reason. Was there a clue, somewhere in this dream version of the island, that I was supposed to be noticing — a structure, or maybe a figure, that differed from the actual photos I'd seen?

Once awake, the kingdom had become important enough that I'd started adding it as a line item in my daily planner each morning, just so that I would have an excuse to keep researching it. No longer was I reading the occasional Marías or Shiel novel and thinking *Hey, that's neat*. Richard Shiell and his Australian care package had shown me that the story of Redonda extended further than I'd realized, and indeed beyond the realm of fiction altogether. At the same time, I felt a growing sense of personal responsibility to the story. If people were willing to entrust me with their Redondan books and documents, the least I could do was put them to good use.

Several of the people I contacted, looking for more documents, responded with a mixture of excitement and relief. Anne Eng, for instance, had been maintaining her late husband Steve's literary archive, which spanned multiple genres and decades, since he passed away in 2014. I had found Steve's writing about Gawsworth nuanced and insightful, and when I told her what I was working on she generously offered to look through his entire archive and send me whatever she could find related to Redonda, free of charge, just as long as I promised to also make it available to other researchers in the future. "Steve would be happy to have the Gawsworth torch carried forward," she wrote. A few months later, I was walking home with my kids from a playground when I got a phone call from an unfamiliar number in the United States. This turned out to belong to Carol Billings Blood, the daughter of Harold Billings, Shiel's biographer. He had also recently passed away, and Blood was still in the process of sorting out the contents of his office in Texas. But she, too, offered to send along anything that mentioned Redonda. That evening, a digital version of *An Ossuary for M.P. Shiel*—the fragmented final instalment of Billings's biography, of which only eighty-five copies were printed, and which I had begrudgingly accepted I would probably never see for myself—appeared in my inbox.

That summer, my family and I took a vacation to England to spend time with my partner's extended family. The trip had been carefully planned out in advance—with the exception of one secret excursion that I had been unable to find the right time to bring up. The University of Reading, located about an hour's drive away, had an extensive collection of material relating to the life and work of John Gawsworth. I was trying to think of a way to casually float the idea of dropping by the university, when the truth was I'd already spent hours on the special collections website, quietly ogling its descriptions of King Juan's old writing notebooks, as well as "a large quantity of correspondence (mainly transcribed), family, personal and business papers, drawings by John Gawsworth and photographs of Gawsworth, his family and friends." The collection had been placed there by Ian Fletcher, the Reading professor and co-executor of Gawsworth's estate. My eventual pitch to Kate had all the forced nonchalance of a used-car salesman's schtick: *Hey, honey, it's no big deal if I pop over for a few hours to take a quick look, right? I think the library is open Tuesday to Friday from 9:30 to 4:00, with an hour closed for lunch ...*

Luckily, I have an understanding family. It didn't hurt that Kate's Uncle Peter, whom we were staying with, was a retired archivist with a weakness for literary puzzles. He even had a minor connection to the Redonda story: his own uncle, Bernard Gutteridge, was a poet, novelist, and playwright who had seen some of his poems published by Gawsworth in the *Poetry Review* in the early 1950s. And it was Uncle Peter's little car that I stepped out of one morning in mid-July, a few minutes before the library opened. As the rest of my family drove off for a day's frolic in the English countryside, I paced back and forth in front of the redbrick building, anxiously fantasizing about what lay within.

Ideally, I would come across something that explained Gawsworth's complete vision for Redonda. Despite all that I'd read so far, the story was still slippery and unreliable. Most of it had been told through a series of fragments and rumours, which were difficult to gather in one place, let alone stitch together into something coherent and definitive. But perhaps there was a single document — a letter, a page from a notebook, even a napkin lifted from the Alma — where King Juan laid it all out. If something like that *did* exist, chances are it would exist in a place like this.

And if that wasn't possible, then I at least wanted to find a copy of Gawsworth's will. The question of who he named as his final successor, if anyone, loomed over much of the confusion that had dominated the realm in the decades since his death. If I could find that, then I would at least have a starting point on figuring out what his true intentions were.

There were warning signs, however. Namely, an email from the University of Reading confirming the details of my visit, which I'd booked (also secretly) in advance. "The Gawsworth collection is quite sizeable, yes," one of the librarians wrote, "and I think it would take much longer than a day to work through if you wished to see everything." I looked again at the listing on the university's website: eighteen boxes of material. Was that a lot?

The doors in front of me unlocked with a click, and I walked down a twisting hallway that the library shares with the Museum of English Rural Life before reaching the special-collections library and its information desk. "You must be here for the Gawsworth material," the librarian said, gesturing over one shoulder, when she saw my foreign driver's licence. Behind her, on the left-hand side of a cluttered countertop, sat three large Bankers Boxes that visibly sagged with material. A fourth sat on a nearby plastic rolling cart.

I signed in, checked my jacket and bag, and lugged the first box over with me to the far end of a communal research table. By this time, several other researchers were getting settled around me with their own books and documents —

every single one of them, I noticed, about Samuel Beckett. It turned out that the University of Reading was renowned for its Beckett material, which, at more than seven thousand items, was the largest such collection in the world. You couldn't really argue with that level of dedication to a Nobel Prize winner. But for a writer of Gawsworth's meagre profile? Even the shelf space required for these eighteen boxes of material suddenly sounded difficult to justify. How often, I wondered, were people really dropping by to look at the rough drafts of poems that, even in their finished state, almost nobody read?

A nearby sign noted that the library closed at 5 p.m. As long as I could get through each box in about twenty-five minutes, I'd be done with time to spare. Besides, I wasn't here to futz around with every single piece of paper — only the ones related to Redonda.

I lifted the lid off the first box and began pulling items out. The first thing I grabbed was a stack of finished books, including Gawsworth's personal copy of his *Collected Poems* — "For Reading, Revising, Annotating," according to a note on the title page — that had been absolutely pummelled with use. Even its illustration of the author had been self-defaced with blue ink. Or maybe the graffiti had been done by someone else; another note on the title page said that the book was, at one point, "*on loan* to author's wife" (emphasis in original). Underneath these books were stacks of newspaper clippings, drafts of essays, and several full notebooks, as well as an assortment of odd documents like faded gin advertisements, restaurant menus, tissue paper, and torn halves of envelopes — all crawling with fragments of unpublished poems. Wherever Gawsworth went, it seemed, he was writing, on almost literally any surface available to him.

Despite my plan to stay on task, I found myself getting distracted, not just by the volume of the archive but also its tactility. This was the first time I'd been this close to Gawsworth's actual handwriting. I hunched over the desk and raised page after page to my face to scrutinize the indents his pen left on the notebook paper, then let my eyes wander down to the corners, which were full of doodles, jotted-down addresses and phone numbers ("Churchill Arms 727-4242"), and banal notes that only Gawsworth himself could have deciphered, or cared to. The man had been dead for half a century, but everything inside the box still held a residual warmth, as if Gawsworth had only just wandered away from his desk and was due to return at any moment.

As I worked my way down to the bottom of the first box, I felt a jolt of voyeuristic giddiness. Being so close to another writer's raw materials was an addictive experience, and I wanted more of it. Every scrap of handwriting, no matter how banal, felt like being let a little further into Gawsworth's private life. These were intimate, fragile documents that existed in one place and one place only; if you wanted to see them for yourself, you had to come to Reading. I thought I was making pretty good time, too, but once I'd reassembled the box's contents and placed the lid back on top, I glanced at my phone and realized that more than an hour had already passed. According to my schedule, I was supposed to be well into box three by now.

I made a silent prayer that the first box had been an outlier, and that the next one would be less tightly packed. Or else that it would contain some kind of system of organization that would allow me, at a glance, to zero in on the Redonda material. No such luck. There *was* a more obvious order to the papers and notebooks inside box number two, but even figuring out what decade a particular piece was written in required study. Then there was the matter of determining what "important" actually meant for my purposes. A copy of *Lyrics to Kingcup*, with a lengthy note to Gawsworth's mother written across the flyleaf, seemed unlikely to be useful, but I had to spend several minutes squinting at Gawsworth's faded, pencilled handwriting to be sure. Letters referencing Shiel seemed essential the first few times I found them, and progressively less so the dozens if not hundreds of times afterwards. Several notebooks from the 1950s and '60s, meanwhile, contained poems with the telltale words "Redonda" or "Juan" in the title. But few of them seemed to contain any significance beyond the use of a familiar nickname. As time went on, I also grew frustrated with myself. As a first-time archive user, I could tell I was making rookie mistakes: stacking folders at random after removing them from boxes and not taking thorough enough notes on those pieces I *had* already looked at. Research, it turned out, was a skill in its own right, and I did not possess it yet.

For his longer correspondences, Gawsworth would rewrite both sides out by hand. Even as I felt more precious minutes slipping away, I couldn't help but consume entire exchanges like the one Gawsworth had in his early twenties with Arthur Machen, endearing himself to his idol by volunteering to snoop around a shop in London that Machen suspected was selling autographed photographs of him obtained under false pretences. Equally revealing were letters from A. Reynolds Morse, detailing on the one hand how thorough he was in assembling his Shiel bibliography, but also giving vent to repellent descriptions of his publisher as a hypocrite and "lousy Jew bastard." I told myself I was reading these letters in case they contained information about the kingdom. Really, I was just snooping.

Each new box in the archive presented untold numbers of potential new discoveries, with thousands of pages to sort through and decipher. At times my task felt so broad as to become paralyzing, though I did my best to not look or think past the page in front of me. Eventually, another bottleneck emerged. When I returned the first batch of boxes to the information desk and asked for the next one, the librarian told me their policy was to only keep four boxes from a single archive in the reading room at once. Swapping out one quartet for another was a process that required a staff member to wheel, at their convenience, the first set of boxes back downstairs and then return with a new batch. I returned to my seat so anxious about this unexpected delay, which took about fifteen minutes each time, and so antsy about the ever-more-dwindling time that remained before closing that I rapped my pencil impatiently against the edge of the tabletop until one of the nearby Beckett researchers had to ask me to stop.

No matter how many documents I sifted through that had nothing whatsoever to do with Redonda—the entirety of boxes three, five, and eight, for instance—the feeling of surprise and delight that accompanied a real find was bracing. In Machen's final letters to Gawsworth, for example, the aging novelist expresses regret at Shiel's recent death and thanks King Juan for "the rich merriment" in being named Redonda's first archduke. "But, stay," Machen adds, six months before his own demise, "there is something that doth appal, in the very sound and figure of that name. When Minos utters his awful doom, let him not thunder both Shiel and myself the word—Redundant." Elsewhere Gawsworth had preserved a collection of some fifty letters relating to Shiel's first marriage to Lina Gomez, which he playfully reinterpreted as a narrative work in its own right, complete with an annotated dramatis personae, a list of Shiel's known whereabouts between 1898 and 1904, and a title that left little doubt as to whom Gawsworth, like Shiel, blamed for the failure of the union: *L'Ouragon Espagnol; or, The Matriarch*. I was also encouraged to see Gawsworth had actually begun work on his biographies of Shiel and especially Machen, which, at one point in the early 1960s, appeared to be under contract with the University of California. The press's eventual abandonment of the project must have been a source of great frustration to him.

By the time I started tunnelling into the third quartet of boxes, which contained hundreds of letters that I only gradually confirmed I had no use for, the material began to take on an air of tragedy. I knew that Gawsworth never published another book after his *Collected Poems*, but the second half of his archive drove home, again and again, that this was not by choice. In the last two decades of his life, Gawsworth never stopped writing poems — they just didn't leave the notebooks. It was painful to observe that he had no idea all of this effort, all of these pages, would turn out to be for naught, as he agitated for a career revival that never happened. The only sign of potential understanding came via Gawsworth's handwriting, which tilted further to one side as the years wore on, before collapsing into near-complete inscrutability.

As closing time approached, I was forced to accept the truth of my situation: I was not going to get through all of the boxes in the Gawsworth archive. Not even close. As I popped the lid on box thirteen, it was already 4:30 p.m. The Beckett researchers had by now all packed up and gone home, content in the knowledge that they could pick back up where they left off the next morning. I didn't have that option; my family and I were off to start a walking tour in another part of the country the next day. Even if I could somehow instantly assess the contents of all four boxes currently in front of me, by the time the final pair was unearthed from storage, I'd find myself right at the brink of closing time. And a librarian at closing time was not someone I wanted to risk irritating.

The prospect of finding some master document that would unlock all the mysteries of Redonda grew dimmer with every new box I opened. Really, it had been foolish to expect, or even to hope, that such a piece of paper existed. All of the most interesting documents I'd found so far had come from Gawsworth's younger years, and I began to suspect that whatever kingdom-related material I hadn't already seen probably wasn't here. It was, if not in private hands, then scattered among the other Gawsworth collections: at the University of Iowa, at the Harry Ransom Center in Texas, at Rollins College in Florida, and even a couple of scraps back home in Canada, at the University of Victoria in British Columbia.

Gawsworth's will, on the other hand? That I still held out hope for. Back in box seven, for instance, I'd already found a copy of Shiel's. Dated June 27, 1938, it decreed that the bulk of his remaining money would go to his sister Harriet, while all of his "manuscripts, papers, books, and copyrights" would go to Gawsworth. It wasn't the key to the kingdom, but it was a significant find nonetheless — and I'd spotted it sandwiched in the middle of a brick of unrelated papers. If I'd been flicking through that pile with only slightly less patience, I might have missed it entirely. Maybe the Gawsworthian equivalent was still out there, too.

Box thirteen contained the usual mountains of letters and poems. But at least this time there was a clear theme: the anthology organized by Charles Wrey Gardiner for Gawsworth's fiftieth birthday. These, I figured, were valuable insights from a wide range of friends and colleagues, so I decided to photograph each one, since many contained personal details about Gawsworth that had never been recounted anywhere else.

"There is no literary figure of importance that is unknown to this arch-Londoner," wrote John Metcalfe.

"John wants the best, even at his worst," wrote Oswell Blakeston.

"In his living presence, the decibels of his voice are apt suddenly to diminish and the poet steals out," remembered Jerrard Tickell, Redondan Duke of Tokay. "I wish he would do so more frequently."

It was more repetitive, methodical, slightly maddening work. Each time I flipped to a new page, laid a device called a snake weight across the top to keep the corners down, took a photo with my phone, and then repeated the process. The danger was in moving too quickly. Each essay had been retyped onto onionskin paper so thin that it would blow right off the table, taking a couple of its neighbours with it, if I so much as turned too quickly in my chair. *Flip, snake, click. Flip, snake, click.*

Soon, however, I heard the gentle but firm clearing of a throat behind me. My time was up. The library was closing. Not only had I not found Gawsworth's will—I hadn't even finished going through the anthology submissions. The page in front of me was a humorous poem from Heath-Stubbs about the Italian writer Benedetto Croce, whom Gawsworth had met during his time in Italy during World War II. That would have to stand as the last word. I reluctantly packed everything back away, where Gawsworth's papers would stay, in undisturbed darkness, for who knew how long until another researcher one day called for their retrieval. Ringing in my head was the advice received by a young Robert Caro, years before he started writing his mammoth biography of Lyndon Johnson: "Never assume anything. Turn every goddamn page." I hadn't done that, and now it was too late. As much as I'd been able to learn about King Juan I over these past few years, some of his secrets were going to stay hidden.

BACK IN EDMONTON, it was time to get methodical. I printed off a copy of John D. Squires's Redondan bibliography, which contained a list of hundreds of books, articles, and pieces of ephemera. I went through the whole thing with a pen, crossing out each item I'd already tracked down. What remained was my shopping list.

I started with Paul De Fortis's *The Kingdom of Redonda: 1865–1990*, a pocket history published by the UK-based Aylesford Press on behalf of something called "the Redondan Cultural Foundation." The book appeared in 1991 as a paperback in pale-blue wraps. On the cover was a hand-drawn Redondan coat of arms that included a serpent coiled around the island, a well-dressed human trapped between its jaws. A Latin motto at the bottom read *Ite ad rem*, or, loosely translated: *Get to the point*. Inside, De Fortis provides an overview of the reigns of Shiel and Gawsworth and reprints kingdom-adjacent material from Lawrence Durrell and Roger Dobson. But from there the text takes a curious turn, endorsing a man referred to as King Cedric as the current ruler. Cedric in turn provides an approving foreword to De Fortis's book, in which he suggests that rightful control of the monarchy all depends on whom you asked. "What, after all, is any nation's history but the version of events which that nation believes?" writes Cedric, who like Shiel grew up on Montserrat. "It is less a collection of facts than a series of both myths and facts which generations have believed and so have come to crystallise as truth."

I was also able to track down copies of some of Reynolds Morse's publications about Shiel. His bibliography had first appeared in 1948, but decades later Morse revised and expanded the project into a four-volume set that he published himself. I managed to find a decently priced copy of the final volume, a hefty essay collection entitled *Shiel in Diverse Hands* that is almost certainly the highest concentration of writing about Shiel in one place. Not long afterwards, I also snagged a hardcover edition of the first volume in the set, which collected offprints of the original serialized versions of *The Empress of the Earth* (renamed *The Yellow Danger* for its book edition), *The Purple Cloud*, and an assortment of short stories.

Gawsworth's work, on the other hand, required a little more strategy. His early poetry collections were issued in such limited runs that they had long since shot out of my initial price range, though I wasn't sure who, exactly, was buying them. After a few weeks of careful sleuthing, I managed to find an affordable (read: crumbling) copy of his 1931 poetry collection *Confession* and was pleasantly surprised to find that it that included a bookplate from Walter de la Mare, one of Gawsworth's childhood heroes. Meanwhile, his essay on book collecting, "Magnetic Fingers: A Bibliophile's Holiday," was first published in a 1949 anthology called *Holidays and Happy Days* and was reissued in the early

1990s by Tartarus Press.[↓] Surprisingly, the original anthology proved easier to acquire, even with its bright-green dust jacket intact. By this point I'd gotten a taste for signed and association copies, which is how I talked myself into pulling the trigger on a book that I'd been coveting for months: John Gawsworth's personal copy of the original version of *The Works of M.P. Shiel*. It was, and remains as of this writing, the single most expensive book I've ever purchased. It arrived showing signs of heavy use, and it didn't have a jacket. But it was thrillingly, unmistakably Gawsworth's. His name and signature (as Juan I) appeared on the front free endpaper, as did his pasted-in Realm of Redonda bookplate. Even more exciting was the fact that Gawsworth had peppered the book with his marginalia, correcting details that Morse had gotten wrong and adding new ones as they came to mind. The most revealing such instance was Gawsworth's handwritten note underneath the text of the eulogy delivered at Shiel's funeral. The scant number of mourners had already been documented in Redondan lore, but Gawsworth had taken the trouble to write all thirteen out by name. Among the attendees was Gawsworth himself, as well as several of Shiel's nieces and nephews, the children of his beloved sister Gussie. Only one name was a mystery to Gawsworth. Next to the seventh mourner, he had simply written "???" followed by "(Shiel's natural daughter)."

> Tartarus, based in North Yorkshire, is an independent publisher of literary supernatural novels, typically in limited editions. They're also one of the few operative presses that has actively helped keep the Redondan story alive. In addition to publishing beautiful new editions of *Prince Zaleski* and *Shapes in the Fire*, Tartarus has overseen several essay collections that touch on the kingdom and, in 2005, the long-awaited first publication of Gawsworth's *Life of Arthur Machen*.

Gawsworth's handwritten list of mourners in attendance at Shiel's funeral.

The Thirteen mourners present were:

1/ Edward Shanks
2/ David C Polden (at organ)
3/ Frederick Carter A.R.E
4/ E.H.W. Meyerstein, FRSL
5/ Mrs E.L. Armstrong (my mother)
6/ Mrs P.F.B.N. Armstrong (my sister in law)
7/ ? ? ? (Shiel's natural daughter)
8/ Dr Cyril Hovsford (Shiel's nephew)
9/ Miss Olive Hovsford (niece)
10/ Miss Muriel Hovsford (niece)
11/ Mrs Cyril Hovsford
12/ Kenneth Myer (editor The W.W.)
13/ John Gawsworth FRSL.

A package of nearly equal intrigue arrived at my front door soon afterwards. The return address said Pasadena, California, and inside was the next step towards my personal Redondan archive, courtesy of Anne Eng. I slid the items out of the envelope one at a time. There was a photocopy of Gawsworth's entry from *The Penguin Encyclopedia of Horror and the Supernatural*, and a copy of his short story "Scylla and Charybdis" from a 1987 issue of *Night Cry* magazine. There was a two-page excerpt from Shiel's novel *The Man-Stealers*, with a faded note in pencil across the top, presumably intended for her late husband, Steve: "From the sixpenny edition. Do you have this?" There were also a variety of letters and emails, most concerned with details of the kingdom; one referred to a biography that Eng was then planning to write about Gawsworth. There was a faded printout from 1998 of a now-defunct website called Caribbean Super Site. And there was an old, thinning, heavily faded newspaper article called "What women don't know about MEN," written by Noel Whitcomb, aka the Duke of Bonafides, which discussed Gawsworth's decision to put the kingdom up for sale in the *Times*. It was a copy — probably a copy of a copy — and the newspaper's masthead had been cut off entirely. A garbled signature at the top indicated that it had once belonged to William Reginald Hipwell, Gawsworth's old landlord and his one-time Redondan successor.

The package also contained two books. On top was a collection entitled *The Defrauding of the Worms*, which contained some two hundred of Steve's own poems, plus one more on a scrap of paper, signed and dated 1982 and tucked mysteriously into the table of contents:

On Learning of a Third Claimant to the Throne of Redonda
Redonda's mystery abides,
Luring soul toward soul
Across Atlantic's calms and tides,
Questing for the goal.
But all is mist. Redonda hides,
Its truth inscrutable upon its royal scroll.

The other book Anne sent was *Toreros*, a collection of Gawsworth's poetry that was published posthumously in 1990. The manuscript had been prepared by Gawsworth back in the 1960s along with his friend Richard Aldington, and it had been part of a larger donation to the University of Iowa — which is where it sat until Steve Eng stumbled across it. *Toreros* was eventually published in a paperback edition of nine hundred copies, each of which bore Eng's name as editor.

The Reynolds Morse Foundation's four-colour map of Redonda.

In addition to being a new Gawsworth title, *Toreros* is noteworthy for how strongly it foregrounds the Redondan legend. It includes not only a poem celebrating Shiel's reign as King Felipe, but also a catalogue in the back listing Redonda-related material available for sale from the Reynolds Morse Foundation, including a history of the kingdom called *The Quest for Redonda* and a four-colour map of the island co-created by Morse.

I turned the pages of this new book carefully. It had always seemed odd to me that, for all the bombast the story had in pubs and in the press, mentions of Redonda in the kings' actual books were rare. So at first it was a surprise to here see the kingdom not just acknowledged but openly celebrated. When I looked a little more closely, however, the shift started to make sense. *Toreros* was published by Centaur Press, a one-person operation run by Jon Wynne-Tyson: publisher, author, literary executor, vegetarian activist, and the reluctant third king of Redonda.

NO FORMAL TRAINING 13

KING JUAN I remained loyal to Redonda to the end. He even asked for his ashes to be mingled with what was left of Shiel's and for the combined batch to be flown down to the Caribbean and spread overtop of the island, which he had still never seen in person. It was to be a lavish send-off befitting a king. (This was quickly deemed impractical, however, and Gawsworth's ashes were instead spread over the crocuses at Golders Green.)

Yet when it came time to hand off the crown itself, Gawsworth's succession plan was a lot less clear. In times of desperation, he had more than once sold the kingdom off for cash, and it was unclear which of these claims would hold up as the legitimate one. First among would-be claimants to the throne was Reginald Hipwell, the landlord who purchased the kingdom from Gawsworth in 1954, but who had predeceased King Juan. Then came Prince Bertil, the Swedish prince who'd put down a deposit after reading the ad in the *Times*, which Gawsworth had only been too happy to cash. And then there was Arthur John Roberts, manager of the Alma, who'd signed a new blood pact with Gawsworth in the 1960s. Following King Juan's death, even more claimants emerged — most prominent among them Dominic Behan, the songwriting brother of Brendan, who claimed Gawsworth gave the kingdom to *him* as early as 1960.

When Gawsworth first received the kingdom from Shiel, it had come along with the title of literary executor. This was an intentional twinning of responsibilities that reinforced Redonda as an artistic realm, in which the current king maintained a duty to uphold and promote the works of the previous one. It was in that same spirit that Gawsworth first wrote to Jon Wynne-Tyson from Italy, in May 1970, and informed him that he and Ian Fletcher were to share the job of being Gawsworth's own literary executors. Along with this task, once again, came the kingdom. Yet Wynne-Tyson claimed that Gawsworth never spelled out this implication while he was alive, and that he only learned of Gawsworth's Redondan wishes when he read about them in his will. By the time Wynne-Tyson realized that it was *he* who was to succeed Juan I, Gawsworth was already dead. There was no time for Wynne-Tyson to discuss the details of the title of King of Redonda — specifically, the fact that he didn't want it.

JON WYNNE-TYSON was born in Hampshire on July 6, 1924. Like Gawsworth, he wandered into the world of publishing at a young age, in his case dropping out of Brighton College at the age of fifteen and cycling through a series of jobs in a high-end art bookshop, a paper merchant, and an international distributor of fashion magazines — what he later termed a "reprehensibly unplanned drift." In 1949 he was hired as a literary advisor for the press Williams and Norgate, and after a year and half on the job was pleased to discover that all of the books he'd recommended for publication, save one, had ended up turning a profit. Wynne-Tyson's first book, a gentle satire about the tribulations of being a renter called *Accommodation Wanted*, appeared when he was just twenty-six.

Despite his early successes, publishing didn't pay enough for Wynne-Tyson to support his growing young family. In 1950 he'd married Joan Stanton, an illustrator and musician who did the illustrations for *Accommodation Wanted*; their daughter, Caroline (nicknamed "Tilly-loo," after a line in Edward Lear's *Calico Pie*), was born the following year. Wynne-Tyson ended up taking a job as a custodian at London's University College Hospital, which, while lacking the glamour of his previous employment, at least gave him enough free time to continue freelancing as a book reviewer on the side.

It was while on shift at the hospital that Wynne-Tyson learned one of his co-workers' fathers owned a local printing company. By this point Wynne-Tyson had written a sequel to *Accommodation Wanted*, and he gave the co-worker a copy of the manuscript for his father to look at. Whatever minor discount on printing fees he was hoping to secure, Wynne-Tyson ended up receiving a much different offer. The co-worker's father didn't just agree to produce Wynne-Tyson's new book. He was so enamoured by the idea of publishing books for a general audience that he offered to underwrite the costs of *four* different titles, so long as Wynne-Tyson agreed to select, edit, design, and distribute them—in other words, to create a publishing company. Centaur Press Ltd. was thus formed in fall 1954, "with no resources," Wynne-Tyson wrote, "other than the loan of £1,000 from a friendly publisher who had faith in my ability to make a go of it."

Wynne-Tyson did not suffer from a lack of confidence. But this wasn't the first time he'd benefitted from family connections. His mother, Esmé, had been a precocious child actor in the West End who was close friends and collaborators with a young Noël Coward, but ended up retiring from the theatre and turning to writing full-time in her early twenties after marrying an air-force pilot named Lynden Charles Tyson and giving birth to Jon a few years later. Lynden, however, abandoned the family for another woman when Jon was still young, leaving the boy in the sole care of his intelligent and possessive mother. Once Jon zeroed in on publishing as a career path, Esmé helped him get one of his first jobs. Again, the request was, if anything, too effective: after being prematurely promoted to advertising manager for the entire company—an arrangement Jon later called "suicidal"—he was dismissed just as quickly, albeit with an improved resumé to show for it.

The jump into launching his own press was just as sudden, and it took Wynne-Tyson some time to settle on a direction as a publisher. Centaur's first offering was an eclectic list that ranged from puppetry plays to a collection of mini-biographies of women who reached their creative peaks in middle age—the latter written by Esmé under a pen name. Subsequent lists dabbled in memoir, philosophy, travel, medical reference (1967's *Dictionary of Symptoms* anticipated WebMD by several decades), poetry, and literary criticism. Centaur also published the occasional work of fiction. Michel Fourest's 1959 novel *Behind the Smiling Moon* was a brooding, self-absorbed work intended to be a parody, though none of its reviewers picked up on that fact; they also had no clue that the book had been secretly penned by Wynne-Tyson himself, as an amusing change of pace from his editorial duties. As Centaur slowly built up its presence in the industry, Wynne-Tyson was also dealing with changes at home. He and Stanton divorced in 1954, and not long afterwards he remarried, this time to a ballet dancer named Jennifer Tyson (no relation). The new couple raised Tilly together and also had a daughter of their own, Susan, born in 1957.

It wasn't until Centaur got into the business of reprints that the press found its niche. The Centaur Classics imprint was designed to bring back into print works of enduring value — some, like *The Itinerary of John Leland in or about the Years 1535–43*, which arrived in five volumes and weighing nearly three kilograms, nearly as difficult to reproduce as they were to find in the original. But readers, and the media, took notice of Centaur's ambitious new project. As sales began to climb, Wynne-Tyson took inspiration from the words of his fellow publisher Fredric Warburg: "A new imprint can establish itself by its willingness to publish books so unusual or so unpopular that the established houses won't touch them with a barge-pole." With its classics line, Centaur would take that advice to heart.

Keeping the company solvent was a full-time job, but one perfectly suited to someone with Wynne-Tyson's temperament. A solitary, introspective man by nature, he relished being his own boss and working in isolation out of his home in Sussex; in lieu of a marketing team, Wynne-Tyson would pack orders of books and catalogues himself, wheeling them down to the post office inside a converted baby stroller. He also loved the quixotic hunt for out-of-print titles that filled small but valuable gaps in British history or that were merely topics that Wynne-Tyson found interesting. Profit was always a secondary concern. Centaur was just as happy to publish Derek Stanford's early, controversial biography of his friend Muriel Spark (which Spark herself hated) as it was monographs on post boxes and chimney pots. In his memoir *Finding the Words*, Wynne-Tyson summed up his approach in those years:

> I had no formal training; rudimentary business acumen; minimal commercial nous; nil independent means; a woozy conviction that small, if not always beautiful, was at least more workable; and a disinclination to cultivate those literary and media moguls who can be helpful on life's ladders.

He was also willing to log long hours in service of that vision, routinely spending evenings and weekends at his desk while bringing eighty titles to market in the 1960s alone.

As Centaur's output became more focused, it also revealed more of its owner's politics — an outspoken progressive bent that ran in the Wynne-Tyson family. Back in the 1920s, after leaving the theatre, Esmé had converted to Christian Science. This led to a serious interest in philosophy and comparative religion that would last until her death, and which she would in turn pass on to her son. One of their shared reference points was the Greek philosopher Porphyry, who wrote an early vegetarian text called *On Abstinence from Animal Food* in the third century. Esmé referred to it in several of her books, and decades later Wynne-Tyson decided to publish a new hardcover edition, long before vegetarianism would become a mainstream political issue. "No major newspaper gave it a line of attention," Wynne-Tyson wrote, "but [they] had not been expected to." A few years later, Centaur published the first serious book of non-fiction written by Wynne-Tyson himself: a polemic on vegetarianism and non-violence called *The Civilised Alternative*. Books like these were never destined for the bestseller list, but that didn't matter. Wynne-Tyson was becoming more and more interested in how humanity could live in harmony with the rest of the planet, and the titles he wrote and published reflected a larger project that he referred to as "humane education." In 1970s England, there was no shortage of learning to be done.

EVEN THOUGH he lived miles away, Wynne-Tyson was nonetheless aware of what was happening in the publishing scene in London. The city was still by far the largest market for Centaur titles, and many future Centaur authors were likely to be found there, too. As a respected but small publisher who often had to woo his writers with a personalized touch, Wynne-Tyson kept a number of contacts in London. Among them was an eccentric but troubled poet named John Gawsworth.

The two had first met in 1949, when Wynne-Tyson was still casting around for a steady career in publishing and serving as one of the managers of the philosophy journal *Enquiry*. Gawsworth, meanwhile, was a seasoned anthology editor who had just published his *Collected Poems*. Intrigued, Wynne-Tyson brought on Gawsworth to edit upcoming issues of *Enquiry*, but the collaboration didn't work out as planned. Rather than seek out new material, Gawsworth filled the journal with rejected submissions from one of the other magazines he edited, the *Literary Digest*. Despite this editorial sleight of hand, the pair remained friendly. That June, Gawsworth dubbed Wynne-Tyson a Knight Commander with the Order of the Star of Redonda in front of bemused members of the press; a few years later, *Science, Life and Literature*, Shiel's posthumous essay collection edited by Gawsworth, was published by Williams and Norgate largely on Wynne-Tyson's say-so. As thanks, he was promoted within the Redondan court to Il Duca d'Immaculado.

In the years that followed, Wynne-Tyson retreated to Sussex to immerse himself in all things Centaur, and from there received only occasional news of his friend's descent into alcoholism. It wasn't until 1968, when an ailing Gawsworth was finally evicted from his apartment at 35 Sutherland Place, that Wynne-Tyson returned to London to help him move his battered archive. A few months later, Gawsworth travelled out to Sussex for an impromptu visit but was so far in his cups that no amount of black coffee could sober him up again; the only thing that seemed to calm his agitation was spending time with Dumbo, the family donkey. The next morning Gawsworth threw up several times, downed a glass of whiskey, and asked Wynne-Tyson to be his literary executor.

Over the next two years, Gawsworth was in and out of hospital and Wynne-Tyson gave little thought to the Kingdom of Redonda or his place in it. But it was clearly on Gawsworth's mind. In 1970, Wynne-Tyson and Jennifer visited Gawsworth as he lay recovering in the Princess Beatrice Hospital to discuss details of his will. Wynne-Tyson privately hoped that Gawsworth's illness meant he'd abandoned his "manipulative Performing Monarch act," but King Juan had other plans. Wynne-Tyson didn't know that Gawsworth was (once again) making arrangements for the future of the kingdom, and he certainly didn't know that *he* was meant to succeed him as King Juan II. That news would only be revealed months later, after Gawsworth's death, when Wynne-Tyson read it in his will. But by then it was too late to argue.

WHY WYNNE-TYSON? Of all the decisions that have shaped the Redondan legend over the years, few have been as controversial as Gawsworth's decision to name King Juan II his final successor — and few have come with higher stakes.

In its early years, the Kingdom of Redonda had a clear and uncontested line of succession from Shiel to Gawsworth. From there, however, the line fractures. Since 1970, more than a dozen different people have claimed to be the one true ruler of Redonda. Most of them traced their claim back to Gawsworth: either to a verbal promise made in a Fitzrovia pub or to one of his dashed-off "irrevocable covenants." By definition, the majority of these agreements cannot be valid. Gawsworth could only give away the kingdom once. So which of these claimants had true authority over the kingdom? And which were just pretenders?

The paper trail was lengthy and scattered, and began with the contract signed at L'Abri back in October 1936. In it, Shiel declared, in the royal third person, "Our sovereignty, upon our death, is his possession to be conferred by him on his death unto such of his blood as he appoints." Here "him" referred to Gawsworth and "on his death" suggested that he wasn't allowed to give the kingdom away while he was still alive. If true, this would mean that Gawsworth's covenants were nothing but more pieces of paper. But already there was a complicating factor. This account of the initial contract is not a direct quote, but rather a reconstruction, supplied by Gawsworth in a letter to A. Reynolds Morse during the writing of *The Works of M.P. Shiel*. So it was possible — perhaps even likely — that Gawsworth was paraphrasing the fine print and tossing in official-sounding language that may or may not have been present in the original. Even he couldn't have imagined that people would still be trying to parse his wording decades later. And what to make of that last part of the quote: "conferred by him on his death unto such of his blood as he appoints"? There are two ways to read it. If "of his blood" meant that Gawsworth could transfer the kingdom to anybody, so long as they had performed the same blood ritual that he and Shiel had, then only one claimant had a case: Arthur John Roberts, the pub manager who mingled blood with Gawsworth back in 1966. But if transference of the kingdom was strictly reserved for Gawsworth's own children, then nobody qualified. At the same time, little else in the Redondan tradition suggested a lineage defined by bloodlines: Shiel was not close with his own children and doesn't seem to have ever considered assigning the kingdom to any of them — even if that's what Matthew Sr. would likely have assumed to be the case when he first claimed the island for the family in the 1860s. When Shiel began leaning into this childhood anecdote, his first priority was leveraging it to sell copies of his novels. Years later, anxious to find a literary executor, he tied the job to the kingdom in order to further entice Gawsworth — who, Shiel knew, would continue advocating for his works after his death the same way he had while still alive.

This is the light in which Gawsworth's decision to pass the kingdom to Wynne-Tyson makes the most sense. As an author and publisher, Wynne-Tyson was better equipped than most to ensure that the Redondan legend would live on. Plus, as someone with stable accommodations outside of London, he was also in a position to safeguard Gawsworth's papers, or what remained of them. Gawsworth's will stated that Wynne-Tyson and his co-executor, Ian Fletcher, should do whatever they could to keep the reputations of the previous kings alive. But in this case, attaching the kingdom to the executorship wasn't a sweetener. If anything, it may have been a liability, since neither Wynne-Tyson nor Fletcher were ones for theatricality. How to choose between them?

Fletcher, who passed away in 1988, never commented on the matter publicly. He did once publish an essay about Gawsworth in a Canadian literary journal entitled "The Aesthetics of Failure." Yet it only glancingly mentioned the story of Redonda and said nothing at all about his own role in it. In fact, Fletcher chalked the entire legend up as a cautionary tale that defined, and then consumed, his late friend. "If it is true that we survive by shaping images," Fletcher wrote, "but that we often become, and disastrously so, the victims of those images, Gawsworth's case might be cited." His widow, Loraine, meanwhile, told me over email she considered the kingdom a "graceful last gesture," offered by an ailing and broke Gawsworth to two of his most loyal compatriots in lieu of something more substantial. And so, in the absence of any publishing expertise on Fletcher's part, the task — and title — fell to Wynne-Tyson.

To this day, Wynne-Tyson's claim to the Redondan throne is disputed by more than one party. (We'll meet them all shortly.) These other claimants argue, for various reasons and with various degrees of insistence, that Gawsworth's transfer of the kingdom to Wynne-Tyson was never legitimate and should therefore not be recognized now. But there is another reason for this disagreement, and that is the near-decade of silence that followed the death of King Juan I. For most of the 1970s, it wasn't clear that the Kingdom of Redonda had survived at all.

"THE DEATH OF GAWSWORTH," writes Wynne-Tyson in his memoir, "did not bring an end to the literary legend of Redonda and its kings, though it might have done if I had been less of an idiot."

Wynne-Tyson, as has been said, had no taste for Gawsworth's tabloid antics. But as a veteran publisher, he had no issues taking on the duties of literary executor, as this amounted to little more than occasional paperwork. In fact, it would be eight years before the first request to reprint Shiel's or Gawsworth's work came across on his desk. This came from Victor Gollancz, the firm that had accidentally kickstarted the entire Redondan legend in the 1920s, with the publication of the "About Myself" pamphlet; now Gollancz wanted permission to reprint two of Shiel's novels, *The Purple Cloud* and *The Young Men Are Coming!*

The exchange had a fitting sense of symmetry to it. Just as Shiel had coyly disclosed his Redondan origins in order to boost media interest, now Wynne-Tyson found himself doing the exact same thing a half-century later. In an attempt to give the re-released books a new topical hook, he informed Gollancz, which by then was being run by Victor's daughter Livia, that he happened to be the island's current king. This was the first time Wynne-Tyson had ever mentioned this fact outside of his personal circles, and, as with Shiel, it set an unexpected chain of events into motion. Livia Gollancz received Wynne-Tyson's secret without much interest, but word of a new king eventually made its way back to A. Reynolds Morse, who was by this point back in the United States and still hoovering up every available morsel of information about Shiel. Morse was overjoyed to learn that the Kingdom of Redonda lived on and contacted Wynne-Tyson right away. The wealthy industrialist knew that the centenary of Shiel's accession to the throne was fast approaching, and he had an idea to celebrate the date by doing something no Redondan king had done for nearly a century: visit the island in person and climb to its top. King Juan II, perhaps sensing the scope of the spectacle already taking shape, immediately started to backpedal. But Morse would not be denied.

To lay the groundwork for the trip, Morse and his wife, Eleanor, flew down in November 1978 to scout out the area. There the Morses met up with poet and Redondan Duke of Tintinnabulation Royston Ellis, who lived in nearby Dominica, and the trio toured Montserrat together, seeking out anyone who knew Shiel's family and confirming details about his early life. At the time, it was only suspected that Shiel's family was part Black, and Morse was dogged in trying to confirm this fact, among others. He also discovered an intriguing alternate account of Redonda's origin story. A Montserratian historian named Delores Somerville claimed that the Shiells' visit to the island in 1880 was for a simple picnic with some friends, during which an Antiguan bishop hit Shiel on the shoulder with a tin can as a joke and named him duke of the island.

"King?" Morse asked.

"No," said Somerville. "Not King. Positively Duke."

The highlight of the Morses' weeklong trip was two excursions out to Redonda itself. First they hired a plane to fly them around the island at dusk, and later they sailed out in a motorboat to see it from sea level. Unfortunately, the waves were too intense during this second effort to attempt landing, so after spending hours just offshore, waiting for the wind and rain to die down, the party was forced to turn around and head back to Montserrat. Six months later, Morse was ready to repeat the entire journey—this time with the reluctant King Juan II in tow. As Wynne-Tyson wrote, "apprehensive reminders that I was a workaholic, single-handed, unclubby, travel-weary, apolitical, low-profile publisher-cum-writer cut no ice with Reynolds Morse."

What became known as the Second Shielian Discovery Expedition took place in April 1979, in the days leading up to the Easter long weekend. This time around, the team included not just Morse and Wynne-Tyson, but also Harvard dendrology professor Richard Howard, Denver museum curator Jack Murphy, Antigua-based yachtsman and historian Desmond Nicholson, Bert Wheeler of the Montserrat National Trust, and Dick Liddle, skipper of the *Nor'Easter*, the sixty-two-foot yacht that would transport the group out to Redonda in considerably more comfortable accommodations than Morse had experienced on his previous attempt.

This time, however, the party encountered an equally difficult obstacle before even leaving port: Caribbean red tape. It started when an Antiguan government bureaucrat named Peter Hilaire got wind of their trip and informed Morse et al. that the group needed multiple special permits—one just to take photographs of the island—before their voyage could go ahead. After spending several days filling out paperwork to acquire these permits, they were told that the Antiguan government was concerned the trip could pose a threat to national security, so Hilaire stipulated that he had to personally accompany the group out to Redonda. And since the trip was official government business, Hilaire also needed a security detail with him. Oh, and his girlfriend wanted to come, too.

The whole situation was as frustrating to the group as it was absurd, though Morse admitted, "Our conjoint inward amusement was far more difficult to conceal." While they waited for their permit applications to be processed, the group members spent their days schmoozing an entirely different group of government officials, who also needed wining and dining before they would approve what was technically an international journey between Montserrat and Redonda. Finally, on the afternoon of Thursday, April 12, the *Nor'Easter* set sail, and after a bumpy night's sleep offshore, the party awoke the morning of Good Friday with the island finally within reach.

The plan was for Liddle to keep the ship anchored about a hundred yards from the rocks while the group climbed into a rubber dinghy that would carry them to shore; each person would then wait for the crest of a wave before leaping onto the closest boulder. As members of the group worked up the nerve to jump, Morse and Wynne-Tyson both noted a conspicuously empty seat on the dinghy. For all of his earlier bluster, Peter Hilaire never left the safety of the *Nor'Easter*.

Considering the island's reputation for isolation, the first thing the group encountered on Redonda may come as a surprise: a building, with a person inside it. Back in the nineteenth century, a post office had been built on the

island for the phosphate miners' use, and in recent years it had been rebuilt near the shoreline as a one-room brick structure on stilts, its shelves bearing stamps produced by the Antiguan government to celebrate the mine's centenary. The post office may have been a little impractical, but it served a strategic purpose, reinforcing Antigua's claim to Redonda in the lead up to declaring its independence from the British Commonwealth a few years later, during which time the smaller island would officially become an Antiguan dependency. Its only employee was a part-time postmaster who, for perhaps the first time, now found himself with a lineup of customers, each seeking a souvenir to bring back home. The group then began their trek up the loose rock path, led by the three Antiguan locals who had been brought along as Hilaire's makeshift security detail. After an arduous climb of about an hour, the men emerged onto the plateau above, where they came across large hunks of rusted mining equipment and clusters of boobies in their nests, each making their distinctive call — a noise that sounded uncannily like a high-pitched "Oh no!" — as the humans approached. The largest remnant of the Redonda Phosphate Company was the manager's house, of which an entire floor was still largely intact, as was a lonely, curved staircase that now led nowhere. Aside from some agave plants in full orange-yellow flower, however, there was surprisingly little plant life, a fact that Professor Howard attributed to the island's half-starved goat population, which was comprised of the inbred descendants of the animals left behind by the departing mining company.

From the plateau, it was an even more difficult hike to the peak, especially under a Caribbean sun that was only getting hotter. Finally, at approximately 10:15 a.m., the group reached the summit, with its panoramic views of the sea and several other nearby islands. It was here that King Juan II, his hair ruffled and his shirtsleeves rolled to the elbows, raised a new Redondan flag made up of three horizontal stripes of blue, brown, and green to represent the ocean, the soil, and plant life, respectively. It was an appropriate gesture for an environmentalist like Wynne-Tyson, and the flag's playful use of materials — a pair of old pajamas, sewn together by his wife Jennifer — was an equally accurate sign of how seriously the ceremony was meant to be taken by the Antiguan government. Then, standing nearly a thousand feet above the waves crashing against the shore below, Wynne-Tyson pulled a piece of paper out of his pocket and read aloud to those assembled. King Juan II's proclamation gave a brief overview of Shiel's claim to the kingdom and announced that his visit was intended to peacefully advocate for a parallel history that was happening alongside the area's recent push towards sovereignty:

With the pending relinquishment of British control over Antigua and her dependencies, it has seemed timely to issue a reminder of Redonda's abiding monarchy. To this end the flag of Redonda has today been planted on the island's summit.

The motive for this action is not to provoke or to contest, but to confirm our right and desire to invite friendly and fruitful collaboration with the government of Antigua on the eve of that island's independence.

Once safely back down at the shoreline, expedition members picked up their stamps from the post office and reconvened on the *Nor'Easter* for a victorious post-summit dinner and drinks. To celebrate the accomplishment, King Juan II awarded a series of dukedoms to his companions — even Hilaire, who was dubbed Duke of Waladli, after one of the Indigenous peoples' names for Antigua.

Until Morse foisted the trip upon him, Wynne-Tyson hadn't really considered the role of the actual island of Redonda within the kingdom's mythology. Like Gawsworth, his primary concern had been the papers and copyrights of its previous rulers. As the first king to stand upon his territory since the teenaged Shiel, however, Wynne-Tyson realized there was a fair amount of overlap between the island's current reality and his personal values; after years of shirking his royal duties, perhaps Redonda wasn't strictly an embarrassing barroom fantasy after all. Not long after the Second Shielian Discovery Expedition concluded, a document was privately circulated among court members, pointing out that Redonda's isolation had the happy side effect of keeping it "totally free of beer cans, paper, plastic, and the other familiar pollutants of 'civilisation.'" Of course,

Wynne-Tyson on top of Redonda.

plenty of humans *had* left their mark on the island, most notably in the form of the mining company that had left behind crumbling machinery and starving goats as soon as their profits dried up. But it couldn't be denied that Redonda was unspoiled compared to any island where humans had settled permanently. While sailing back to Montserrat, Morse and Wynne-Tyson agreed that it was in the kingdom's best interests to keep it that way. The realm ought to remain a figurative kingdom, an idea that lived in the minds of its court members and well-wishers, fuelled by books and poems and other documents, and celebrated always in absentia. The island itself should remain free of all future development and exploitation.

Redonda, they agreed, was for the birds.

WHILE JOHN GAWSWORTH likely named Wynne-Tyson his literary executor because of his experience running Centaur Press, King Juan II also fit the bill as a writer — and his taste for mystique and pen names, which were kept so private that even Gawsworth may not have known about them, turned out to be entirely of a piece with the Redondan legend.

Wynne-Tyson wrote a dozen books; but, for much of his working life, only one, his first, appeared under his real name. The follow-up to *Accommodation Wanted*, which appeared in the first slate of Centaur titles and was the impetus for the formation of the press in the first place, was another collaboration with his first wife, Joan, this time about life with a young baby. Yet Wynne-Tyson's name was nowhere to be found on the cover of *Grin and Bear It*, which, he admitted ruefully, went on to become one of the most popular titles Centaur would ever publish.

Something must have appealed to Wynne-Tyson about trying on other identities while obscuring his real one, because for the next decade, that's how all of his fiction appeared. In 1959 Centaur published the aforementioned *Behind the Smiling Moon* under the pen name Michel Fourest; this was followed in the 1960s by *Square Peg* and *Don't Look and You'll Find Her*, a pair of social satires written under the new pseudonym Jeremy Pitt. These all received positive but modest receptions, confirming Wynne-Tyson's belief that, since he didn't have time to pursue both writing *and* publishing full-time, he had at least chosen the right one to extract a salary from.

Alter egos, of course, had long been an unofficial tradition within Redondan ranks. A recurring feature of King Juan I's state papers was the bestowal of new titles upon high-ranking members of his court. These titles tended to include an oblique reference to literature, geography, or some aspect of the member's civilian life, and in Gawsworth's later years were one of the few rituals he never abandoned. While whimsical, these alter egos allowed Gawsworth to tap into a sense of grandeur and elegance that his actual everyday life had never been able to provide.

There was also a pattern of pseudonyms among the Redondan kings' writings. One could argue that this dated all the way back to the day M.P. Shiel dropped the second L in his last name when submitting his early short stories, perhaps in an attempt to disguise his Caribbean heritage. Later in his career, Shiel teamed up with fellow pulp writer Louis Tracy to publish a series of stories and novels under at least two different pen names, and their mutually tangled bibliographies suggest there may be other secret collaborations yet to be identified. Gawsworth, meanwhile, built his entire career on the strategic use of pseudonyms. The man born Terence Ian Fytton Armstrong was known to write stories under one name and acquire them for his anthologies under the other. But his penchant for disguises went back further than that. One of Gawsworth's very first poetry chapbooks, 1931's *Snowballs*, appeared under the cacophonous alter ego Orpheus Scrannel, a name that was created by combining unrelated words from John Milton's pastoral elegy "Lycidas." *Snowballs* is a charmingly riled-up booklet of poems that takes aim at some of Gawsworth's more successful peers, as in the following, from "Fait Accompli":

> This bad poet
> sees his books
> through a thousand
> editions.

Surely he can
come to terms
in Hell on royalty
conditions?

When Wynne-Tyson started experimenting with fake names to assess his true worth as a novelist decades later, he turned out to be in surprisingly good company.

Beginning in the late 1960s, Wynne-Tyson's tastes as a writer gravitated towards non-fiction — and in particular the social and environmental activism that had been instilled in him by his mother as a child. These books brought a return to the use of his real name, borne of a real-life anxiety that came with raising daughters during the height of the free-love movement. Fortunately, Wynne-Tyson was confident that a natural correction was already on the horizon. "There is every indication," he writes in the introduction to 1972's *The Civilised Alternative*, "that more and more [young people] are discovering that the negative answer of retreat into obsessive drug-taking, loveless sexuality and gestures of society-rejection that nevertheless are only possible while that society exists to be used and abused, is unsatisfying, inadequate and deeply frustrating to any idealistic and creative impulse." Three years later, Wynne-Tyson focused his thoughts further into *Food for a Future*, a book-length case for vegetarianism. And he spent much of the early 1980s assembling *The Extended Circle*, a centuries-spanning compendium of quotes about animal welfare and human compassion more generally. The *Times* declared it "angry and sorrowful, but also full of beauty."

Wynne-Tyson returned to fiction exactly once during this era, and that was to pen a novel inspired by his trip to the Caribbean with A. Reynolds Morse. *So Say Banana Bird* was the first work of fiction to appear under Wynne-Tyson's real name and was published in 1984 by Pythian Books, a Centaur imprint created expressly for this purpose. It tells the story of one Matthew Braine, a washed-up novelist who sails away from his home in England solo in order to quietly kill himself at sea. But his plans are thwarted in part due to a stowaway kitten, and he ends up sailing across the Atlantic. His first sighting of land is a mysterious island in the West Indies, roughly a thousand feet tall, that is ringed with steep, jagged cliffs. "The rock was grey," Wynne-Tyson writes, "he supposed volcanic, relieved here and there by drifts of green and streaks of white." On impulse, Braine decides to climb the island, making his way up a treacherous gully to a plateau where he runs into a thicket of prickly cacti and, in the distance, a wild goat traversing the rocks with ease. "It would not have been difficult," writes Wynne-Tyson, echoing *The Purple Cloud*, "to sell himself the fantasy that he was the last man alive in a mysteriously abandoned world." Here the island is called Zafada, but its true identity is obvious to anyone able to read between the lines.

Other locations in the novel are decoded just as easily. "Monesterio," the much larger and more-populated island nearby, is Wynne-Tyson's stand in for Antigua; "Port St. George" is his version of English Harbour, on Antigua's southern tip. The real-life version of that harbour was, in fact, where Wynne-Tyson wrote much of the novel while returning to the area for a vacation in the winter of 1980. He was inspired, if you want to call it that, by the comical amounts of political meddling he'd endured in Antigua the previous year, and his protagonist finds himself enmeshed in a similar web of scandals and low-level corruption. But as the novel progresses, the legend of an odd kingdom surrounding Zafada, begun by a science-fiction writer and carried on by a run-down poet, begins to occupy more and more of the narrative. Wynne-Tyson adds a new wrinkle of family drama to his semi-fictionalized version of Redonda by making its third king the son of the second, and resentful of his father's choice to participate in this bizarre story in the first place: "Instead of being remembered as a first-rate writer, he chose to die a down-market king."

For our visiting narrator, however, Zafada is a source of wonder and creativity. While in the Caribbean, Matthew feels the long-dormant spark of inspiration returning and begins compulsively writing what he suspects might be his best novel yet. Yet artistic fulfillment comes with a price. *So Say Banana Bird* ends with Matthew fleeing a group of local toughs and taking refuge on top of Zafada once more — only to realize, too late, that the worker at the post office below has given away his location.

To readers already versed in the Redondan legend, *So Say Banana Bird* contains several clues and winks, including an island-top proclamation and a homemade pajama flag. But to most, Wynne-Tyson's novel was their first introduction to the kingdom, and the book gained a new level of intrigue once word got out that Wynne-Tyson was its real-life king. The *Sunday Express Magazine* announced Redonda as "the world's weirdest monarchy" and opened its story with a scene of King Juan II rummaging around in his fridge for a beer. "The queen is knocking up some bread and cheese," he cheerfully told the reporter. "She'll be along in a minute." Yet Wynne-Tyson quickly realized, as Shiel had before him,

Wynne-Tyson pointing out Redonda on a map of the Caribbean.

that media attention resulting from Redonda was a mixed blessing. It might help with book sales, but it also led to confrontation with other claimants to the throne, many of whom had no idea until then that Wynne-Tyson was one of them. Following his appearance on *Midweek*, a prominent show on BBC Radio 4, producers received phone calls from four different people claiming to be the *real* king of Redonda, and each upset that a pretender like Wynne-Tyson was allowed to perpetuate his false claim on the air. One threatened legal action against the network after hearing a promotional spot advertising Wynne-Tyson's appearance.

"A fruitcake?" the producer asked Wynne-Tyson.

"Has things a bit out of proportion," he replied.

Privately, however, Wynne-Tyson couldn't discount the possibility that each of these callers could very well have in their possession another irrevocable covenant signed by a desperate King Juan I.

REDONDA MAY HAVE given Wynne-Tyson material for a novel, not to mention a pair of memorable Caribbean vacations, but he still wasn't thrilled to be occupying its throne. As a man of his word, however, he continued dutifully performing royal tasks when necessary. In 1982, Wynne-Tyson published an essay outlining the basic history of the kingdom, and concluded, "The legend of Redonda is, and should remain, a pleasing and eccentric fairy tale; a piece of literary mythology to be taken with salt, romantic sighs, appropriate perplexity, some amusement, but without great seriousness." He also stood up for local interests, alerting readers of the British *Daily Mail* to an unsightly and "irresponsible" housing development set to take place near Antigua's historic Nelson's Dockyard. Wynne-Tyson also supplied the foreword to *The Dragon of Redonda*, a picture book written by Jan Jackson and illustrated by Frané Lessac. In it, three children get shipwrecked on the shores of an uninhabited Caribbean island — its king, we are told, is nowhere to be found — and rescue a dragon named Rupert who is trapped inside a nearby volcano. "The pictures are splendid," King Juan II writes, "but perhaps they make Redonda rather prettier than it really is, for in fact it can be a quite frightening place, especially at night under the full moon when the wind (or could it be Rupert?) roars between the peaks." Above the foreword is an illustration of Wynne-Tyson in formal dress, smiling at a booby standing on an open book, with a crown floating a few inches above his bald head. The illustration is accompanied by a slogan written in Latin, also provided by Wynne-Tyson. *Ride si sapis*, it read, which translates to *Laugh if you are wise*.

THERE WAS a heat wave in Alberta that summer, so I'd gone downstairs to sleep on the couch in my living room. Not that it had helped. When my phone alarm finally went off at 5 a.m., I was staring at the ceiling, with no memories of achieving anything you'd call a functional sleep state and no dreams, Redondan or otherwise. But I also didn't feel tired. I was far too excited for that.

I'd recently received an email from Tilly Vacher, the eldest daughter of Jon Wynne-Tyson. She bore some sad news: her father had passed away a few months earlier, at the age of ninety-five. Vacher was the one who had first told me that Wynne-Tyson was living in an assisted-care facility and therefore not available for an interview, but she had been kind enough to answer a few questions about the kingdom on his behalf. Now, with his passing, Wynne-Tyson had left behind a literary archive that rivalled even Gawsworth's: thousands of books, typescripts, photographs, and correspondence, as well as the entire working history of Centaur Press, all kept carefully organized and intact. It was the product of an entire life devoted to literature, and his family had decided to put it up for auction. Most of the three-hundred-plus lots would have no trouble drawing interest, but Tilly had thought of me specifically because of the half-dozen that had to do with Redonda. "All a mixed bag," she cautioned. "I simply didn't have time to read through every sheet of paper, sadly. But lots of fun stuff."

She attached a link to an itemized preview, and as I clicked through the descriptions, I felt my cheeks flush. In all the time I'd spent trawling the internet for books connected to Redonda, the rarest and most expensive were inevitably the ones that had passed through the hands of a king. I had one such book in my possession already, and it had cost me an amount I was still embarrassed to say out loud. Now I was looking at photographs of hundreds of them, casually lumped into piles.

One of the lots Vacher had flagged for me was a collection of fifty-three books by or about M.P. Shiel and Arthur Machen. The next was a set of roughly sixty titles by Javier Marías, in both English and Spanish, most of which had been inscribed by King Xavier to his royal predecessor. A third contained correspondence between the two men—including, I could only assume, the letters detailing their Redondan transfer back in the mid-1990s. Yet it was the final two lots that I kept going back to. One was a box of books and documents related to Wynne-Tyson's tumultuous friendship with Gawsworth, which was said to include critical Redondan pieces like signed copies of King Juan I's state papers and a copy of Gawsworth's elusive will—the same document that had eluded me back at the University of Reading. The other was simply titled "Kingdom of Redonda." To most people, it probably looked like a bunch of vacation mementos; to me, it was a one-of-a-kind piece of literary history. This lot contained all of Wynne-Tyson's personal scrapbooks and photo albums from his trip to Redonda in 1979, along with piles of press clippings and several envelopes' worth of related documents and correspondence. Tucked into the back of one folder was the hand-sewn pajama flag that had once flown from atop the place now known as King Juan's Peak.

In all, these five lots represented the most thorough and well-documented collection of Redondan material I'd ever seen. The only comparable I could think of was from back in 1995, when Wynne-Tyson auctioned off the beat-up boxes of Gawsworth's papers that he'd been safekeeping, and which had sold at Sotheby's for a reported £10,000.

I didn't have anywhere near that kind of money. But I had a hunch that I might not need to. As I clicked through the rest of the auction, it was clear that the most attractive lots had nothing whatsoever to do with Redonda. So while most people were busy competing for signed correspondence from W.H. Auden, or a run of signed first editions by Dodie Smith — whose book *The Hundred and One Dalmatians* was supposedly inspired by a suggestion from Wynne-Tyson — maybe I could sneak past and end up with the Redondan material more or less to myself. Plus, the auction house had provided estimated values for each lot, and the ones for the Redondan ones seemed very reasonable. If I were able to land the Shiel collection even at the high end of the estimate, I could cover my costs by flipping a couple of the titles I didn't want or already owned. That would make the rest of the books, essentially, free. Near as I could tell, just two of the Machen books on offer were worth the lot's total estimated value of £100–£150. Ditto the signed Marías collection. My initial napkin math was so encouraging that it scared me a little. Was it possible I was going to buy *everything?*

Antiquarian bookseller Roy Harley Lewis once wrote that the auction room meant different things to different people: "lifeblood to the professional dealer; an awesome spectacle to the novice buyer, frightened to breathe in case the movement of his shoulders be misrepresented; a source of amusement to students of human behaviour." That basic framework seemed to hold up, even though this particular auction was being held online, on UK time. By 5:02 a.m., I had the kettle on and was seated at my desk, triple-checking that I wouldn't accidentally press the wrong button and either end up bidding on the wrong item or shutting my entire computer down by mistake.

I'd never been part of a live online auction before, so I used the first few lots as an opportunity to get familiar with the process. As each lot was introduced, a picture of it flashed onto the centre of the screen. Underneath was the opening price, plus a black button indicating the amount of the next available bid, which turned grey whenever someone made it. The difference between this and an eBay auction was the audio feed, which piped the auctioneer's rapid-fire encouragements — and occasional gentle prodding — into my office from halfway around the world.

The main thing I noticed, though, was how quickly everything moved. This was, of course, by design. Even if each lot took only a minute from start to finish, that added up to more than five straight hours of auctioneering. It was in the house's interest to keep things moving, which was why more than a dozen lots were already gone in the time it took me to get my bearings. The rhythm was hypnotic, actually: a lot would pop up on the screen, float there for a few seconds as the auctioneer coaxed higher and higher bids out of his virtual audience, and then disappear, claimed, back into the ether. I wasn't sure if it was good or bad news that the Auden letters I'd spotted earlier ended up selling for £1,550, significantly more than their estimated value. So, too, did copies of the short-lived Vorticist magazine *Blast*, edited by Wyndham Lewis. Yet other items garnered few bids at all, and I didn't know enough about most of them to spot a pattern; Wynne-Tyson, it seemed, was a man of many interests, from the history of Sussex to fine automobiles, and all of these were represented in the auction.

Before I knew it, the first Redondan lot appeared in the on-deck circle in the corner of my screen. I'd already written out my plan on a piece of notebook paper, ranking all five lots in terms of priority, as well as how much I was willing to spend on each one. Luckily, the one I wanted the most was also the first up: Lot 74, the "Kingdom of Redonda" collection featuring Wynne-Tyson's vacation photos and pajama flag. I wasn't sure if there was such a thing as auction strategy in the online world, but I decided I wasn't going to risk playing it cool. My mind was full of images of my internet connection suddenly crashing just as I went to finally place my bid. No way was I going to chance it. As soon as the button went black, I clicked.

"And we've got an online bid to kick things off," the auctioneer purred.

For a brief moment, everything stood still. I was listed as the highest bidder, and nobody was kicking me off the perch. *Is that it?* I thought feverishly. *Am I the only one who wants this?* But then the next-bid button turned grey again, and my fantasy of waltzing away uncontested was dispelled.

I bid again. So did the other person. Within the span of a few seconds, we'd gone back and forth three times, in the process pushing the price right into the middle of the house's estimated value. Each time I saw I no longer owned the highest bid, I clicked whatever new amount showed up immediately. As this was happening, I couldn't help but wonder who it was I was bidding against. For whatever reason, I had a hunch it wasn't just some profit-seeking dealer on the other side of the screen. After all, there were no *books* in this lot. Nothing in the lot held any conventional resale value at all—unless you were looking specifically for the history of Redonda.

I pressed the bid button again, and this time we were up to £500. This was now past even the high end of the estimate, and right at the ceiling of what I'd told myself I was willing to spend. But I didn't feel as though I had a choice. If I missed out on this, I knew I'd regret it for years.

And then something unexpected happened. The button turned black—and stayed that way. My bid stood on the screen, untouched, for a second, then two, then three. *What's happening?* The auctioneer gave the room one last chance, then said: "Sold!"

By this point, it was past 6 a.m. my time, and the sun was starting to come up. Awoken by a series of only half-stifled noises coming from the main floor of the house, my son Finn wandered down to find me with my arms raised above my head and letting out a small whoop at my desk. I tried to explain what I was doing, but the auction was already moving on, so I just whisked him up onto my lap so that neither of us would miss what was about to happen next.

The next lot was the one about Shiel and Machen, and if I had any daydreams about flipping half of the titles to pay for the other half, they were quickly squashed. A dozen bids poured in as soon as the lot went live, more than tripling the estimate within the first minute. I knew Shiel had devoted fans, but this was more passion than I'd planned for. Still, there was no time to wallow in my disappointment. It was time to get ready for the second most important item on my list.

Lot 79 was the Gawsworth-Redonda collection. Once again, it wasn't so much the books I was interested in as the miscellaneous documents and papers — which, I hoped, might shine a new light on how the kingdom was understood by Juans I and II; at the very least, they were pieces of literary history that were worth preserving. As soon as the button went black, I returned to my strategy of click first, click often, and once again found myself in competition with at least one other bidder. Finn had by now figured out the rules of the game, and he started cheering me on as if we were playing a video game together. "Do another one!" he said. "Are you going to do another one?" Soon enough, I didn't need to. The lot was mine for £460.

Finn was excited, too, but he looked at the price in confusion. "Uh, how much is that in dollars?" he asked. When I gave him a rough estimate, his eyes went wide and he went back upstairs to break the news to his mom, who was still asleep.

The final two lots I was interested in exploded their estimated values before I even had a chance to place a bid. For the auctioneer, this was all a blip in his day, and he moved on to the next one without ceremony. But I felt as exhausted as if I'd just finished an entire day's work. I closed my laptop and redid the math. Including auction-house fees and the cost of shipping everything to North America, this was more money than I'd ever spent on anything that I couldn't drive or live inside. I stood up and went to the kitchen to put the kettle back on, giddy. Jon Wynne-Tyson's Redondan archive was intact, and it was headed my way.

TWO MONTHS LATER, a pair of large, heavy boxes arrived at my front door from the auction house in the UK, weighing forty kilograms in total. One of the boxes had a label taped on top that simply read: "HEAVY!" Inside was more Redonda material than I'd even dared hope.

There were press clippings. There were photographs. There were royalty statements and business cards and typescripts. There was the original document formalizing the transfer of Shiel and Gawsworth's literary executorship from Wynne-Tyson to Marías, signed at the bottom by both men. There was a document suggesting that Shiel had once been the secretary of Florence Nightingale. There were letters and postcards. There was a photocopy of Gawsworth's 1928 report card from Merchant Taylors' School, in which he placed fifth out of twenty-seven students in English literature, but twenty-third overall, owing in part, his teachers wrote, to a lack of focus. (The reverse of the report card was covered in Gawsworth's doodles of soldiers, judges, and a talking tree.) The range of information was so wide as to be completely overwhelming. It took me weeks to go through all of the material, and to this day every time I open it back up I find something fascinating that I seem to have missed every other time around.

Even on first glance, however, the contents were electrifying. On my first trip to England, I'd booked a morning at the British Library so I could see King Juan I's State Papers — now I was holding more than twenty copies of the three instalments, each of them signed by Gawsworth. There were photos of both Gawsworth and Wynne-Tyson I'd never seen before, a stack of blank Redondan bookplates, and multiple copies of rare titles related to the kingdom. (I nearly had a heart attack when I unearthed a copy of Dylan Thomas's Redondan

poems, only to realize that they were reproductions.) Tucked into the back of one of Wynne-Tyson's photo albums was *the actual flag* he'd planted on top of Redonda during his visit in 1980. To try to make sense of it all, I invited over my neighbour Jeff, who also happens to work in a special-collections library. We stood together over the mass of folders and binders spread across my kitchen table, and he made several good suggestions about how to retain Wynne-Tyson's organization system while also updating some of the more unstable materials, like the thicker and dangerously sticky plastic King Juan II had stored his Redondan photos inside. But he warned me to be careful. With photos this old, if I removed the plastic too quickly, Jeff said, parts of the image might stick to it and the entire picture would be ruined. I thanked him, said goodbye, and then gingerly put everything away as if I'd just purchased forty kilograms of explosives instead.

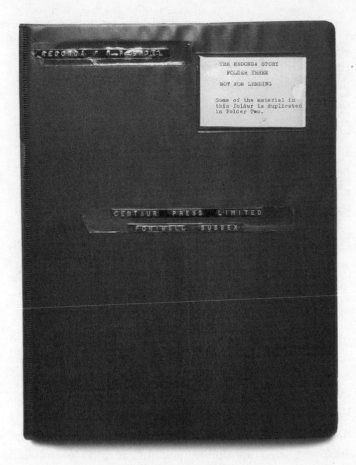

The following was detected on the folder label:

THE REDONDA STORY
FOLDER THREE
NOT FOR LENDING

Some of the material in
this folder is duplicated
in Folder Two.

The Redonda Story, *folder three,*
from the Jon Wynne-Tyson archive.

Perhaps the single most important document I found in the Wynne-Tyson archive was a copy of Gawsworth's elusive will. This was the document that would, at long last, confirm whom Gawsworth intended to be his successor to the throne, and it was sitting inside one of a series of folders prepared by King Juan II as a sort of Redonda crash course.

"THE REDONDA STORY, FOLDER THREE," the cover read. "NOT FOR LENDING." Inside, following a copy of the sheet music for "O God Who Gave Our Island Soil" and a press release for *So Say Banana Bird*, was a document that began, "This is the last Will and Testament, cancelling all previous Wills, of Terence Ian Fytton Armstrong, known as 'John Gawsworth' ...." The document had been written in Italy on April 24, 1970, and named Ian Fletcher and Jon Wynne-Tyson his co-literary executors, responsible for cooperating to their "utmost capacity to keep my memory green." Gawsworth also requested that they edit two books: a new collection of his poems, as well as a collection of letters that Gawsworth had received from other famous writers over the decades. (It's unclear whether either of these projects was pursued, but neither was published.)

There was just one problem with the will: it didn't mention Redonda at all.

THROUGHOUT THE 1980s and '90s, Jon Wynne-Tyson grew increasingly irritated by how much of his time was being taken up by a small but committed group of Redondan obsessives around the world—including multiple competing claimants to the throne, few of whom showed any signs of understanding that the kingdom was a fantasy, with a unique history that wound its way through an increasingly neglected corner of English literature. It wasn't simply a title up for the taking. Privately, Wynne-Tyson *was* interested in finding a replacement. But that person needed to fit two different sets of criteria: they would have to assume responsibility for both previous kings' literary estates, and they would also have to take over the supervision of a story that, while not meant to be taken literally, had nonetheless built decades' worth of mythology around it. It was a complicated task, and Wynne-Tyson wasn't convinced he'd ever find the right candidate.

Fortunately, across the channel, a rising star in the world of Spanish literature sat at his typewriter, smoking cigarettes and working on a novel featuring a memorable appearance from Redonda's most infamous fallen king. The publication of Javier Marías's *Todas las almas* would once again set the kingdom on a wild and unexpected new trajectory.

MARÍAS WAS BORN in Madrid on September 20, 1951, into a family of intellectuals. His mother, Dolores, was a translator and publisher before becoming the full-time parent of five sons, of which Javier was the fourth. His father, Julián, meanwhile, was a well-known philosopher who opposed Franco during the Spanish Civil War and was thrown in jail after a friend betrayed him by reporting—and exaggerating—his political leanings to the new dictatorship. After his release from prison, Julián was barred from teaching or publishing in Spain. Instead, he was forced to seek out work in other countries, and the rest of his family would travel along with him; Javier's first memory was of the snowy New England landscape, where his father was teaching at the time. Yet no matter where the Marías family lived, or for how long, their house was always crammed full of books, to the point that little Javier got used to elbowing piles of them out of the way so that he could play his own games. The home was also a site of endless discussion and debate. Even as a boy, when Javier had finished making his point, Julián would always push him to follow his argument further and see where it led. "You've just started, what else?" he would ask. "Keep on thinking, keep on thinking, keep on thinking ..."

As a teenager, Marías fell in love with literature. But he wasn't particularly interested in what was being published in Spain, instead finding himself drawn to the more exotic worlds of English and American fiction. In addition to devouring foreign adventure novels one after another while on family summer vacations, he started writing stories of his own, publishing his first piece, "The Life and Death of Marcelino Iturriaga," in a Barcelona newspaper when he was just fourteen. He wrote his first novel the following year. Marías believed his interest in storytelling could be traced back to the toy soldiers he had played with as a child. "When you think about it," he wrote, "those games in which — by following certain rules or conventions, and trying always to keep within the bounds of plausibility — one decided the fates and vicissitudes of soldiers or dolls were probably a first decisive step towards writing fiction." For this reason, Marías kept rows of little tin and plastic soldiers lined up on his bookshelves well into adulthood — a reminder to never take his profession too seriously.

The only thing that rivalled Marías's love of literature was his love of film. As a teenager, he developed a routine of going to the movies several times each week, and at seventeen he headed off to Paris to live with his uncle, the film director Jesús Franco, for six weeks. In that time Marías watched nearly one hundred different films in Parisian cinemas, and also wrote the bulk of what would become his first published novel, *Los dominios del lobo*, set during the golden age of Hollywood.[†] To finance his film habit, Marías saved money by eating a diet of mostly bread and mustard. He also earned some extra cash by busking along the Champs-Élysées, where he sang songs by North American acts like Bob Dylan, Leonard Cohen, and Crosby, Stills & Nash.

If local literature didn't excite Marías, then he was at least willing to add to the body of work available in his native tongue by becoming a translator from English to Spanish. His first job was a series of horror film scripts commissioned by his Uncle Jesús, but when he graduated from university in 1972, Marías set his ambitions higher. (By this time he'd also published his second novel, the adventure pastiche *Travesía del horizonte*, or *Voyage Along the Horizon*.) Over the next few

Curiously, despite its setting, this is one of the few Marías novels yet to be translated into English.

years Marías would translate short stories by Thomas Hardy and John Updike, poems by Vladimir Nabokov, Frank O'Hara, and Robert Louis Stevenson, and, most notably, *The Life and Opinions of Tristram Shandy, Gentleman*. It took Marías four years to complete his version of Laurence Sterne's famously complex and inventive eighteenth-century novel, but it proved to be time well spent: the published version won accolades across Spain, including the national award for translation in 1979. Juan Benet, a Spanish novelist who also acted as Marías's literary mentor, compared his young protege to the Renaissance scholar Erasmus. For his part, Marías relished the opportunity to so deeply inhabit another writer's prose. He believed the careful, meticulous work that went into translation in turn strengthened his own writing, which he was still working on between translation gigs.

Because Marías's early novels were inspired by the English and American traditions, they didn't intuitively fit into the Spanish literary landscape, and it took time for his work to become accepted in his home country. One local academic described him early on as a "goddamn Anglosaxonist," a comment that amused Marías to no end — in part because his books had an equally difficult time finding a home at an English-language press. By the time one of his novels was finally translated into the language he'd long admired and translated from, Marías had been publishing for twenty years. To introduce Marías to English readers, the UK's Harvill Press selected a book set in a familiar city, and which also featured the reflective, middle-aged male narrator archetype that would appear in many other Marías novels to come.

By 1989, when Marías wrote *Todas las almas* (*All Souls*), his sixth novel, he had already known about John Gawsworth for some time. Four years earlier, Marías described for the

Spanish-language newspaper *El País* coming across signed copies of Gawsworth's work while travelling in Oxford and feeling a strange sense of connection to this forgotten writer. That interest would be passed on to the fictional narrator of *All Souls*, who, like Marías, is struck by the notion that someone could be an acclaimed poet—and self-proclaimed king—one day and homeless the next. Gawsworth appears in Marías's novel as a minor figure, but a useful one. The narrator first learns about him thanks to an encounter with a book collector, based on the real-life collector Roger Dobson, and with Gawsworth's name now planted in his head, the narrator finds himself looking for it on the shelves of every bookshop he visits.

Over the course of the novel, Gawsworth's name also becomes shorthand for a kind of cautionary tale. Marías's narrator takes regular walks around Oxford and notices, at first only glancingly, that the city has a large homeless population. As these walks continue, he starts to recognize some of the beggars individually, and in some cases he learns details about the lives they led before falling on hard times. Homelessness obscures a person's past accomplishments, and even Gawsworth's lengthy literary resumé and status as a war veteran became invisible to those who came across him in his final years, asleep on a park bench. The narrator of *All Souls* shares certain interests with Gawsworth, too, chief among them book collecting, which by the narrator's own description has a "morbid" quality to it. So why does this poet, "a man with a false name whom I never met and whose writings—which are all the visible remains I have of him, that and the photographs of him alive and dead," hold such fascination? Because the narrator is worried that he might one day become him.

ALL SOULS proved to be a savvy way to introduce Marías to the English-speaking world. Reviewers in the UK and North America alike were impressed by the elegance of his prose (as rendered in Margaret Jull Costa's translation) and hailed the book as "stunning" and "a dazzling example of the Oxford novel." BBC Radio interviewed Marías in 1992 to promote the book, and one of the people who happened to be tuning in was Jon Wynne-Tyson. King Juan II was intrigued when he heard the initial description of Marías's novel, and outright shocked when he heard the Spanish novelist mention his late friend by name. Later that year, Marías and Wynne-Tyson's paths crossed more directly, and once again the cause was Gawsworth. This time Wynne-Tyson discovered that Marías had published one of Gawsworth's short stories, "How It Happened," in a Spanish-language anthology of fantastic stories called *Cuentos únicos* — without permission from Gawsworth's estate, aka Wynne-Tyson himself. As a formality, Wynne-Tyson wrote to Marías to let him know about the oversight, as well as to introduce himself and provide an update on the state of the Kingdom of Redonda. Marías wrote back right away, delighted to learn that the kingdom lived on.

A few years later, Wynne-Tyson decided it was time to finally divest himself of the beat-up archive of papers and memorabilia he had inherited from Gawsworth before his death. Eleven large boxes were listed for sale with Sotheby's in July 1995, where they were purchased, over the phone, for an estimated £10,000. The identity of the winning bidder was kept anonymous, and even Wynne-Tyson didn't know at the time that it was none other than Marías himself, flush with cash from a recent literary prize (though he claims he paid much less than the reported sum). When he realized the truth of what had happened, Wynne-Tyson wrote, "the pieces began to fall into place." Once again, his thoughts were turning to succession. But this time a clear candidate was emerging.

What followed was a courtship so subtle that both parties found themselves at times driven to confusion. Wynne-Tyson wrote letters hinting that he was perhaps considering abdicating the Redondan throne, and Marías responded sympathetically and with interest, but unsure what, exactly, was being proposed. The two went back and forth like this, with Wynne-Tyson comparing their exchanges to a delicate dance and wondering, "Perhaps I should come down on my heels more audibly." Wynne-Tyson had grown tired of debating with "pretenders," and he hoped that Marías's interest in Gawsworth's eccentric, tragic biography was enough to convince him to take the whole endeavour off his hands.

It didn't hurt that Marías's writings also contained a decidedly Redondan streak. His early novel *Voyage Along the Horizon*, for instance, includes among its cast a sea captain who once discovered a previously unknown island in the Pacific. The island, Marías writes, in Kristina Cordero's translation, "seemed to have a mysterious hold on him, calling him away for countless trips and long, unexplained absences." Meanwhile, the anthology that first brought Marías and Wynne-Tyson into contact, *Cuentos únicos*, contained several pieces that Marías had retrieved from the old ghost-story anthologies edited by Gawsworth in the 1930s. In addition to these pieces, Marías had included work by Lawrence Durrell and even Sir Winston Churchill, as well as a writer named James Denham, whose biographical note indicated he died in combat in North Africa in 1943. In reality, "James Denham" was Marías himself — another pseudonym to add to the list.

Eventually, Marías picked up on the increasingly overt hints being dropped in Wynne-Tyson's letters. The good news was that Marías *was* interested in the throne. But he wanted to be clear on the terms of the transaction before accepting. What duties would he be responsible for? Wynne-Tyson explained that any future King of Redonda had to oversee the estates of Gawsworth and Shiel, as he had been doing for the past twenty-five years. They would also have to keep the Redondan legend alive—which wouldn't be difficult for Marías, because in a sense *All Souls* was already doing that, as the novel continued to find new readers around the world. Beyond that, however, the new king could interpret his role however he saw fit. Privately, Marías was charmed by the whole proposition and felt he had no choice but to accept the offer when it was finally presented in full. As he told the BBC, "I shouldn't be termed a real novelist if I didn't accept the novel-esque in my own life when it came."

In April 1997, Marías and Wynne-Tyson met for lunch at London's Basil Street Hotel to discuss the transfer of power. Wynne-Tyson wanted to confirm in person that Marías would be a suitable match for the throne, and the pair got along well enough that Wynne-Tyson ended up bringing Marías back home with him to meet his wife, Jennifer. "I had the feeling," Marías wrote later, "that Jon needed Jennifer's approval or go-ahead, as if he trusted her judgment more than his own." She, too, signed off. And so, on July 6, 1997—the date of his seventy-third birthday—King Juan II officially abdicated the Redondan throne. Taking his place was Javier Marías, now known as King Xavier.

PALACES and PASSPORTS 17

WYNNE-TYSON couldn't have been more relieved to have found a successor. "I had to pass on the title at some stage," he told the *Redondan Cultural Foundation Newsletter,* a sporadic publication (with a tongue-in-cheek title) founded by Roger Dobson and Mark Valentine in the early 1990s to gather all news about the kingdom in one place. "Now I'm in my mid-seventies, and while I still have my marbles, the time seemed right. Javier is the best candidate for the role. He has an international reputation as an author, and his writings about Redonda have raised the profile of the legend considerably." Marías, for his part, accepted the title gracefully, and called Redonda "a charming fantasy."

As a ruler, King Xavier—the spelling derived from the way Marías's mother used to spell his actual first name— vowed up front not to spend any time whatsoever squabbling with the other claimants to the throne. "I am not going to discuss 'legitimacies' with anyone," he said. "The truth is, I do not think 'kings' should be giving interviews at all." He was, however, willing to write another novel about it. *Negra espalda del tiempo* was published in Spain barely a year after the coronation; it appeared in English in the UK and

North America as *Dark Back of Time* in 2001, where it further bewitched readers, especially those in search of simple answers about Marías's newfound claims to royalty. Wendy Lesser, for instance, reviewing the novel for the *New York Times*, spent an entire paragraph mulling the reality of this supposed island kingdom:

> *Dark Back of Time* mentions that Marías, like John Gawsworth before him, has become king of Redonda. If you go to the Web site of the Redonda Foundation, at www.redonda.org, you will see that there is actually a dispute involving Javier Marías's sovereignty over this tiny Caribbean island. The English-speaking disputant employs the word "impostor," which happens to be a favorite Marías word. Has Marías himself set up the whole dispute — perhaps the whole Redonda site — as yet another literary game? Probably not: Marías claims in *Dark Back of Time* to be completely computerless, and for some reason I believe him. But the uncertainty is nonetheless tantalizing. It is impossible to know, with anything Marías has touched, who is whose fictional creation.

Intrigued uncertainty is, of course, a defining feature of the entire Redondan project, and in that sense Lesser was closer to the truth than she realized.

Perhaps, at one time, further clarification was intended. *Dark Back of Time* contains multiple references to a planned third book on the kingdom. More than twenty years later, it has not yet appeared. And yet this absence, too, is appropriately Redondan, for the kingdom is as much a story of *missing* books as it is of finished ones. Shiel had teased readers with his concept of four linked novels, each supposedly based on a found notebook, but he only ever published three, leaving the contents of the final one open to speculation. Gawsworth's career, meanwhile, was full of ideas that never made it to print, none more tantalizing than those works of non-fiction that could have further illuminated the kingdom: his planned biography of Shiel, his hospital-penned memoir, and even, at one time, his history of Redonda as a whole. Marías had also participated in his own way, reminding readers in *Dark Back of Time* that Gawsworth's poems had been collected "between 1943 and 1945 in six volumes — most of them printed in India — but, peculiarly, the fourth volume appears never to have been published, though it has a title (*Farewell to Youth*). It simply does not exist."[*] Considered within the overall Redondan oeuvre, each of these missing titles only added to the ambiguity at the centre of the story. When Shiel and Marías left gaps in their stories, and then drew our attention to the fact that they were doing so, it fell to the reader to fill in those gaps for ourselves. But we will never know for sure what they were intended to contain. How much of the kingdom are we meant to take seriously? What is it all supposed to mean?

As a novelist, Marías was well acquainted with ambiguity. In fact, the first thing he ever published about Gawsworth, in *El País* on May 22, 1985 — years before he became tangled up in Redonda — was a column in praise of the unknown. "What I want to point out," he writes, "is that, no matter how much we know about the lives of illustrious men and women, the shadows will always surpass greatly the parts upon which

This is true, and matches an entry in *The New Cambridge Bibliography of English Literature*, from which it was presumably taken.

light can be cast." For a forgotten poet like Gawsworth, that ratio of darkness to light was even more pronounced, and even more impenetrable. And it wasn't just people who could never be fully deciphered, either. In *Dark Back of Time*, Marías refers to the island itself the same way. Redonda "can be located and does figure on certain maps," he writes, "but not on others." It all depended on how closely a person was willing to look.

READERS WEREN'T the only ones unsure what to make of Marías's claim to the Redondan throne. His friends and peers were puzzled, too — especially those who now found themselves being offered titles and positions in his royal court. It was the fulfillment of a promise he'd teased near the end of *Dark Back of Time*. "I'll have to name my own peers," he wrote, "since I must now play along with the game."

Marías gave out his first batch of titles in 1999, and in the years since has faithfully continued John Gawsworth's vision of Redonda as an "intellectual aristocracy" of writers, artists, and other creative people whose work he admires. Among those inducted into the court of King Xavier are filmmakers Pedro Almodóvar (Duke of Trémula) and Francis Ford Coppola (Duke of Megalopolis), poet John Ashbery (Duke of Convex), sociologist Pierre Bourdieu (Duke of Uprooting), and novelists Arturo Pérez-Reverte (Duke of Corso and Royal Fencing Master) and A.S. Byatt (Duchess of Morpho Eugenia). As in Gawsworth's time, these titles were received with the same playfulness with which they had been assigned: to use Marías's term, it was all understood to be part of the game, requiring only a sense of play and a gentle suspension of disbelief. "It is to me a pleasant diversion," Byatt told the BBC about her place within the Redondan court. "Javier is such an extraordinary contrast, between the more deeply serious than anybody I know, and the elegantly frivolous. So I take it seriously because I take him seriously. The fact that he — in this strange, precise, determined, profound way — continues to conduct the business of this imaginary realm, I just feel privileged to be part of it."

Again, as with his predecessors, Marías didn't bestow titles along with much in the way of actual duties, though several of his more design-minded dukes and duchesses contributed pieces of royal paraphernalia. The American architect Frank Gehry, as the Duke of Nervión, submitted a sketch of an imaginary Redondan palace, with an abundance of doors to emphasize its open nature. A fanciful throne and crown were conceived by industrial designer Ron Arad and jeweller Helena Rohner, respectively. The Spanish artist Javier Mariscal created a design for a new, sea-blue Redondan flag, with a jagged edge and striking pattern resembling brown-and-red grains of rice, while Italian designer Massimo Vignelli created a Redondan passport featuring two different shades of ocean blue and a simplified coat of arms. In a nod to Redonda's name, this coat of arms was round, as was Alessandro Mendini's set of Redondan coins, which came in different sizes, depending on the denomination, and could be arranged to fit one inside another like concentric circles. King Xavier even approved the kingdom's first official mode of transportation: the bicycle, as proposed by Australian industrial-designer Marc Newson. This was an environmentally friendly choice — Jon Wynne-Tyson would surely have approved — but also a playful and contrarian one, as bicycles would be of limited use on the island itself.

There was, for a time, one mandatory task that Marías asked of his court each year. In 2001, Marías created the

Kingdom of Redonda Prize, which was awarded to a distinguished writer or filmmaker who worked in a language other than Spanish. "We have hundreds of literary prizes [in Spain]," he told the BBC. "I thought it could be nice to have one at least that could be given to foreign authors or filmmakers." The award came with a Redondan title, as well as a not-insignificant cash prize, and the winner was selected by the current members of the court. Each member submitted, by mail, the names of three candidates whose work they admired, and whoever received the most votes won. The initial recipient of the Kingdom of Redonda Prize was the South African novelist J.M. Coetzee, who was dubbed Duke of Dishonor; subsequent winners included German filmmaker Éric Rohmer (Duke of Olalla), Italian novelist and critic Umberto Eco (Duke of the Island of the Day Before), British novelist Ian MacEwan (Duke of Black Dogs), and Canadian short-story writer Alice Munro, the latter of whom issued a rare public statement in accepting her title. "I am honoured and delighted to receive this award," Munro said. "And it is a special privilege for me to accept a distinction from Spain, a country with a wonderful literary tradition. I accept, therefore, with great pleasure the title of 'Duchess of Ontario.'" It was more good fun, but unfortunately it didn't last. Despite having a jury that Marías considered as strong as any in the world, the prize was discontinued in 2014, due, according to King Xavier, to a lack of interest from the Spanish press.

In the years since ascending to the Redondan throne, Marías's output as a novelist has not slowed down. Following *Dark Back of Time*, Marías spent much of the 2000s writing his most ambitious work yet, *Tu rostro mañana*, or *Your Face Tomorrow*, a thousand-page continuation of *All Souls* that was published across three separate volumes. Other books have appeared at a steady pace since, many of them continuing Marías's habit of inventing narrators who earn their living by, as he once put it, "renouncing their own voices." One is an opera singer, singing other people's lyrics. Another is a ghostwriter. Others work in translation, reinterpreting language and leaving the original speakers unsure of how their statements are now being presented. This last profession is the specialty of *Your Face Tomorrow*'s narrator, and he soon finds himself being recruited out of Oxford and into the mysterious world of espionage and MI6 — a joke from *All Souls* now brought to fruition.

In fact, in the years since the publication of *Your Face Tomorrow*, spying has become one of Marías's most revisited subjects.ᵗ His 2017 novel *Berta Isla*, for instance, is about a woman whose husband is similarly recruited by MI6 during his time in Oxford — in his case, to avoid being framed for the murder of a woman he was sleeping with while away from Berta, who remained back in Spain. Berta's husband, whose name is Tomás Nevinson, is even recruited by a younger version of the same man, Bertram Tupra, who later in life supervises the narrator of *Your Face Tomorrow*. Other signs of a shared Maríasian universe abound: from the brief appearance of a man with a dog scouring second-hand bookshops for supernatural fiction (the same Dobson-like figure who would go on to introduce the narrator of *All Souls* to Gawsworth) to an alias that Nevinson is given later in the novel — Cromer-Fytton, a reference to both another character from *All Souls* and to Gawsworth's actual middle name.

> Given how casually he added material from his actual life into *All Souls* and *Dark Back of Time* and then called it fiction, it is tempting to conclude that Marías either has firsthand experience with espionage, or he is daring his readers to assume so.

At one point in the novel, Marías gifts Berta another piece of his real-life biography with a Redondan connection. As she considers meeting up with a man she'd once had a youthful affair with, Berta thinks:

> I couldn't be bothered to go over to his part of town again, an area I'd never liked and to which I'd only gone back once since that January in 1969, to talk to the people at Ediciones Siruela about possibly publishing an anthology of strange, fantastic English tales, a project that never came to anything.

Except, in reality, it did. *Cuentos únicos* was indeed published by Ediciones Siruela, but with Marías's name appearing on the cover as editor, not Berta's. Included in that real-life anthology was John Gawsworth's story "How It Happened," which is what brought Jon Wynne-Tyson, as Gawsworth's literary executor, into Marías's life. Finally, it's impossible, if one is even vaguely attuned to Redondan frequencies, to read a book like *Berta Isla* and not take note of the fact that the titular character's last name is the Spanish word for *island*.

Marías, however, has resisted the idea that his books constantly return to the same material. Rather, he believes that all novelists tend to share the same habits and interests. "Those subjects, or those things, in many of my novels are so ample, are so general, are so meaningful, are so important, to everyone, I think, that you wouldn't be able to say 'This is a subject,' really," he said in a video interview in 2012. "Things like treason, secrecy, the impossibility of knowing things for sure, the huge difficulty of knowing people or even one-self, persuasion, suspicion, marriage and love as well. All of those things are, I would say, the matter of literature." The difference, then, is in how they are considered and then expressed.

As Marías's bibliography has grown, so, too, have the accolades. The year he was coronated as King Xavier, Marías and his long-time English translator Margaret Jull Costa shared the International Dublin Literary Award and its hefty purse of £100,000 for his novel *Corazón tan blanco*, or *A Heart So White*. In 2008, Marías was elected to a lifetime appointment with the Royal Spanish Academy, a government organization dedicated to the preservation of the Spanish language. Each seat in the academy corresponds to a particular upper- or lower-case letter from the Spanish alphabet. His father, Julián, held the capital-S seat from 1965 until his death in 2005, while Marías holds—in a touch fit for a Redondan king—the capital-R seat. Marías's work has become so well respected that his name inevitably appears each fall on lists of betting favourites to win the Nobel Prize for Literature, with odds as high as ten-to-one.

Whether the Swedish Academy recognizes him or not, Marías is already the most accomplished of any of the kings thus far. Not only is his work more critically acclaimed and more popular around the world, but he has also written the most about the kingdom itself. In addition to the two novels already discussed, there is "An Epigram of Fealty," a short story first published in 1989 and included in Marías's English-language collection *While the Women Are Sleeping*. In it, a manager at Bertram Rota's antiquarian bookshop in London is startled to discover a ragged-looking homeless man standing outside on the sidewalk, staring at something in the store's window display. The item turns out to be a rare sheet of little-known poems by Dylan Thomas, "printed privately," the manager reads in a catalogue, "for the members of the Court of the Kingdom of Redonda." Curious, the manager goes outside to speak with the homeless man, who has a scruffy red beard and what looks like a broken nose, and a pair of others standing near him. "Can I be of any assistance?"

"Yes, you can," the man says, brandishing a half-empty bottle of beer. "Tell my two friends here who the King of Redonda was. You must know."

The question catches the manager off guard, and he struggles to hide his confusion. After a bit of back and forth, the homeless man triumphantly reveals himself to be that man: John Gawsworth, also known as King Juan I, and the original publisher of the poems that Rota was now trying to sell for £500. Irritated at being so blatantly lied to, the manager shoos the entire group away, goes back inside, and locks the front door of the shop for good measure. Yet the story ends on a moment of doubt. *What if he was telling the truth?* In that case, the manager really should have gotten the homeless man to sign the pamphlet, thus increasing its value. Just as Marías's fictional characters reappeared throughout his work, hinting at a larger universe just off the page, so, too, did Gawsworth and the crown he once wore.

Aside from his literary output, King Xavier's most enduring contribution to the kingdom may be the founding of his own publishing company: the aptly titled Reino de Redonda. The company was announced at a press conference held by Marías on July 7, 2000, and was initially founded as a way of introducing Spanish-language readers to noteworthy books connected to his new realm — his duty, as pledged to King Juan II. The first title published by Reino de Redonda was a collection of Shiel's short stories entitled *La mujer de Huguenin*, or *Huguenin's Wife*. It also included, as an appendix, a thorough list of Redondan titles and peerages awarded from the 1930s to the present day. Each subsequent Reino de Redonda title included this same appendix (updated as King Xavier named new members to his court), as well as a uniform cover design featuring an art-nouveau arrow inspired by the first British edition of Shiel's novel *The Lost Viol*. Some of the books chosen for Reino de Redonda had a connection to the kingdom, such as *The Purple Cloud*, a story collection by archduke Arthur Machen, and a reissue of Marías's *Cuentos únicos* anthology. But the press has also published titles that Marías simply likes, including work by W.B. Yeats, Thomas Hardy, Isak Dinesen, and Thomas Browne. As of this writing the press has published approximately forty titles, yet remains a leisurely two-person operation, with Marías selecting the titles and Carme López Mercader, an editor in Barcelona, overseeing the press's day-to-day operations.[↓]

Reino de Redonda is a fulfillment of Marías's responsibilities to the kingdom, but also a convenient way for him to celebrate and keep in print the books he loves. He has admitted that few of the titles published by Reino de Redonda have turned a profit, and those most directly tied to the kingdom have sold worst of all. Yet Marías, whose own work has never wanted for confidence, remains unfazed here as well. King Xavier deals with his company's precarious financial situation by deliberately ignoring the details and pushing ahead anyway.

Mercader and Marías are also romantic partners who were in a long-distance relationship for two decades before finally marrying—though still not settling in the same city—in 2018.

IN THE COURT *of* KING XAVIER 18

WHEN MARÍAS assumed the Redondan throne, he vowed never to speak with journalists, playfully noting that they were beneath a king's attention. But in the years since he'd nevertheless talked to several different media outlets about this strange conjunction between his novelistic and real worlds, so I figured I had to try. Through his literary agent, I sent Marías a message, asking if he would consider speaking to me about his kingdom.

A few weeks later, I received an email with a PDF attachment. True to his old-fashioned reputation, Marías had typed out a letter on his electric typewriter, signed it, and sent it to his agent, who then forwarded it to me. It read:

Dear Michael Hingston,

A brief reply, as I am about to leave Madrid for three weeks, and am currently trying to write a new novel, with no time for anything else.

That is, by the way, the reason why I would not be able to "participate" [the word I had used in my initial request] in your book on Redonda, or speak to you in the next many months. I am sorry. But I have written enough about Redonda and my connection to the legend.

Marías listed all of the places I could find his writing on the kingdom, including *All Souls*, *Dark Back of Time*, and "An Epigram of Fealty," as well as a couple of smaller pieces that I hadn't yet come across. He also mentioned the chapter in Jon Wynne-Tyson's memoir, *Finding the Words*, which explained Redonda from the weary perspective of King Juan II. He added:

> I have never "claimed" the title, by the way. I just received it from Wynne-Tyson, and have never argued with any other real claimer. You can never take seriously this very nice legend, still less enter "dynastic disputes," generally with rather crazy, solemn people.

It was a gracious response, albeit a disappointing one. But that was OK. If King Xavier wasn't interested in speaking with me, there were plenty of other people who were.

IT DIDN'T TAKE LONG — just a few minutes sitting on a London patio, sipping ginger beer in the afternoon sun — before the subject of murder came up.

"I offered to kill these pretenders," said Marius Kociejowski, more or less unprompted. "I'd like to think of Redonda as a peaceful kingdom. But I was quite prepared to assassinate them."

There was a pause. Then he started to laugh.

The joke, of course, was that the man sitting across the table from me did not appear to be the murderous type. A slim, well-dressed man in his seventies, Kociejowski had steely eyes but a soft voice, which he used with precision. Over the past thirty years he had published poetry, travelogues, and essay collections. But just as important to him was his career as an antiquarian bookseller. Kociejowski joined the trade in the 1970s, and it had brought him into contact with a variety of characters — some he was fond of, others less so. "Indeed," he wrote in one of his essays, "there was much pleasure to be had in *not* selling a book to someone thought undeserving of it." Kociejowski entered the bookselling world too late to meet John Gawsworth, but during his time working at Bertram Rota's, there was another regular customer who piqued his interest. "The most mysterious thing was this Spanish fellow," Kociejowski told me, "who looked like a kind of toreador, coming in and buying Gawsworth pamphlets. It was rather intriguing."

This was in the early 1980s, when Javier Marías was teaching at Oxford and subconsciously gathering the material that would later be modified (or not) for *All Souls*. From afar, Kociejowski admired Marías's refined yet inscrutable taste. Up close, however, the two ended up in the kind of standoff typical of men who can't decide whether their shared interest will render them friends or enemies. Kociejowski worked at a desk located near the shop's front door, and every time Marías entered or exited, the Spaniard would give him a pointed glare. In his book *The Pebble Chance*, Kociejowski characterized their dynamic as "a measured hostility such as usually exists between two wild animals straying into a new, unpissed-upon space." For two years, neither man actually spoke a word out loud to the other — until Marías's teaching stint at Oxford ran out, and he came back down to London for one last visit. "It was rather touching," Kociejowski remembered. "He said, 'I'm going back to Spain, and I'd like to say goodbye.' I was completely taken aback."

Kociejowski didn't even realize that Marías was a writer until years later, when he recognized his name in an anthology—and, at the same time, recognized a version of *himself* in the accompanying story, "An Epigram of Fealty," as the humourless bookseller who shoos a homeless Gawsworth away from his display window. In the early 1990s, when *All Souls* appeared in English, Kociejowski spotted another personal connection. The death mask that Marías reproduces in his novel was taken from the cover of *Some Poems*, a pamphlet issued after Gawsworth's death; Kociejowski remembered that Marías had bought his copy from him.

Once this connection had been made, and their rivalry was replaced by a tentative friendship, the two men began corresponding with each other. Marías would send Kociejowski copies of his new novels, and Kociejowski, in turn, would show Marías his poetry. Then, in 1999, Kociejowski received a fax. Marías had recently assumed the throne as King Xavier and was looking to fill out his royal court. The message contained a surprising offer: Would Kociejowski be interested in the title of Poet Laureate of the English Language?

"I guess he liked me," Kociejowski said, looking out over the busy square. "There's a quiet eccentricity to Javier. He's a little bit formal. But so well spoken, you know. It was wonderful having the odd conversation with him." The offer to join the Redondan court, Kociejowski said, came out of "a kind of friendship, which—I don't know if it ever fully materialized. But we do write to each other twice a year." Marías's fax stressed the lighthearted nature of the kingdom and the hope that Kociejowski wouldn't find the request embarrassing. But King Xavier needn't have worried: Kociejowski happily accepted the position, responding with a mock-formal tone that would have made Gawsworth proud.

As Redonda's official English-language poet, Kociejowski has no regular duties or obligations. But King Xavier did once ask him for a list of the ten greatest poems ever written in English. In response, Kociejowski nominated Richard Stanyhurst's famously incompetent sixteenth-century translation of *The Aeneid*, which was ridiculed in its time for its "foule lumbring boystrous wallowing measure" and later by C.S. Lewis as "barely English." The other nine poems submitted were written by Kociejowski himself.

I wanted to speak with Kociejowski because he knew Marías, and because his essay on Stanyhurst had been included as an appendix in some of Marías's Reino de Redonda titles, meaning it was now part of the larger Redondan canon. But Kociejowski, though charmed by the legend, admitted he hadn't studied it in detail. He treated the kingdom, he said, as a "distant rumour." Threats to assassinate other would-be monarchs notwithstanding, Kociejowski was more interested in pursuing his civilian life as a writer, reader, and bookseller. I soon witnessed his skill in the latter field firsthand. Once our conversation was finished, we walked back to Peter Ellis bookseller, in Cecil Court, where Kociejowski handsold me, in a matter of seconds, a signed collection of Gawsworth's early poems and a copy of Shiel's 1905 novel *The Lost Viol*.

A FEW MILES AWAY, in London's northeast, was an artist who had thought about the kingdom in considerably more detail. "It was such a big part of my life," said Stephen Chambers, shaking his head. "Certainly the eighteen months it took to make, and then the year that the exhibition ran. To some extent I've put it behind me, but it keeps coming back."

Chambers is an acclaimed painter in the UK who was named to the Royal Academy of Art in 2005. His work is visually striking, using a rich palette of yellows and oranges to represent scenes of rural life, and often feels like an

intentional anachronism: he likes to combine the flattened perspective you'd find on a Greek vase with a rough, aged technique, as if the paint itself were about to flake off. The paintings also have an understated comic element, and are often formally ambitious. Chambers's series *The Big Country*, for instance, consists of dozens of screenprinted panels that can be reorganized in a variety of ways, thereby leaving its overall meaning malleable and subject to change.

In 2017, as part of the Venice Biennale, Chambers unveiled one of his grandest projects to date: a suite of 101 different portraits, each depicting a fictional member of a fictional court of a (perhaps) fictional kingdom. The paintings were done with oil on wood panels, giving them a feel of pragmatism, as if they'd been made with whatever materials were closest at hand. The individuals depicted, too, are not your typical royals. Instead, Chambers's court is an ethnically diverse group of working-class people with titles like "Pensive Milkmaid," "Harold the Bum," and "Bold Belinda of the Stables." Their eyes are calm but studious, their mouths containing just the hint of a smile.

"I'm not really a portrait painter, in a conventional sense," Chambers told me as he ushered me into his Hackney studio. "If you wanted to sit down and have me do a painting of you, you'd look a little bit off." For a project like *The Court of Redonda*, however, that technique was a perfect match for its subject.

FACING Guardian of the Guano, *by Stephen Chambers.* ABOVE *The Court of Redonda, as shown at the Venice Biennale in 2017. Courtesy of Stephen Chambers.*

Like Kociejowski, Chambers was soft-spoken, but his stubble, black-rimmed glasses, and dishevelled white hair gave the impression of a professor on sabbatical. Like many visual artists, he seemed more comfortable showing me his work than talking about it. Unfortunately, at that moment, the entirety of *The Court of Redonda* was sitting in storage in the south of the city, awaiting another exhibition, or perhaps, finally, a buyer.

The Kingdom of Redonda had always been an escapist fantasy, and as such, it was a convenient framework around which Chambers could imagine an alternative to a distasteful political reality. By taking a painterly treatment that was usually reserved for the wealthy, and instead applying it to the working class, Chambers was, in his words, "bringing to the High Table those that would normally be fed in the garden shed." More specifically, the idea for class inversion came in response to the ongoing political debacle over whether the UK should leave the European Union, where voting intentions broke down largely along long-entrenched lines of class.

And in case *The Court of Redonda*'s politics were too subtle, the suite of paintings was displayed in Venice alongside another large work called *State of the Nation*, which depicted, in three stages, a rider getting bucked off of his own horse. As critics noted, when you placed Redonda and the UK next to one another, it wasn't difficult to see which of the two monarchies Chambers preferred.

Given the project's scope and technique, as well as the resumé of its creator, *The Court of Redonda* turned heads within the art world. Yet news of the project also made it back into the realm of literature. One evening at the exhibition, Chambers met an elegant Venetian woman who had made a point of coming over to introduce herself. She said she was the Italian ambassador to Redonda, and it was then that Chambers realized she'd been sent by King Xavier. "He was clearly reading the press," Chambers said with a smile.

It was fitting that Javier Marías would eventually make contact, because Chambers had first learned about Redonda by reading Marías's novels. In fact, when he first conceived of the idea for the project, Chambers wrote to King Xavier, telling him that he was a fan and explaining what he intended to create. "From the correspondence that has ensued," Chambers said, "I get the feeling that had it been a straight fan letter, I might not have gotten an answer." In Marías's replies, it was clear that he was protective of the kingdom. Redonda may have been a fantasy, but it also had a fixed story at its core — it couldn't simply be rewritten, and especially not by an outsider. At the same time, Marías understood that Chambers wanted to riff on the kingdom in a way that was different than simply painting overtop of Marías's court; to Chambers, Redonda was a placeholder for the *concept* of a fictional nation, rather than any one dreamland in particular. As such, Chambers's paintings represented a sort of parallel-dimension Redonda, similar in spirit to Marías's intellectual aristocracy but in practice far different: a place where hierarchies of all kinds were dissolved, and where the shed and the palace were interchangeable.

Looking through the catalogue of the finished series, there wasn't a lot of obvious overlap between Chambers's version of Redonda and the island realm of Shiel et al. (The one exception was a tired-looking gentleman in *The Court of Redonda* dubbed "Guardian of the Guano," a nod to the former mine.) But by choosing to name his portraits after Redonda specifically, Chambers had assumed a certain level of responsibility to the kingdom, even just to explain its influence on his own work. Once the Venice exhibit opened, Chambers started getting questions from the media about Redonda the literary kingdom, and it was then that the letters from Madrid began to arrive more frequently. "[Marías] would write to me to correct my inaccuracies, of which there were many," Chambers said. "If he thinks I've made an error, he's not slow in telling me. There's no soap. He doesn't say, 'This is really interesting, but ...'"

In the end, King Xavier was pleased enough with the final project that eventually Chambers, too, got the call to join the court. It was a flattering, and slightly surreal, moment. "I'm not terribly interested in or impressed by handles," Chambers said, "so one that's completely fanciful appeals to me as much as, or more than, most of the other ones I have." The only question was what his Redondan title would be. It turned out Marías had a self-imposed rule whereby painters were only eligible to become viscounts, so in honour of the exhibit's debut, he suggested the possible title of "Viscount Biennale." Chambers considered this, then sent back a list of

alternatives he liked better. From there, he didn't hear anything until one day he came across an article in which Marías
referred to him as Viscount Hue and Dye — one of the options
from his list. There was no formal ceremony, as Gawsworth
would surely have done. But once the title appeared in print,
both parties considered the matter settled.

Since its debut in Venice, *The Court of Redonda* has been
exhibited at Downing College in Cambridge and at a gallery
on England's south coast. The prospect of one day selling
the collection, however, had proved difficult, as a suite of 101
pieces would not go cheap and Chambers refused to sell the
portraits individually. He even considered creating a contract stipulating that anyone who purchased the series was
legally barred from breaking it up in the future.

Prospective buyers can at least take heart in knowing
that they're getting a bonus painting thrown in at no extra
charge. At the same time that *The Court of Redonda* was
being exhibited at the Biennale, Chambers was separately
hired to paint a portrait of an art collector who owned several
of his other works. Chambers ended up painting two different pieces and sold the more handsome-looking one to the
collector's wife, who had commissioned it. But he remained
fascinated by the other version. "It was actually the more
interesting painting," Chambers told me. "The jowly-ness was,
I thought, kind of fantastic. So I added him in." When *The
Court of Redonda* departed Venice, it contained 101 portraits;
when it arrived in Cambridge, it had 102. Chambers never
told anyone about the extra painting, and he says nobody
seems to have noticed. Does the art collector, at least, know
that he's been covertly added to the court — along with the
new title of "Warden of the Turtles"? Oh yes, Chambers said.
"And he's terribly proud of it."

TALKING TO CHAMBERS and Kociejowski had been instructive. It was clear that both saw the kingdom strictly as a realm of fantasy, with little interest in or awareness of the actual place. For the painter, Redonda provided the imaginative scaffolding for a new formal challenge and political statement; for the poet, it was a fanciful continuation of the bookish rapport he had already established with King Xavier. Both of them also understood Redonda's inherent sense of play, which verged at times on a shared game of improvisation. Kociejowksi didn't have to ask Marías whether it was appropriate to submit a bad poem as the pinnacle of the form in English — he simply intuited that the Redondan ethos would always have room for one more oddity with a good story behind it.

In the months that followed, I tried to reach other members of Marías's court from back home in Canada. A.S. Byatt's secretary confirmed her Redondan title but said she, too, was busy completing a new novel and had decided to "withdraw entirely from public life" until it was finished. Many of Marías's earliest appointees from the late 1990s had since passed away, and in recent years few new ones had replaced them. Was the court of King Xavier perhaps winding down for good? But then, in December 2021, I noticed an announcement on a blog linked from Marías's official website naming a new member: the novelist, professor, and historian Marina Warner. I wrote to Warner's agent and soon heard back. She was happy to talk.

Warner was in her mid-seventies, and a sharp and intimidatingly well-spoken professor at the University of London's Birkbeck college. The author of dozens of books, including novels, picture books, memoirs, and essay collections, her best-known work focused on mythology and fairy tales; the

"Honours and awards" section of her Wikipedia entry — which included an appearance on the Booker Prize shortlist, several Oxford fellowships, and being named a Dame Commander of the Order of the British Empire — was so lengthy that it didn't all fit on my computer screen at once. (A more whimsical achievement: she was likely the inspiration behind the Dire Straits's 1979 single "Lady Writer," talking about the Virgin Mary on British TV.)

It was Warner's experience at All Souls College, where she has been a distinguished fellow since 2019, that first brought her into contact with Redonda via Marías's novel of the same name. "The book is not popular in the college, so you're not supposed to mention it, but actually I rather loved it," she told me over video chat. "I don't mind that it isn't an accurate picture; to me it captures some fabled mystery of the place." Intrigued, Warner moved on to *Dark Back of Time*, where she tried to follow the story of the kingdom but found herself unsure where Marías's artistic licence ended and reality began. "My first impression was that I liked this inverted colonization," she said. "The fact that an island had been left bare, in a very colonized part of the world, but named by Columbus — it all seemed a space of fantasy, really. It had been created and identified by these people. But I wasn't sure whether these people really had created it. When I read those books, I thought Javier Marías might have created it."

In 2017, Warner was named the president of the Royal Society of Literature, a charity and learned society in the UK that dates back to the early nineteenth century — the first woman to ever hold that title. A few years later, Marías was named one of the twelve inaugural members of the RSL International Writers program and Warner wrote to congratulate him. Over the course of a just a few letters in the fall of 2021, Marías offered her a Redondan duchy in recognition of her own work. Warner suggested her new title refer to the area in Italy where her mother was born, but Marías overruled her and dubbed her instead the Duchess of Phantasmagoria: a nod to her wide-ranging 2006 book about the representation of spirits throughout history, but which also contains an appropriately Redondan double meaning as the uncertain, dreamlike space between illusion and reality.

Warner says her new title delights her. "It's a little bit like fiction itself," she told me. "The Kingdom of Redonda magnifies people's personalities. It sharpens the taste of them by the way it casts them."

ULTIMATELY, all of these conversations sent me back to books, the true Redondan currency (apologies to Alessandro Mendini's interlocking coins). No matter what else I did in pursuit of the kingdom, I kept reading. As my son swung on the monkey bars at the park, I sat on a nearby bench, frowning my way through the acrobatic opulence of Shiel's early story collection *Shapes in the Fire*. While my daughter's play rehearsals finished up, I waited in my car with the dashboard lights on, eager to see whether Prince Zaleski would catch his man. I was looking for references to Redonda, even oblique ones. I had never quite understood how a man so desperate for material that he used to lift lines from letters to his mother and put them in the mouth of a character addressing his lover had never once adapted this readymade story from his youth for print. But I thought I saw glimpses, particularly in his use of islands as a dramatic setting. His ghost story "Vaila," for instance, was set on a remote Nordic island; originally part of *Shapes in the Fire*, it was later reworked as "The House of Sounds" and acclaimed by H.P. Lovecraft as "the most haunting thing I have read in a decade." Shiel's final published novel, 1937's *The Young Men Are Coming!*, was a supernatural story that took place in part on a flying island. Perhaps these fictional places were simply drawing on Shiel's childhood on Montserrat. Or perhaps not. He also wrote about monarchies, most explicitly in *The New King*, a historical novel about rival brothers in a fictional European country that never saw publication during the author's lifetime. As far as I could tell, the only time Redonda explicitly showed up on the page was in a single throwaway passage.

I kept up the same approach, as best I could, with the other Redondan kings. It turned out that the special collections library at the University of Alberta owned copies of more than a dozen of Gawsworth's scarcer poetry chapbooks from the 1930s and '40s — kept in a temperature-controlled room just a short bike ride from my house. The staff at the Bruce Peel weren't sure why, or how, the library got hold of them. But I was welcome to come take a look. That's how I got to hold pieces like 1931's *Twilight*, a faded, autographed poem printed on blue paper (number 82 of 100), as well as several of Gawsworth's wartime pamphlets, which appeared while he was stationed in Italy (the Peel's copy of *Cleopatra* being number 13 of just 30). The most surprising item in the library's holding, however, was its copy of *Marlow Hill*, a collection published by Grant Richards in 1941, which contained not only the poem "Self-Portrait" written out in full in Gawsworth's handwriting, but also an inscription to his first wife, Barbara. How on earth did this copy get here, to a corner of the Canadian prairies where few would even know to look for it? When I opened the book, I laughed out loud at the serendipity. But that, I was learning, was the true power of book collecting. Marías had called it morbid — but it felt to me more like a form of time travel. For a few minutes that afternoon, I had one foot in the present, and another in the London of the 1940s. And it would stay that way for as long as I kept that copy of *Marlow Hill* open in front of me.

Wynne-Tyson, meanwhile, wrote in multiple genres, but, with the exception of his Redondan novel *So Say Banana Bird*, focused most of his attention on unrelated — and, to this reader, unconvincing — non-fiction. While well-intentioned and morally sound, *The Civilised Alternative* is broad to the point of vagueness, while also offering odd generalizations like the idea that eating meat is wrong because children "naturally" don't enjoy the taste. (Has he ever tried giving them a vegetable?) Given Marías's relative popularity in North America, his books were the easiest of all to acquire, and they never failed to delight with their elegance and languor. The more I read, the more I appreciated the hints of a shared universe: I started to identify references to real-life Gawsworth experts he'd been in touch with, as well as a pair of nods to Marius Kociejowski, in the first volume of *Your Face Tomorrow* and in the later novel *Thus Bad Begins*, in which Marías's poet laureate had crossed over into the fictional realm, becoming an alias-adopting figure being tracked by MI6 and a travel agent specializing in the Middle East, respectively — the latter a nod to a pair of travel books Kociejowski had written about Syria.

The other side effect of this research was that my personal Redondan library grew apace. When I finally purchased a new glassed-in bookcase to keep all of the kingdom-related titles safely in one place, I was shocked to discover that it now took up two entire shelves, and most of a third.

The IMPOSTOR'S CLUB 19

IN HIS TWENTY-FIVE-YEAR REIGN as King Juan II, Wynne-Tyson reluctantly fielded letters and phone calls from other claimants to the Redondan throne. When Marías took over, he vowed not to make the same mistake:

> Never to pay any attention to any of them; never to worry about them; never to take any of them seriously; never to discuss, let alone dispute or contend with any of them; never to disavow their claims, as this would entail their consideration; accordingly, ever to respect their freedom, as I respect my own to leave them alone and to ignore them, as that would seem the only "kingly" thing to do.

This turned out to be a wise decision. Since the death of John Gawsworth in 1970, more than a dozen people have claimed to be the one true King of Redonda. Wynne-Tyson, for his part, never doubted his choice of successor. "Javier's 'accession' is just the shot in the arm that the Redondan story has been needing," he wrote in 2002, adding that Marías's writings "are lifting the legend to a level deserving of wider interest. A better class of stars are there for the counting." Yet even if Marías has refused to engage with these so-called "pretenders," their claims have nonetheless proliferated— especially in recent years. The rise of the internet means that, these days, staking a claim to the Redondan throne is as easy as making a website and uploading a manifesto.

OF COURSE, any discussions of rivals, impostors, and pretenders to the throne must begin with Gawsworth, the boozy and bombastic King Juan II, without whom the Redondan legend would never have taken hold in the first place. By following his scattershot approach to royal succession, we can find the origins of much of the present-day confusion.

The first claim dates back to June 29, 1954, when, on his forty-second birthday, Gawsworth signed the kingdom away to his landlord, William Reginald Hipwell, in exchange for forgiveness on rapidly accruing unpaid rent. However, this "irrevocable covenant" clearly stated that it came into force upon Gawsworth's death; until then, Hipwell was merely a king-in-waiting. It's unclear how seriously Hipwell took Gawsworth's covenant, though evidently seriously enough to threaten legal action when Gawsworth tried to sell the kingdom a second time, via the front page of *The Times*, a few years later. Mostly, Hipwell believed in the kingdom insofar as it enabled him to make money producing and selling Redondan stamps (the Antiguan government would get the same idea a decade later). Either way, this claim was rendered moot when both Hipwell and his son, David, passed away before Gawsworth did. The first "irrevocable covenant" never came into effect.

The next case, however, was a little more complicated. In 1966, with the kingdom now back in his possession, an ailing

Gawsworth once again started casting around for successors. He considered passing the mantle to Caroline Brill, the teenaged daughter of his long-time companion Eleanor Brill, even going so far as to draw up a proposed "Court Council for Queen Caroline" that August. But Gawsworth was talked out of this idea following a spirited debate with members of his court, and that October he instead decided to bequeath the kingdom to Arthur John Roberts, a Redondan grand duke and manager of one of the court's preferred Fitzrovian pubs. Once again an irrevocable covenant was signed, and a blood pact was performed, similar to the one done by Shiel and Gawsworth in the 1930s. This time the contract was set to kick in on a predetermined date: February 17, 1967, which would cap Gawsworth's reign over Redonda at twenty years to the day. To prevent any later accusations of illegitimacy, Roberts made sure that several other Redondan court members were present; he also demanded that Gawsworth stay sober for a full two weeks ahead of the signing (it is arguable whether he succeeded in doing so). Shortly thereafter, Gawsworth met Roberts and a historian named William Gates at the White Hart to hand over several boxes of Redonda-related documents, correspondence, and newspaper clippings. When the fated day finally arrived, Roberts and Gawsworth threw a party that attracted a reporter from the *Evening Standard*, whose story bore the headline "The Abdication of King John." From that point onward, Gawsworth started referring to himself in letters as "ex-king" and "Juan as was." According to a history of Redonda written by Gates under a pen name, "By this time it was clear to all who knew him that Gawsworth's career, as a poet, man of letters and a king, was over."

The whole arrangement sounded above board—except for the fact that Gawsworth's original agreement with Shiel stipulated that he could only confer the title upon his death. In his hunt to find a quick buyer, Gawsworth may have glossed over his own fine print. Still, there was an argument to be made that when Gawsworth died in 1970, the title actually transferred to an entirely different man than has been popularly believed. According to some reports, Roberts was as ambivalent about actually ruling over Redonda as Wynne-Tyson was. He sold his pub in Fitzrovia and moved with his wife to the north of England, where he lost contact with most of the members of Gawsworth's old court. In his book *The Kingdom of Redonda: 1865–1990*, Paul De Fortis wrote that Roberts continued claiming the title "in a quiet sort of way" until January 1979, "when he announced on BBC Radio 4 that he had given the island to the United Kingdom."

Yet this particular claim doesn't end there. Remember Roberts's friend, the historian William Gates? Well, he and Roberts kept in touch throughout the 1970s, during which time Gates developed more and more of an interest in his friend's title. As it happened, years earlier, Gates had also received a royal title from Gawsworth, following a lively night of drinking: Baron L'Angelier de Blythswood, a reference to a sensational nineteenth-century murder in Scotland in which a woman poisoned her lover by putting arsenic in his cocoa. In the years following Gawsworth's death, Roberts set up the Shiel Literary Trust Fund to continue his mission of supporting struggling writers and poets. Gates, meanwhile, wrote to Ian Fletcher, Gawsworth's co-executor, and asked if there was a way for the two parties to work together to keep the fallen kings' legacies alive. Fletcher was trying to do right by his late friend, but on this point may have been confused about Gawsworth's intentions. Fletcher told Gates he wasn't interested in collaborating, since, he said, the executorship was meant to stay separate from the kingdom — the exact opposite of how the title had worked during Gawsworth's reign.

In fairness to Fletcher, the 1970s was a period of confusion for virtually all Redondans. With Gawsworth dead, most believed the kingdom lay in a state of near-fatal uncertainty. There was no central authority to definitively rule in any one candidate's favour. Wynne-Tyson wouldn't publicly assert *his* claim to the throne until the very end of the decade. In the meantime, Roberts and Gates believed there was a clear path forward. "In London," Gates wrote, "the old Redonda gradually faded from public knowledge, and many who had known of it in Gawsworth's time came to regard it as defunct or even extinct." In its place was a new branch of the kingdom, "quietly flourishing further north." According to Gates, Roberts was more active than some have thought, establishing his own court and continuing Gawsworth's practice of making new members swear oaths of allegiance to the realm. He also published a Redondan newsletter and held regular meetings of his court, which was open to practitioners of the humanities and the arts, "regardless of colour, class or creed." Roberts named his court the Fellowship of the White Hart, after the pub in London where he and his wife had first met Gawsworth.

It wasn't until Wynne-Tyson went public, and then flew to the Caribbean with A. Reynolds Morse in 1979, that the two factions came into direct conflict. On his way back home to America, Morse received a message from the *other* King Juan II (Roberts went by his middle name), and the two men agreed to meet at Roberts's home in Oxfordshire. But neither party was willing to back down on its claim. If Roberts had already gifted the island to the UK, at this meeting he showed no signs of having given up on his title as king. Roberts had what he saw as an indisputable paper trail leading back to Gawsworth, while Morse was fighting for more than just the truth — he was fighting for his pride. After all, he had just organized a massive intercontinental coronation and was about to publish a book-length account of the adventure. Accepting the legitimacy of another candidate now would mean throwing all of that away. Instead, Morse grew defensive. He couldn't deny the irrevocable covenant between Roberts and Gawsworth, but he could cherry-pick language from Shiel and Gawsworth's original contract — arguing, for instance, that the phrase "at his death" (which would nullify Roberts's claim) was inviolable, but "of his blood" (which would invalidate Wynne-Tyson's) could be safely glossed over. Morse also called into question the validity of Gawsworth's later decisions as king, reframing the entirety of the 1950s and '60s as a quasi-legitimate period he called "Almadonda." In the end, Morse did acknowledge Roberts's claim in *The Quest for Redonda* but concluded that "Shiel cannot be effectively revitalized unless the tradition is continued of combining in one person the literary executor with the fictional kingship." For the sake of King Felipe, "[t]oday Shielians are rallying around the literary executor."

From this point, most histories of Redonda follow Morse and Wynne-Tyson's claim and relegate Roberts's to the sidelines. This is likely due to Wynne-Tyson having the higher literary reputation, and because the saga of travelling to the Caribbean and climbing the island simply made for a better story. But nobody has ever found conclusive grounds to disprove Roberts's claim. At worst, his covenant from Gawsworth functioned as an old version of a will, valid up until the moment a newer version was drafted. And in 1989,

244 | *Try Not To Be Strange*

when Roberts decided to finally give his title away to his friend and Redondan colleague Gates, the kingdom added its most combative claimant yet. For the next three decades, the prickly King Leo refused to yield an inch.

In fact, Gates has appeared in this story already. Whenever Wynne-Tyson, Marías, or any of the media who covered their respective reigns received an angry phone call, letter, or email, it was most often King Leo on the other end. Gates was also the proprietor of redonda.org, the website that tripped up Wendy Lesser as she tried to detangle Marías's claim to the throne in the *New York Times*. This site, which for years remained one of the top search results for the kingdom, not only outlined Gates's claim to the Redondan throne, but also spent an equal amount of time denouncing who he viewed as pretenders, in statements with titles like "Delusions of Grandeur" and "The Impostor's Club." While perceived by Wynne-Tyson and Marías as a killjoy who had taken a joke too literally, King Leo's correspondence also revealed a woundedness at feeling left out of the joke altogether. He continued adding to the Redondan court he inherited from Roberts from his home in Norwich, organized events to honour the memory of Shiel and Gawsworth, and maintained the sizeable royal archive inherited from his King Juan II. To his credit, King Leo also took steps to keep the lighthearted Redondan spirit alive, naming for the first time an official mascot of the realm (a seagull with a broken wing) and even becoming, briefly, the patron of an unusual pub sport called toe-wrestling. But people like A. Reynolds Morse simply weren't interested. Several years into their correspondence, before he had even been named Roberts's official successor, Gates was still trying to get the basic details of their claim recognized. "I must admit that I am getting a little tired of repeating the FACTS based on EVIDENCE to people like yourself who prefer to ignore them," he wrote to Morse in 1985, "but I have not the slightest intention of allowing someone like you to have the last word in the matter."

William Gates passed away on January 2, 2019, at the age of eighty-four, at which point control of the Kingdom of Redonda passed, according to a statement on his website, to his wife. Queen Josephine politely answered my initial emails looking for information and always signed off with a royal flourish. But as soon as I asked for an official interview and copies of certain documents, she stopped responding. I'd privately wondered whether Leo's version of the story was perhaps not quite as iron-clad as he'd always claimed — why publish his history of Redonda under a second pseudonym, if not to create a false aura of objectivity? — and nobody outside of his court had ever verified the contents of his archive, so far as I knew. But perhaps in Josephine's eyes I had simply become the same kind of busybody who had bothered previous monarchs from afar in years past.

At the same time, I was learning that uncertainty dogged more claims to the throne than just the one advocated by Roberts and Gates. When I'd discovered Gawsworth's will, my excitement had turned to confusion when I saw that, contrary to what Wynne-Tyson had implied in his memoir, it made no mention whatsoever of giving the kingdom to him and Fletcher along with the literary executorship. This meant that the transfer of power was a lot less clear than previously thought. Roberts, at least, had a slightly aged irrevocable covenant; all Wynne-Tyson had was his word on what the will contained, and it turned out he'd misrepresented the most crucial detail. That discovery brought back to mind a poem I'd found back in the special-collections library at the University of Reading. Entitled "Unannounced State Visit," it was written during Gawsworth's final months in hospital and was about "King Juan the Second and Queen Margaret" visiting their "abdicated predecessor." In my haste, I'd just assumed this referred to Wynne-Tyson, since he did visit Gawsworth in the hospital to discuss his estate, and moved on. But with the discovery of the omission in Gawsworth's will, something new occurred to me: Roberts's middle name was John. Could it be that the Juan of this poem referred to *him* instead? I went back through my photos from that day in Reading and realized I'd completely overlooked something even more telling in the poem's very first line: *Wynne-Tyson's wife wasn't named Margaret.* Despite the abrupt cut-off in our earlier communication, I emailed Queen Josephine again, keeping most of what I knew hidden, and asked if she happened to know what Arthur John Roberts's wife name was.

This time she wrote back right away: "Her name was Margaret."

Now I had to reconsider much of what I knew about the dispute between the two factions. Wynne-Tyson wrote that "it had been John's wish that I be saddled with the thankless (I was yet to learn how thankless) role of being the next king." But if this wish wasn't in Gawsworth's will, then where was it? The window in which such a request could have been made was shrinking. There were just five months between the date on the will and Gawsworth's death, during which time he could have made any number of other requests. But if Wynne-Tyson had seen a later document that spelled out the succession plan more clearly, why wouldn't he have placed *that one* in the official Redonda folder? Why highlight the one that only confuses things further? And if Gawsworth's request wasn't tied up with a final will, but was instead brought up in person, perhaps during one of those hospital visits, wouldn't Wynne-Tyson have simply turned it down like he'd always claimed he'd wanted to?

That night, after my kids were asleep, I put the kettle on and pulled the boxes of the Wynne-Tyson archive back out of the storage cabinet in my office. I opened a faded red folder marked "REDONDA, MISCELLANEOUS LETTERS ETC" and came across a curious sheet of paper: a typed journal entry dated January 30, 1979. This was after Wynne-Tyson went public with his claim to the Redondan throne, but three months before A. Reynolds Morse convinced him to fly down to the Caribbean. In the entry, Wynne-Tyson wrote that he'd received a phone call from an editor at the *Daily Mail* newspaper, which had recently run an article about Wynne-Tyson and the kingdom. In response, the editor had received an angry message from a man named Arthur Roberts, who claimed that *he* was the real king. This was exactly the kind of bickering that Wynne-Tyson later said he loathed being roped into, but here his response was much different. "I said I was delighted," Wynne-Tyson wrote, "had hoped for just such a development, and would abdicate as soon as a Deed of Accession was produced."

Wynne-Tyson then called Roberts directly and affirmed how relieved he was to learn of Roberts's status as king, since this would free Wynne-Tyson from having to continue in the role. "Asked him to send copy of the deed of accession," he wrote. "Told him I'd be delighted to 'hand over' [the kingdom] but am literary executor for Gawsworth and Shiel and am therefore concerned that any new King should continue to handle Redondan matters with an eye to furthering Shiel's work." The next day, Wynne-Tyson writes, Roberts went on BBC Radio to announce that the matter was now settled, and that he was giving the island to the UK, which controlled it until it was named part of the newly independent state of Antigua, Barbuda, and Redonda two years later.

If Roberts and Wynne-Tyson weren't in conflict after all, and in fact agreed that, once the covenant was produced, Roberts would be the uncontested third king of Redonda, what changed? In a word: Morse. The wealthy American industrialist was aggressive and used to getting his way. After going to the trouble of arranging—and financing—the cinematic coronation of Wynne-Tyson atop Redonda's peak, there was simply no way he was going to then concede it all in favour of some unknown publican. No wonder Wynne-Tyson was reluctant to participate in the ceremony. He had already agreed with Roberts to relinquish his claim, yet soon afterwards he changed his mind and went along with Morse's plan, in the process discrediting one of Gawsworth's most important "Almadondan" decrees in favour of a story they happened to like better. The more I read, the more I realized King Leo may have had good reason to be angry.

SEVERAL OTHER contenders to the Redondan throne traced their claim back to a similar encounter with Gawsworth, but without the written documentation to back it up. Following Jon Wynne-Tyson's appearance on BBC Radio to promote *So Say Banana Bird*, at least four different people called in to assert themselves as Redonda's true king, including the Irish writer and songwriter Dominic Behan, brother to Brendan, who allegedly claimed that Gawsworth had given *him* the kingdom back in 1960. Then there was Max Leggett, a Canadian whose parents briefly rented a room to Gawsworth in the early 1950s following his divorce from his second wife. Leggett's mother was pregnant at the time, and Gawsworth apparently promised that if the couple named their baby after him, then he would become the next king of Redonda upon Gawsworth's death. Max Juan Tonge Leggett was born shortly afterwards, and Gawsworth was named the boy's godfather, despite having since moved away. In fact, godfather and godson would never meet in person. Leggett outlined his claim on a GeoCities webpage in the 1990s: the Kingdom of Redonda's first appearance on the internet.

Other claims are even more tenuous. In 2002, a Canadian reporter for the *Hamilton Spectator* named Steve Buist wrote a travel story about visiting Antigua, where he learned about an unusual kingdom on one of the nearby islands. In a sidebar piece accompanying the story, he then revealed himself to be King Steven the First of Redonda, "following a bloodless coup." But his claim ended with the filing of his story — a fact that Buist confirmed to me over email. The horror and fantasy writer William Scott Home, meanwhile, at least had a loose Shielian connection. As a young man Home had studied Shiel's work, at times consciously emulating King Felipe's style in his own stories; one such tale, "Dull Scavengers Wax Crafty," prompted a reviewer to declare Home the "reincarnation" of Shiel. When Home later learned that Gawsworth had died, he mistakenly believed the throne vacant and assumed the title himself as Guillermo I. Home justified this decision on the grounds that he happened to be flying past Redonda in November 1970, a few months after Gawsworth's death, and this, he said, was a sign that the throne was fated to be his. For many years King Guillermo has run his version of the kingdom from his home in Skagway, Alaska, naming a cabinet, pegging the Redondan doubloon to the American dollar (at a conversion rate of 1 = US$4.60), and introducing his own national motto: *Pro se quisque*, or *Everyone for himself*.[↓] Paul De Fortis, in his history of Redonda, lists several other mysterious claimants, including a bartender named Ferdinand, "whose present whereabouts is unknown."

CLAIMANTS TO the Kingdom of Redonda can be divided into two groups. One is comprised of those seduced by the idea of the Redondan "intellectual aristocracy," as it has evolved since the 1930s, and who then pledged to help extend and protect that story in the years to come. The other consists of people whose allegiance is to the actual place. One group is interested in the imaginative possibilities of the island, the other its measurable dimensions and properties. Or, to put it another way: the first group is devoted to the map, the second to the territory.

Most of the kings we've met to this point, especially Gawsworth and Marías, have been devotees of the map. Redonda was appealing to Kings Juan and Xavier precisely *because* it was too far away to seem real. Shiel and Wynne-Tyson, as writers who accepted the mythology but also had firsthand knowledge of Redonda's physical charms, fell somewhere in the middle. Even someone like King Leo agreed that,

In late 2021, I finally got in touch with Home via email. In his eighties, he still lived in the Alaskan wilderness and had to drive into town in order to use a computer. Home referred to his Redonda as a "sovereign buccaneer kingdom," and said his claim would be far better known were it not for the meddling of a woman who, he said, borrowed some of his original documents in order to update the kingdom's Wikipedia entry, then claimed the documents were "boring" and threw them away. He promised to send me other material in the mail, but nothing bearing the seal of King Guillermo has yet arrived.

no matter his issues with the other kings, the actual island was not part of the dispute. As Leo told the BBC:

> The title of "King of Redonda" is a valid legal entitlement which is known in law not as intellectual property but incorporeal property — property without substance, just the same as the title of lordship of a manor. That means it is unique. That is why Redonda is in a field of its own. We don't claim the island — that has been run by Antigua for many, many years. But the title remains valid.

Yet if anyone is truly overlooked in the history of the kingdom, it is those contenders who are primarily concerned with the territory — the people who were inspired to act by the island itself. Largely, this is due to their lack of documentation. To which they might reply: Why bother? What was the point of publishing novels and poems about Redonda when they could simply look across the water and see their kingdom for themselves?

First up in this category is the flamboyant Aleph Kamal, which was the nom de plume of the South African artist and clairvoyant Hennie Boshoff. He started his career as a psychic and tarot-card reader in London, and went on to do semi-mystical consulting work with musicians like Peter Gabriel and Tina Turner, enriching, as he put it, "their emotional and spiritual souls by unlocking their creativity." When Sting flew down to Montserrat to record at George Martin's famed AIR Studios in the early 1980s, Kamal was in the group that went with him. There, he and some of the others developed a fondness for the uninhabited island in the distance, and together they formed a collective called the Council of Ten of Redonda.

Kamal's pursuit of the throne, however, didn't begin until 1986, when Frané Lessac was trying to set up a launch event for the new picture book she'd illustrated. Lessac wrote to Wynne-Tyson, who as King Juan II had already supplied the foreword for *The Dragon of Redonda*, and asked if he could attend the event at London's Commonwealth Institute. Wynne-Tyson wasn't available but suggested Lessac hire a stand-in. "Kids won't look into his credentials," he assured her. Lessac ended up asking her friend Kamal, who she knew was already a fan of the island, to serve as the replacement king, and from there he simply refused to relinquish the title. Kamal created his own coat of arms (this time including a goat and a rat) and asserted his kingship largely through articles written about him in the in-flight magazine of a Leeward Islands–based airline. In subsequent emails to the magazine's editor, Kamal asserted that Wynne-Tyson had been deposed by Council of Ten for "laxness" (refusing to attend Lessac's book launch) and bribery (offering a friend a knighthood if she could sell paperback rights to *So Say Banana Bird*). In a follow-up story, Wynne-Tyson flatly denied the charges, including the idea he had been deposed. "I mean, one would know, wouldn't one?" he wrote. Aside from this public exchange, Kamal's royal business appears to have been limited to naming Lessac a princess of Redonda and Sting an archduke. He later returned to his native South Africa, where he reverted to his birth name and turned his attention to making art full-time until his death in 2017.

Sting's PR representative: "He appreciates the invitation, though I'm afraid we're unable to accommodate your request [for comment] at this time."

Cedric Boston's attachment to Redonda was also based on first-hand experience. Like Shiel, Boston was born on the nearby island of Montserrat, visited Redonda as a child, and moved to England to pursue his education — this time, studying law and politics on his way to becoming a barrister. Unlike Shiel, however, Boston's reign had an overtly political agenda. He claimed the throne on February 11, 1984, and announced the creation of a Redondan Cultural Foundation (not to be confused with the identically titled group run by Mark Valentine and Roger Dobson the following decade), as well as the kingdom's first university, which claimed to offer faculties of study including arts, music, medicine, law, science, divinity, and "vampyrology." The mailing address for these institutions was a pair of private residences in England, suggesting that in-person meetings and classes were the exception, not the rule.

King Cedric's claim to the throne ran directly through Paul De Fortis, whose history of the kingdom was produced under Cedric's oversight and was, unsurprisingly, a full-throated endorsement of Cedric himself. "Nobody could describe the claim of King Cedric as legitimist," De Fortis admitted, "but by stepping in to the breach caused by the muddle of the succession to Gawsworth he has effectively breathed new life into a kingdom in danger of atrophy or death." From his new home in London, Boston revived Gawsworth's habit of hosting rousing royal gatherings at the Fitzroy Tavern, where his court left literature behind entirely and instead debated fanciful issues like whether Santa Claus, that "dangerous heretic and lunatic," should be banned from the realm permanently. Those in attendance at the court's inaugural meeting were said to include Hilary Machen, who had inherited the title of Redondan archduke from his father, as well as one of the physicians who had attended to the late King Juan I.

One of the key planks of King Cedric's administration was seeing Redonda returned to a ruler who had a personal connection to the island. As he saw it, the reigns of Kings Juan I and II had turned Redonda into just one more colony overseen by a bunch of foreign white guys. At the same time that other Caribbean islands were fighting for independence, King Cedric decided it was time for Redonda, too, to return to its roots. At his first gathering at the Fitzroy, Boston made a point of emphasizing Redonda as not just an island, but a *Caribbean* island. And that, he felt, went hand in hand with the man sitting on the throne.[↓]

The next claim was the result of a good old-fashioned bloodline. In May 1993, a reporter from the UK's *Daily Mail* teamed up with Redonda historian Roger Dobson to track down Margaret "Maggie" Parry, the only known surviving grandchild of M.P. Shiel—and therefore, the reporter reckoned, Redonda's current ruler and first true queen. Parry's father was Caesar Kenneth Shiel, who was born to Shiel and Lizzie Price in 1914. As a girl, she had heard stories about the

> Boston's belief that Redonda needed to get away from its colonial past was actually more complex than it first appeared. Aside from the fifty-year occupation by the American phosphate company, the island had no history of permanent human settlement to speak of. It had a European name, courtesy of Columbus, but no subjects, enslaved or otherwise. When Boston said he wanted Redonda to become an independent state, he didn't just mean kicking out British rulers-in-absentia like Wynne-Tyson, but also Antigua and Barbuda—the neighbouring Caribbean islands that had held actual governmental control of the island since 1981. If these people were all colonizers, what did that make Boston, who was from Montserrat? For Redonda to truly achieve independence, was there any human at all who could claim to represent it?

kingdom from her mother, but the closest she'd ever come to the island was a one-time holiday in Barbados. By the time the media caught up with her, Parry was in her forties and living in a small city on the east coast of Spain. When the reporter presented her with their idea, she quickly warmed to it. "Perhaps I was always destined to be royal," she said once the recorders were on. "After all, I was born in the hospital where the Princess of Wales gave birth to William and Henry and my Dad once ran a general store in Prince of Wales Road, Battersea ..."

The tabloid's story ran on the top of page three, with the headline "New Chapter in a Bizarre Literary Saga." Two weeks later, the newspaper ran a follow-up story, in which the *Daily Mail* actually flew Parry down to the Leeward Islands, dressed her up in a robe, crown, and scepter, and took her out in a speedboat so she could see her domain in person. After climbing to the plateau and posing for photos, Queen Maggie mused on the possibility of opening the island to private businesses like supermarkets and hotels. "We could have a two-hole putting course on the only flat bit," she added. Of course, little in the Redondan tradition suggested that the title automatically passed down through a family tree, or that it could be picked back up after two generations of inactivity. As Parry herself admitted, "My father and grandfather did not get on." But in a sea of conflicting claims, Queen Maggie's seemed as straightforward — and therefore as likely — as any.

With its abundance of harbours, and its central location in the Caribbean, Antigua has become a hub for the international yachting industry. That influx of largely white, largely affluent sailors to the area has created another subset of Redondan kings, who discovered the island the same way: as an obstacle to navigate around. In 2010, a California attorney named Michael Lawler was nearing the end of his three-year cruise around the world when he came across Redonda and heard a version of the story of the kingdom. He decided to make a brief pit stop, anchoring his forty-seven-foot sailboat before making his way onto the shoreline and declaring himself king. When Lawler returned home to the United States, he began regaling members of local yachting and travellers' clubs with bits of the island's history while wielding a homemade crown and sword.

The two most prominent names in this mini-fraternity of sailors, meanwhile, were in a class of their own. If anyone lived a life charmed and colourful enough to match Redondan mythology, it was King Bob the Bald, who, along with his successor, King Michael the Grey, gave the kingdom an injection of new life in the same part of the world where it first began.

THE BALD
and THE GREY

20

ROBERT WILLIAMSON was born in 1940 in Regina, Saskatchewan, and raised in Toronto. His father was a miner, and each summer Williamson would follow him up to Northern Canada to go prospecting; by the age of twenty, he was already overseeing his own syndicate in Yellowknife. Back in class at the University of Toronto, Williamson studied art and engineering, but the highlight of his post-secondary years was the time he decided, on a whim, to buy a boat with a friend and sail together to the Bahamas. The thirty-four-foot schooner set sail from Lake Ontario, navigating through the Erie Canal and on down the Atlantic coast — despite the fact that Williamson had no previous sailing experience and, in fact, did not know how to swim, a detail he only revealed to his co-pilot midway through their journey.

After a four-year stint at the Ontario College of Art, Williamson moved to Cannes, where he managed to land a job working under Pablo Picasso, helping the aging artist convert his paintings into large mosaics. The work wasn't challenging, but it paid well, at least for his boss: Williamson estimated Picasso spent approximately ten minutes on each mosaic, then turned around and sold them for tens of thousands of dollars apiece. When that gig ran out, Williamson relocated to London and started his own advertising agency, where he produced designs for everything from airline logos to ravioli cans.

No matter where Williamson was, his sense of humour was always on display. His pranks, in particular, were so detailed and imaginative that they seemed plucked straight out of a Roald Dahl story. "When he worked in London, there was this real asshole working with him," his daughter Tamara remembered. "Everyone hated this guy—a pretentious English twat who came in wearing a bowler hat each day. So my father decided he had to get him. He got a pool together in the office, and with the money went out and bought three of the same bowler hats in slightly smaller sizes. Every week or so, he would replace this guy's hat with a slightly smaller hat."

That childlike energy extended into the family home. Williamson, his wife, Judy, and their four children lived in Putney, in southwest London, in a converted stable. Yet rather than renovate the space, or even have the horse feeders in the corners removed, Williamson piled on more eccentricities: a custom stage, a swing, a rocking horse, decorative antlers and snowshoes, and more than one *Space Invaders* arcade machine from ... well, nobody was quite sure where Bob got those. He kept chickens in the backyard and bees on the balcony; he also dabbled in making his own ginger beer, which more often than not ended in an explosion. As a kid, Tamara used to invite friends over from school and watch their eyes widen as she nonchalantly skateboarded through the living room.

I reached Tamara by phone at her home in Ontario. She is a veteran musician who spent much of the 1990s as the frontperson of the Canadian band Mrs. Torrance. On the day we spoke she was preparing her hybrid rock-theatre piece *The Break-Up Diet* for a tour of Fringe Festivals across the country, but she was happy to share stories about her larger-than-life father. "He didn't have much concern for safety, or for normal behaviour," she said. "He wanted to live like he was a hero. And he sort of did."

When she was fifteen, Tamara's parents got divorced. Williamson was by then in his mid-fifties and took off with a woman who was several decades younger. To the rest of the family's surprise, Williamson's new relationship ended up lasting a full decade, but that girlfriend ultimately left him in 1994. Williamson did not take it well. He sold his business, leaving most of the rest of his old life behind him and taking off to Russia. When he returned, he was standing atop the brightly painted schooner he'd just bought.

"The tall ship, oh my God," said Tamara. "He wasn't a young guy when he did that."

Williamson had purchased the schooner in St. Petersburg after falling in love with its eccentric history and appearance. The boat had been built by hand according to blueprints for an eighteenth-century Baltic trader and was painted with bright horizontal stripes of red, yellow, and green. Williamson dubbed the boat the *St. Peter* and sailed it right up the Thames River, where he threw a party in London's Chelsea Harbour in the hopes that his ex-girlfriend would show up. When she didn't, a doubly spurned Williamson decided it was time to leave England for good. He aimed the *St. Peter* straight across the Atlantic — an unintentional echo of the plot of *So Say Banana Bird* — and, after nearly a month of sailing in zigzags in order to avoid tropical storms, found himself in the Caribbean.

Williamson's claim to the Redondan throne was based entirely on an encounter he claimed to have had with Jon Wynne-Tyson in Antigua. He recounted this meeting in a newspaper article from 1998:

> Not so very long ago I met the reluctant monarch over tea and asked "Who will be the successor when you abdicate, Your Majesty?"
>
> "I've drawn up a shortlist and number one is a very rich Spaniard who recently bought all the regalia from Sotheby's," he replied. I barely refrained from asking why he'd sold all the royal gear — after all, it belongs to the nation, doesn't it? But instead said "What? Thousands of lives and millions of pounds sterling were spent kicking the Spanish out of the Caribbean and now you're planning to give a bit of it back?"
>
> "Oh, heavens" he replied, "I didn't think of that."

Williamson claimed that he and Wynne-Tyson then exchanged letters, in which King Juan II admitted that he had already promised the kingdom to Javier Marías, but now regretted that decision. "He suggested," Williamson wrote, "that, if I would become King Robert of Redonda it would let him off the hook with the Spaniard."[↓]

That May, Williamson made plans to sail over to Redonda and invade it. A few days before setting off, however, he made a phone call back home to Canada to announce his intentions publicly. "The day after tomorrow, sixty-five of us are sailing

Wynne-Tyson, for his part, vehemently denied ever speaking with Williamson about Redonda, let alone agreeing to hand him the kingdom, leading many to believe that Williamson simply made the whole exchange up.

King Bob the Bald, courtesy of Tamara Williamson.

over," Williamson cheerfully told the CBC Radio program *As It Happens*, "and we're going to invade the island and plant the flag." To Williamson, it wasn't even technically an invasion since he claimed to have the permission of the current king. "I'm five foot six," Williamson said he told Wynne-Tyson, "so please put me on the short list."

Conditions on the morning of the invasion were picturesque, and the crew members were able to drop anchor and make their way ashore without much trouble. From there, Williamson sent a smaller party of about a dozen to hike to the top of King Juan's Peak on his behalf, while he stayed behind to drink beer in a cave near sea level. He renamed himself King Bob the Bald, after a distant French ancestor named King Robert the Bold, then issued his first royal orders: declaring a two-hundred-mile exclusion zone around the island and establishing a fee schedule for violators (ten cents per yacht foot per year). This, King Bob figured, would be an easy way to start cashing in on his new domain, calculating his future Redonda-related income at "around $35 million USD a week. Or maybe a day—my Chancellor hasn't worked it out yet."

FOR THE MOST PART, Williamson was content for the Kingdom of Redonda to be a local legend, confined to the area around the island itself. During his ten-year reign, King Bob was a constant presence on nearby Antigua, spending hours at coffee shops telling stories to locals and tourists alike and puttering down the street in his old black Mazda 323, on whose roof he had attached a crown hand-painted gold.

But he and his court didn't mind flirting with the larger world when an opportunity presented itself. In 2007, the UK implemented a sweeping new law banning all cigarette smoking indoors. Among the displeased parties was a pub in Southampton called the Wellington Arms, one of whose regulars was a friend of King Bob's and had previously been named Redonda's official cardinal. He came up with a brilliant longshot idea: if the pub could be designated an official Redondan consulate, then it would qualify for diplomatic immunity and therefore be exempt from the new law. The pub's scheme made headlines across England, with the government, at least initially, unsure of its exact legal footing. "The smoke-free law will not be enforceable against premises that have diplomatic status," admitted the Department of Health. In the end, however, the idea was abandoned, in part because of a lack of sustained pressure from Redonda's king. When reached for comment about the Wellington Arms, Williamson said distractedly, "I'll look them up sometime."

Not long afterwards, Williamson's health began to decline. In 2009 he returned home to Canada to receive medical care and be closer to his family, and that summer he passed away from complications due to diabetes. "On August 27th my father, King Robert the Bald, set sail on his final voyage and into uncharted waters," Tamara wrote in a mass email. She remembered her father as a larger-than-life figure whose personality remained undimmed even in his final days; he insisted on bringing his Redondan regalia with him to the hospital and could be seen in his wheelchair, rolling around the grounds in a crown and cape, with a toy sword sheathed at his waist.

To Tamara, Williamson's appointment—or perhaps self-appointment—to the Redondan throne was merely the latest in a long list of escapades. "My dad did so many incredible things in his life," she said. "I think he loved the fact that [Redonda] was lawless—that he could go and become king, and then knight people. But it was all in good fun. If it wasn't in good fun, it would be stupid."

So, I asked, when he first told you about the invasion, you weren't surprised?

"God, no," she said with a laugh. "It was perfect, really."

Williamson's illness developed so quickly that Tamara was overwhelmed by how much there was to deal with. One of the things she regretted was not making more time to celebrate the kingdom. "A lot of times when people die, you're so exhausted that the whole handling of the ceremonial side is difficult. You just don't have enough energy." She paused. "Although I did prank the audience at his funeral."

For years, Williamson had insisted he didn't want any kind of public service. But after he died, Tamara felt she had to do something. So, as a kind of spiritual compromise, she decided to throw her father the kind of funeral he might have appreciated. Things started out normally enough, until the priest asked if anyone wanted to say something about the deceased. That's when a man whom nobody had ever seen before put up his hand and marched to the front of the room, where he announced that he was Williamson's long-lost brother. "This guy started talking about how he'd never met Bob, but had heard about him all his life, and on and on," she said. Only at the very end of his speech did the man reveal the truth: he was an actor hired by Tamara to play one grand, final joke on everyone. From there, she said, the funeral turned into "one hell of a party" — and an apt send-off for King Bob the Bald.

BUT WHAT OF Redonda? Before leaving for Canada, Williamson had handed administration of the kingdom over to a man named John Duffy, who was involved in several nautically minded organizations around the island. As Duffy considered the state of the kingdom, the detail that most weighed on him was that King Bob had told him he didn't have any successor in mind. Just in case, Duffy wrote to the Antiguan minister of tourism and asked if the government would be interested in helping find a new king of Redonda when the time came. Duffy had watched the kingdom under King Bob become a legitimate tourist attraction that always delighted visitors to the area when they learned about it — a lighthearted story that was aided, in turn, by the occasional sighting of the royal Mazda puttering around English Harbour. Duffy didn't want their quirky local legend to disappear, and he believed it had economic opportunities, too. The minister, however, was uninterested, and told Duffy to take care of it himself.

Once news made it back to the Caribbean that King Bob had died abroad, Duffy turned to the Royal Naval Tot Club for help. This was a local group in Antigua that met each evening to toast the Queen and listen to readings from naval history. The Tot Club considered its options, but in the absence of any clear direction ultimately decided to treat the kingdom like any other organization with a vacant job posting. They created a questionnaire and put out a call for applicants.

Distributed under the title "Application for the Title of the King of Redonda," the form was concise, taking up just one side of a single sheet of paper. In addition to basic biographical details, it asked for a list of the applicant's published works, including publication dates and sales figures. The form also asked whether applicants were willing to attend a crowning ceremony in Antigua and to raise their standard atop Redonda itself. At times it was no different than a standard job application: one question read, "What qualities do you think set you apart from other applicants?" Before long, the Tot Club was receiving applications from all over the world.

Meanwhile, other parts of Williamson's legacy on Antigua needed more immediate attention. For years, his schooner, the *St. Peter*, with its rickety yet distinctive appearance, had drawn attention from tourists and locals alike. In the early 2000s, it had even caught the eye of film scouts who were in the area looking for vessels to populate the background of Disney's upcoming *Pirates of the Caribbean* movie. The *St. Peter* went on to appear in the first two instalments of the blockbuster franchise, and at one point Disney tried to purchase it from Williamson outright. Rather than sell, King Bob thought it was funnier to rope production staff along by continually raising his asking price. By the time the number hit a million dollars, Disney gave up, and Williamson retained the *St. Peter* as part of his Royal Redondan Navy instead.

Since King Bob had left for Canada, however, the schooner had been sitting in a place called Jolly Harbour, unattended and unmaintained. Now it seemed at risk of actually falling apart, and management wanted it gone—immediately. While Duffy and the rest of the Tot Club tried to figure out how to transport the *St. Peter* from the west side of the island down around to English Harbour, staff at Jolly Harbour decided they were done waiting and took the vessel out to sea, where they sunk it to the ocean floor.

Before the *St. Peter* went down, however, workers did at least look around the inside of the vessel for any items of value. Alongside the usual assortment of boating supplies and equipment, they came upon a chest containing some of King Bob's personal effects. Among these was a piece of paper, smudged with dirt and discoloured at the edges; originally written on a computer, it had since been printed out for the purposes of being signed. At the top was a three-colour flag and a phrase curved around it, written in blue with a yellow outline: "Kingdom of Redonda." Nobody onboard knew what this document was, but it sounded vaguely like something the Tot Club might be interested in. The document read:

> I, King Bob the Bald of Redonda, successor to King Juan II and King of Redonda since the title was passed to me on 1st April 1997 at which time I raised my standard atop my Kingdom thereby asserting my right to the succession hereby bequeath my title to my successor to rule benignly and in peace and uphold the literary traditions of the founding King Felipe on his accession to the throne.

> I, King Bob the Bald, appoint Mr Michael Howarth of Salisbury, England as my successor on condition he raises his standard upon the Kingdom within one year of my parting from this mortal soil and continues the timeless friendship with the neighbouring island of Antigua.

The bottom of the document had been signed and sealed by King Bob and witnessed by Sir Nicholas Montlake, commander of the Redonda Land Forces.

When he read the letter, Duffy breathed a sigh of relief. King Bob had named a successor after all. The Tot Club's search could be called off, and the Kingdom of Redonda, with its unpredictable, zigzagging lineage, would live on.

There was just one problem: Who was Michael Howarth?

WITH THE DISCOVERY of the succession document, Duffy's task changed—but it didn't get any easier. In fact, the Tot Club had been just about ready to wrap up their search, as they'd already received an application from someone they believed would make a capable replacement for King Bob. Now Duffy had to go looking for one particular person, and it wasn't at all clear how he was supposed to find him. Locals on Antigua didn't recognize the name Michael Howarth, and Duffy hadn't been close enough with Williamson to know much about King Bob's many friends and acquaintances, especially those who lived off-island. The only other clue Duffy had was the rule that Redondan monarchs needed to be writers. In addition to a memoir about his quixotic sailing trip to the Bahamas as an undergrad, Williamson had published an art book about mosaics (a by-product of his time with Picasso) and, later, two collections of short stories and cartoons entitled *Bunk* and *Double Bunk*, respectively. Presumably his successor, too, was a writer of some sort.

Duffy began by searching public directories in Canada and the UK. The early results weren't encouraging, but eventually he found someone who seemed like he might be a match. This man had known Williamson, had expertise in the boating world, and made his living as a journalist.

The name wasn't quite a match, but Duffy figured it was close enough. So he scanned King Bob's succession document onto his computer, and started writing him an email.

WHEN MICHAEL HOWORTH got the news that he had been named the new King of Redonda, late that Sunday evening in November 2009, he wasn't sure what to make of it. On the one hand, he was flattered to be entrusted with an entire kingdom, especially one with so much history behind it. Surely there was generosity behind the gesture. Mostly, however, Howorth was filled with trepidation. What did it actually mean to be the king of a Caribbean island? Could one do the job from afar? And if he accepted the title, was he unwittingly wandering into some kind of international incident in the making?

Howorth had first gotten to know King Bob in the 1990s, for professional reasons. As a freelance writer covering the yachting industry, he was unable to personally attend the many events and shows that took place all around the world. Howorth and his wife, Frances, made a point of travelling to Antigua once or twice each year to cover the major races and trade shows. In between, he hired Williamson as a local stringer to keep him informed whenever yacht-related news broke. Over time the two men became friends, meeting up in person whenever Howorth was in English Harbour and corresponding via letter for the rest of the year.

Before responding to Duffy's email, Howorth tried to bring to mind everything he'd ever heard about Redonda. Of course, he was familiar with King Bob's claim to the throne. Anyone who'd spent any amount of time in Antigua had seen Williamson's Mazda with the crown on top. But Howorth knew more about the island than most. His formal introduction to the area came back in the 1970s, when as a young man Howorth served as a cadet on cruise ships, many of which passed through the Caribbean. One of his duties was helping chart safe passage through the Leeward Islands, which required carefully navigating around a tiny island located almost exactly between Nevis and Montserrat. Up until King Bob's posthumous offer, Howorth's main experience with Redonda had been as an obstacle in his path—as he called it, "a little splodge on the charts."

Howorth's initial response to Duffy was guarded and written in the third person. "'Gosh,' he said with his tongue firmly implanted in his cheek, 'I had no idea that King Bob was such an avid reader of all the twaddle I write in the glossy magazines. I am truly humbled.'" Yet Howorth admitted he was intrigued by the idea, and together he and Duffy discussed what taking over the kingdom would entail. Howorth also wanted clarification on some of the language Duffy had used—specifically, the postscript "I am just helping to perpetuate the whole fraud"—to make sure they were all on the same page. "The use of the word *fraud* suggests some criminal misdoing," Howorth wrote, "while *mischievous fakery* does not ... I cannot allow myself to be associated with illegal wrongdoing" (emphasis in original). Duffy assured him that the government of Antigua and Barbuda had no legal problem with the kingdom, and before long Howorth was reconsidering his plan to skip that year's Antigua Charter Yacht Show. Maybe there was a reason to attend after all.

GETTING TO THE Caribbean was the easy part. But how was Howorth going to get out to Redonda, which had always been difficult to reach, and particularly so now, at a time of year when most boats in the area were already booked for show-related business? Howorth knew there was no point doing this halfway. If he was truly going to become the new Redondan king, then he had to show that he meant it. He had to go to the island, and he had to get to the top.

Fortunately, through his writing Howorth had met many of the owners of the yachts and superyachts that would be in town for the Antigua show. After some consideration, he set his sights on a sixty-five-foot yacht called the *Allure Shadow* that in a previous life had been a support ship for an oil rig in the Gulf of Mexico. It was available on the date Howorth had in mind, and as a bonus, its captain was a Greek man named Costas who already knew the story of the kingdom. Once Howorth arrived in English Harbour from the UK, however, he was told there was a problem: the yacht's owner had changed his mind and didn't want the *Allure Shadow* to leave Antigua during the show after all. For a few despondent moments, Howorth worried he was about to fail King Bob's task — and then he spotted the helicopter. Summoning his best attempt at a royal tone, Howorth called the owner back and told him that if the yacht was unavailable, then he would be forced to commandeer the helicopter and take *that* over to the island instead. The owner relented, in exchange for an honorary Redondan knighthood. And on the morning of December 12, 2009 — three and a half months after the death of King Bob — a group of four piled inside the Robinson R44 waiting on the deck of the *Allure Shadow*: Howorth; his wife, Frances; Costas (who was also a certified pilot, and who received the rank of high admiral of the Redondan Navy for his troubles); and John Duffy, as a representative of both King Bob and the Tot Club. Howorth rechristened the helicopter *Air Farce One* for the duration of the journey, and they took off towards the rocky cliffs of Redonda.

The flight from Antigua took only a few minutes, but by the time they were about to land, the wind had picked up. Costas was nervous about damaging his boss's expensive helicopter, especially since the plateau was still littered with rusted bits of old mining machinery, but he eventually found a clear section and brought *Air Farce One* down to a safe landing. With the wind still whipping past, Costas told Howorth to hurry. Howorth leapt out of the helicopter, along with a large Redondan flag that his wife had sewn especially for the occasion. Frances pulled out her camera and snapped a couple of suitably majestic shots of her husband bearing the royal standard. Once that was done, the newly inaugurated Redondan high admiral announced that it was time to leave. With Frances and Duffy cheering his approach, Howorth climbed back inside and the helicopter lifted off, victorious.

Next came the crowning ceremony. This took place back on Antigua, at a scenic lookout in the ruins of the old Fort Charlotte. In contrast to the modest quartet that travelled out to the island, the coronation drew approximately fifty people: some who knew the story and others who'd just heard a king was being crowned and wanted to see what that meant. The ceremony was overseen by Terry Bowen, a former Tot Club president who had been hastily ordained as a Redondan archbishop ahead of Howorth's arrival.[↓] The two stood on a path of old cobblestones, in the shade of a tall, leafy tree, as dozens of yachts bobbed in the waters of English Harbour in the distance. The archbishop read aloud from his prepared text.

"Will you solemnly promise and swear to govern the Peoples of Redonda according to their respective laws and customs?" Bowen asked Howorth.

"I solemnly promise to do so," Howorth replied.

"Will you to your power cause law and justice, in mercy, to be executed in all your judgments?"

"I will."

The bishop then presented Howorth with the Sword of State (in reality, Duffy's old fencing sabre), followed by the royal orb and sceptre (a pineapple and a freshly cut piece of sugar cane, respectively). Next a royal salt shaker was produced, which Howorth took a pinch from — as this, the bishop told the crowd, was how the entire Redondan legend must always be taken. Howorth, wearing a royal-blue cape overtop of a button-up shirt and khaki cargo shorts, kneeled as the crown was placed upon his head. Then the audience of friends, acquaintances, and curious strangers yelled out their cheer in unison: "God save the king!"

Howorth's preparations for the required regalia were similarly last-minute. "Have visited emporium called King's Supplies here in Sint Maarten," he wrote to Duffy from another of the Leeward Islands in the days before the ceremony. "Disappointing selection of orbs and maces and absolutely nothing in the way of crowns!"

WHEN I STARTED INVESTIGATING the Kingdom of Redonda, Howorth's name was one of the first I came across. He'd published lighthearted accounts of his ascension to the throne in trade magazines and lived a double life online, maintaining both a professional website (along with Frances) called *The Yachting Experts* and a separate site dedicated to the kingdom and its tangled history at kingdomofredonda.com. The Redonda site had received less attention over the years than the one that actually paid Howorth's bills — the page called "The Court," for instance, was still full of placeholder text (unless Howorth's court was full of titles like "Lorem Ipsum," a joke I wouldn't put past any Redondan king). But as far as I could tell, Howorth still retained the title.

I sent him an email, and to my surprise he wrote back right away, brightly agreeing to an interview.

The next morning, I booted up Skype with some trepidation. I wasn't sure what the protocol was for speaking with royalty, especially when said conversation was conducted over video chat. I had a list of questions written down for King Michael the Grey, but a new one came bubbling to the top just as the call connected.

"Uh, before we begin, how should I address you?"

A grin slowly spread across the face on my computer screen. "I think it's only right and proper that you should say 'Your Majesty,'" he replied. Then he paused, as if reconsidering the logistics. "But ... once you've done it once, I'll let you off the rest of the time."

Formalities established, I told Howorth that I'd been interested in the history of the Kingdom of Redonda for some time. "To be honest," I said, "it's a story that I love but one that I still don't fully understand."

Now he laughed outright. "Join the club!"

Michael Howorth, now in his early seventies, had settled into his role as king with an air of relaxed bemusement. He knew more about the island than many who had been associated with Redonda over the years, and his allegiance was decidedly to the territory. In addition to his coverage of the yachting industry, Howorth told me he had roots in fiction as well. Back in the 1970s, when he was a cadet on cruise ships, Howorth wasn't allowed to leave his cabin after 10 p.m. To pass the time, he would write semi-fictional short stories in which an idealized version of himself went off on various adventures around the world. "Of course, I always got the beautiful woman in the end," he said. The stories were written to amuse himself, but one day Howorth met a passenger who edited a magazine called the *Australian Women's Weekly*. She asked if she could publish Howorth's stories, and for the next several years he produced new tales of romance and adventure for his far-off audience.

The first time Williamson told Howorth about his kingdom, he was interested, but, like many, unsure of how it actually worked. He did, at least, appreciate that, if Redonda had a king, it should at least have one as odd as the island itself; in that sense, Williamson was an ideal candidate. Similarly, since his own ascension, King Michael the Grey hasn't shied away from having some fun with his position. In 2014, for instance, he and Frances were travelling in Argentina when they learned of another island called Redonda, this one located off the country's southern coast, in the Beagle Channel.[↓]

> Sometimes it wasn't so much a coincidence as a direct influence. One of those island doppelgängers, located off the north shore of Tasmania, was mapped at the turn of the nineteenth century by a British Royal Navy officer and named Rodondo "from its resemblance to that rock, well known to all seamen in the West Indies."

In itself, this wasn't so unusual. "If you look on the bloody charts, there's a Redonda in just about every Spanish-speaking country," Howorth said. "I mean, it means 'round island.'" But the Argentine Redonda was special. Like its Caribbean counterpart, it had its own post office (this one operated more conveniently from the shores of the mainland) as well as its own parallel government in the form of Carlos de Lorenzo, who claimed to be the Redondan prime minister in addition to his actual job of postmaster. The two men arranged for an official diplomatic meeting, where they held up Lorenzo's red and yellow–striped flag and posed for Frances's camera.

Howorth also incorporated Redonda into his daughter's wedding. The reception was held in Michael and Frances's garden in England, and Howorth used his father-of-the-bride speech to inform the groom that there was no way he was going to let his daughter marry a commoner. "I had to make him a knight—the Knight of Goat Point, I think," Howorth said. "And that prompted everybody at the wedding to want to know more."

I asked him what his daughter thought about his impromptu ceremony.

"I am indulged by my family," he admitted.

Whenever Redonda came up in conversation, Howorth found there were only two reactions: wide-eyed curiosity and total indifference. Yet once people started to learn more about the kingdom, even the skeptics inevitably became intrigued. "Everybody who starts to dig into Redonda gets captured by it," he told me. "And I can't really explain why." Howorth said he receives semi-regular emails from other people who've landed on the island's shores, excited by the difficulty of the task and equally eager to let the king know they'd been there. "I always write back and say, 'On this occasion we'll waive the landing

fee,'" he said. "I've always done it with humour. I never call people stupid—but I do caution them about trying to land, because it looks pretty dangerous to me. I landed in a helicopter, which is infinitely safer than going by boat."

Our conversation so far had been pleasant, but I wanted to go deeper. Was this all just a joke to him? Or was there more to it? "Take me back to when you were standing on the island and raising your standard," I said. "Did you feel a connection in that moment to Shiel and the century of history behind the legend?"

He wrinkled his nose slightly. "No, probably not."

That took me by surprise. "Really?"

"It was just a bit of fun," Howorth said. "I was going up in someone's private helicopter! How cool is that?" Howorth also thought the trip was a great opportunity to study the detritus left on the island from the mining operation. But once the party was back aboard *Air Farce One*, they agreed that it was no wonder the island was so neglected. "It's hostile," Howorth said. "There's no little bay, no quaint little anchorage, no gorgeous sandy beach. None of that. It's a hostile island."

I kept pressing. "But John Duffy must have felt relief, at least," I said. "He'd finally fulfilled King Bob's last wish."

Howorth looked at me through his laptop camera kindly, but with an edge of trepidation, as if worried that what he was about to say would come off as condescending. "You're trying to make it a little more serious than it is," he said. "Would they really have fretted if they didn't find me? I think they would have thought it was a shame. So they were perhaps relieved, but not hugely relieved. If Bob had not named me, what would have happened? I don't know. Would someone have been appointed by the Tot Club? I don't know. Would I have done anything about it? Certainly not. Because I wouldn't have known anything about it. All I can remember thinking was that the King of Redonda's dead, and that's a shame."

"But," I said, "this is a story that's lived on continuously for —"

"And so it shall," Howorth said with a nod. "That's my only responsibility, to make sure that I find a successor who I think will look after the kingdom. And I often think about it. But do I do anything about it? No."

"Right," I said. "Your responsibility is to the title, but also to the story."

He nodded again. "That is what I took on: the perpetuating of the story. Because there's nothing else to do, really. I am just a custodian of a title, and my prime responsibility is to pass that title on to somebody who won't fritter it away or forget it, and who will take it at least as seriously as I do — which isn't all that seriously."

Howorth wasn't delusional. He knew he wasn't actually royalty, and that what King Bob had given him wasn't a kingdom but rather access to a quirky tradition that pre-dated them both and — with any luck — would outlive them both, too. "I'm just the holder of the title, and that in itself is fun, because of who has gone before me," he said. "And in four or five generations' times, the title might be even more intriguing. So, therefore, it is my responsibility to make sure it survives. That's perhaps my *only* responsibility."

AT A CERTAIN POINT, interviews about Redonda had their limits. So, too, did the books that were still piling up in my office. It was never as simple as picking up a new title and pulling the relevant information out: each had to first be placed in context, assessed not just for what it said about the kingdom but also who was saying it, to what end, and in the service of which claimant to the throne. The same went for the people I'd spoken to, most of whom had only been told part of the story and happily fudged whichever details they weren't sure of. Other parts of the story seemed lost entirely, printed on long-crumbled newsprint or taken to the grave by a series of unreliable men. The further I dug, the more convinced I was that a truly complete accounting of the kingdom was not possible.

Javier Marías once compared Redonda the island to Transylvania, in that "it has a not inconsiderable reputation as the abode of monsters and beasties of every sort, as a setting for strange tales of many inexplicable events." Another thing the two places had in common was that they had been covered over by layers of mythology; it was possible, even likely, to be familiar with them through story and not realize there was an actual territory to go along with the dot on the map. Studying those layers had value. But I came to see that I really hadn't given the place itself—the territory that had given rise to the mythology in the first place—its proper due.

I'd waited long enough. It was time to go see the island in person.

WOOL SOCKS *and* GOAT WATER   21

IT TAKES THREE different planes and nearly a full day of
travel to get from my wintery corner of Canada to the birthplace of M.P. Shiel. The first leg begins just before midnight
local time, and by the time I land in Antigua late the following afternoon, I'm exhausted and loopy. The outdoor temper-
ature has jumped a full sixty degrees Celsius since I last set
foot outdoors, and as I take my first breath of warm, heavy
Caribbean air, I know one thing for sure: I am the only person
here wearing wool hiking socks.

The final flight of the trip is a twenty-minute hop from
V.C. Bird International Airport over to Montserrat. I'm waiting
in line to get something to eat when I hear my name called
unexpectedly over the loudspeakers, and a minute later I'm
being shepherded out onto the tarmac along with a handful
of other travellers, one of whom is not helping my disorien-
tation by talking loudly about, of all things, the Canadian
hockey player P.K. Subban.↓ It's only when I spot our plane
that I understand how far out of the way Montserrat is, even

Subban's mother, I only gradually manage to eavesdrop, was born
and raised in Montserrat before moving to Ontario.

within the Leeward Islands. It can hold eight passengers, pilot included, and yet even at rush hour there's an empty seat.

Our little plane lifts into the air as effortlessly as a piece of dandelion fluff, and we curl around to the south of the island. From the sky, Montserrat soon appears in the foreground over the pilot's shoulder, and it occurs to me that I might be able to spot Redonda from up here, too. I crane my neck to look out my little side window, and — oh my god — there it is: tall, jagged, and magnificent. Seeing the island so unexpectedly, and so nonchalantly, I make a noise that I don't think I've ever made before. The place I've spent years thinking about is suddenly — there. And not in the sentimental, poetic way that it's often described. None of that *On a perfect day, with no clouds, you just might catch a glimpse...* stuff. In this moment, Redonda is as clear as day.

The woman sitting next to me notices my astonishment (my nose may have actually been pressed up against the glass). She leans over and shouts over the engine noise, "That's only Redonda. Nobody goes there." I nod politely — and when I turn back to the window, the weather has changed. In just a few seconds, a swath of low cloud has rolled in and swallowed Redonda up. Then the plane turns once more, and we begin our descent into Montserrat. Like a magic trick, Redonda has vanished just as quickly as it appeared.

MONTSERRAT IS A teardrop-shaped island eighteen kilo-metres long and eleven wide. It has a population of fewer than five thousand people, and with its lack of resorts and even basic corporate branding, the island leans into its repu-tation as a place largely unspoiled by capitalism: as many people refer to it, *the Caribbean the way it used to be*. Most of Montserrat's businesses are small independent shops and bars on the side of the road, and which can be identified by their colourful paint jobs and distinctive signage. The island's steep hills and lush jungles make for stunning views but also a challenge in terms of transportation. There's one main road that winds its way around the island, and at times its incline is so sharp that cars make high-pitched whines as they careen down and back up again.

Montserrat was Shiel's home, a place he described to Londoners as "a mountain-mass, loveliest of the lovely, but touchy! uncertain! dashing into tantrums—hurricanes, earthquakes, brooks bubbling hot, 'Soufrieres' (sulphur-swamps), floods." He may have exaggerated the dangers of everyday life in the Caribbean, but not by much. In September 1989 the Category 5 Hurricane Hugo passed over Montserrat, destroying hospitals and schools and wiping out nearly all of the island's fresh-water reserves. Few buildings of any kind survived unscathed, and 90 percent of the island's population was left homeless. It was a massive disaster, but Montserratians rallied around one another and set to rebuilding— only for something worse to happen just a few years later. In 1995, the country's largest volcano, Soufrière Hills, erupted after centuries of dormancy, burying the capital of Plymouth up to its neck in lava and ash and rendering the entire lower half of the island uninhabitable. This time the devastation was too much for many residents to take. Some relocated to the northern half of the island and started rebuilding again, but an estimated three quarters of the population left for good. A series of smaller, follow-up explosions occurred sporadically over the next fifteen years, with an exclusion zone still in effect around the volcano's blast range. The majority of the southern half of the island—including Shiel's birthplace in Plymouth—remains sealed off to the public to this day.

A few minutes after I get off the plane, a van pulls up in front of the Montserrat airport's lone terminal, and a woman with her hair in a long grey braid leans out the window and yells, "Michael! Hop in!" Clover Lea and her husband David are Americans who have run a villa on the island called Gingerbread Hill for the past twenty-five years. David is a videographer who has carefully documented each of the Soufrière Hills explosions; Clover is a musician and artist whose homemade soaps can be found in all of the villa's guest bathrooms. By the time we arrive, the sun has set and we're plunged into darkness. As we wind our way up the vertigo-inducing driveway, past a sign that reads "IGUANA CROSSING," Clover warns me that there might be a bit of noise in the area. Montserrat, she says, is in the middle of a national election that has drawn a record number of candidates, many of whom are hosting promotional events at rum shops and nightclubs around the island. "The place you might hear music coming from," Clover adds, "is actually owned by a Shiell." In the end, though, what keeps me up are what sound like hundreds of tree frogs, their croaks so clear and steady that it sounds like they've got me surrounded.

THE NEXT MORNING, I walk from Gingerbread Hill to Hilltop Coffee House, Montserrat's one true café. The path takes me uphill along a grass path strewn with coconut husks and yellow hibiscus petals, then past a shaded rest area made out of a repurposed satellite dish. I turn around to take a picture of the view down to the water and am surprised to see Redonda staring back at me. A few minutes later, I walk by a small church with a goat tied to a leash out front, grazing in a lonely, perfect circle, and pull out my phone again — only to find Redonda once more in the viewfinder. From this angle and distance, the island appears accessible, almost inviting. The shimmering horizon gives the illusion that the island's rocky face gently descends down to the water; in reality, the cliffs are more like a castle wall, sheer and unrelenting nearly all the way around. It's now clear to me why Shiel's father was drawn to Redonda. When you gaze out across the sea, it is the first thing that stares back at you.

The walk to the coffee shop takes less than ten minutes, during which the weather changes as if on a timer, cycling from sun to cloud to rain and back again. This squares with the experience of one of Montserrat's best known visitors. "On no island I have ever lived," wrote the American anthropologist Margaret Mead in 1966, "has there been such simultaneity of microclimates, all visible at once." By the time I arrive at Hilltop, I'm somehow both soaked and sweating, and the last thing I feel like is espresso. That suits David Lea just fine. A slim man with combed-back hair, a light beard, and glasses, he pops up from his chair to give me a tour of the shop, which also contains a makeshift history of the island. On one wall is a stark grid of framed photographs, showing Plymouth before and after the Soufrière Hills eruption: hundreds of buildings, now almost entirely buried. Over time, David says, the ash generated by the volcano combined with rainfall to form a mud-like slurry called lahar, which, once it sets, becomes as hard as cement. As a result, most of the bottom half of Montserrat is now functionally set in stone. "People used to say the north [of the island] is where God turned His back," David says. "Then they all had to move here." Another wall of the café is lined with albums produced at George Martin's recording studio, including Jimmy Buffett's *Volcano*, from 1979, whose prophetic title track considered what might happen should Soufrière

Hills ever erupt. A third is dedicated to the life and music of Alphonsus "Arrow" Cassell, the Montserratian musician whose song "Hot Hot Hot" became a global hit in the 1980s.

Like many locals, David has been into the exclusion zone several times, even though it is technically not allowed. The results of those trips are on display on Hilltop's patio, which has become a kind of museum dedicated to the former capital. It's full of everything from hand-painted signs to a large metal clock face to a bingo machine retrieved from the old Montserrat Springs Hotel. The sight of these items, David says, still brings locals of a certain age to tears, even if all of the details haven't survived the transition: on one shelf sits a metal trophy, the writing on its plaque worn completely clean.

I'd been told David is also an expert on Redonda, and, sure enough, Hilltop has a bookshelf of local-interest titles, including a copy of the 1970s reissue of *The Purple Cloud*, Wynne-Tyson's *So Say Banana Bird*, and *The Dragon of Redonda*. Outside, alongside artifacts from the exclusion zone, hangs a framed map of Redonda produced after Wynne-Tyson and Morse's visit in 1980. And nestled among pictures and mementos on the Hilltop bar, sitting inconspicuously next to a box of vanilla caramel tea, is a photograph of Shiel and his first wife, Lina.

David tells me that he's been over to Redonda in person multiple times, though not recently. On one such trip, he and his children came across a goat that kept kicking rocks down at them, as if trying to prevent them from climbing up the gully. "He knew that if you were coming up, you were coming to bother him," David says. In addition to being the setting for a fun daytrip, he believes the island can have a deeper, almost spiritual effect on people. Before opening Gingerbread Hill, David was a prison chaplain, and in the

Hilltop Coffee House, Montserrat.

1980s he petitioned the Antiguan government for permission to bring a group of prisoners out to Redonda to restore some of the old mining buildings and set up a ham radio station. The plan never came together, but he thinks it would have had a profound effect on whomever signed up. "Once you get away from your situation, and you can actually look back on it and see it from a distance, it changes your perspective," he says. There was no better place to do that than on Redonda.

David walks into a back office and returns with a clear plastic pouch divided into six sections. "These," he says, tossing the pouch onto the bar, "are the only coins in the realm." I look more closely, and discover that they are, in fact, Redondan. One coin shows a scene of the island with fluffy clouds overhead; others depict fish, birds, a coat of arms, and even Christopher Columbus himself, under a banner that reads "Santa Maria La Redonda 1493." Their stated denominations range from a penny all the way up to ten dollars.

I look up, mystified. "Where did you get these?"

"Oh, you can write away to the Chinese and they'll make anything," David says. In fact, he adds, he has a Redondan title to go along with the coin collection: His Excellency the Chancellor of the Ex-Chequer. But he doesn't tell me who gave it to him, or which came first, the title or the cash.

That evening, I've been invited to attend the launch for this year's Alliouagana Festival of the Word, Montserrat's annual literary festival. The route to the cultural centre is simple enough—there's only one road, after all—but without a car, I have to resort to hitchhiking. Several people have assured me this is common practice on Montserrat, though the protocol here is a little different than in North America. I stand on the side of the road, feeling more than a little self-conscious as I stick out my pointer finger and waggle it theatrically in the direction I want to go. A few minutes later, a shiny SUV bearing the green-and-grey logo of the Montserrat Volcano Observatory approaches and pulls over. When I go to open the back door, a young boy is sitting there, strapped into a booster seat. His eyes go wide when he sees me. "Get out of here!" he yells, and smacks me in the chest with his water bottle.

"Oh, don't worry about him," says the woman in the front passenger seat. "Come on in. Where are you headed?"

"Little Bay?" I say, cautiously sliding into the other seat. It turns out the mother and son, whose name is Maxwell, are headed to the same event I am; Maxwell's dad, whose clothing also bears the observatory logo, is dropping them off. As the SUV winds its way towards our destination, I want to ask them what they know about Redonda, but it's impossible to get more than half a sentence out without Maxwell jumping in—my mysterious sins now mysteriously forgiven—

to tell me about how there's no KFC on Montserrat, but this one shop sells chicken that's almost as good, and anyway it doesn't matter because his birthday party was still really fun. The longest stretch of silence from Maxwell's corner of the car lasts approximately a minute, and that's only because he's used that time to lean over and latch onto my left shoulder with his teeth, holding eye contact and refusing to let go until the SUV pulls up to the cultural centre, at which point I thank his parents and slip away into the crowd.

The Alliouagana Festival is an annual celebration of writing and storytelling in Montserrat that was founded in 2009. Even though Shiel has been dead for more than seventy years, I'm curious whether he's still considered part of the island's tradition. At the entrance of the cultural centre is a large pyramid made of metal scaffolding, with a bright vertical LED tube inside to represent magma. A series of double-sided vinyl banners have been hung around the pyramid, showcasing stories of the 1995 eruption from the perspective of those who lived through it. "I've never seen anything so black," reads one. "You put your hands out in front of you and you can't even see your hands." The exhibit has been put together by a team of visiting scientists from the University of East Anglia, and they've announced they are donating it to the island so that it can live on in Montserrat permanently. Inside the building, several local singers perform Calypso songs, all of which in some way reference the eruption, followed by an address by Justin "Hero" Cassell about his late brother Arrow.

The evening's main event is a stirring keynote address from Dr Clarice Barnes, a local academic who speaks candidly about the biases and limitations of researching other cultures. She brings up Margaret Mead and her work on

Montserrat, but cautions against the tendency to treat out-siders as definitive or even neutral observers. Questions of power dynamics and consent, she says, need to be constantly unpacked and re-evaluated. If the people you want to study are uncomfortable with how the information will be used, how do you proceed? Is scientific research an inherently col-onial project? These are difficult questions, and even though they're not aimed at me—some of the scientists from East Anglia are shifting on their feet uncomfortably—I start to reconsider the role I might be unwittingly playing when it comes to Redonda. The last time a white author flew in from afar and attempted to write about the island in the hopes of understanding the kingdom, it didn't go well. In his 1979 book *The Quest for Redonda*, A. Reynolds Morse repeatedly went out of his way to diagnose what he considered to be the lesser intellect of the locals on Montserrat and Antigua. "The blacks—the natives—are separated from savagery only by Coca-Cola and a thin veneer of gasoline and tires," Morse wrote, "both imported." It was ugly. Grossly hypocritical, too, considering Morse relied on those same locals at every turn during his trip, including his ascent to Redonda's peak with Wynne-Tyson. Obviously, this kind of thinking is nauseating to me. Then again, the Kingdom of Redonda is clearly a story that has prioritized the fantasies of white foreigners; even its name defaults to a tossed-off observation from Columbus, rather than its previous Indigenous title of Ocanamunru. Did it matter that Shiel's family was a mix-ture of the African and Irish populations that had lived on Montserrat together since the seventeenth century? Or that Redonda itself was a kingdom with no subjects, and therefore no people to claim sovereignty over, jokingly or otherwise? (Shiel himself had written, in "About Myself": "For what is a king without subjects? Certainly if I am a king, my kingdom is 'not of this World'...") Could the term *sovereignty* even be applied to a piece of rock that has been ignored by humans for most of its existence? Or, as Cedric Boston had put it, was Redondan sovereignty *only* possible if humans everywhere simply left it alone? As the crowd applauds Barnes then lines up for cups of a local dish called goat water, I find myself wondering whether I've made a mistake in coming here at all.

Eventually I make my way over to the podium and introduce myself. Barnes seems pleased to learn what I'm working on. Redonda, she says, doesn't receive as much attention as it should, even from locals. As she gets ready to join the goat-water lineup, she tells me something that takes me by surprise: her grandfather was one of the men who lived on Redonda and worked the guano mine a century ago. Over the years I'd seen the occasional blurry photograph of the workers, but I had never stopped to consider their individual identities. Now it feels like a small portion of those photographs has been brought into sharp relief. We say goodbye, and I stand there alone for a minute, delighted to have found such an unexpected connection to the island's past. In a very real way, Barnes's family knows more about Redonda than any of its kings ever will.

WHEN I'D MENTIONED to the organizers of the Alliouagana festival that I had been researching Redonda, they asked if I would be interested in visiting a local school and talking to some of their students about what I've learned. So early the next morning I find myself standing in front of a classful of children in full school uniforms despite the sweltering heat. The kids are aged between eleven and fourteen and have all grown up within eyesight of the island, so I start by asking how much they know about Redonda. The answer, across the board, is: nothing. To them, the island is just another part of the scenery, as unremarkable as an individual tree in your backyard. But they're a goofy yet attentive audience anyway, making exaggerated gagging sounds at the story of Gawsworth serving Shiel's ashes to his dinner guests and cackling with delight at Wynne-Tyson's homemade pajama flag.

We move on to questions, most of which are the usual things kids want to know about this line of work. *Do you like being a writer? What's your favourite book? How much money do you make?* In the near-decade since I came across that used copy of *All Souls*, my professional life has come a long way. Instead of a headache-inducing cubicle, I now work from the comfort of my home office and write more or less full-time. I've published two books under my own name and co-written a third. I've also grown a beard, which is already starting to show flecks of grey. There is still so much time ahead, and every day is littered with errands and petty grievances, but if I could show all this to my anxious younger self, I am not sure he would believe how fortunate we ended up. Throughout it all, Redonda has been a constant presence, occupying much of my thoughts but always remaining too strange and unwieldy a topic to bring up in conversation. Sometimes friends or acquaintances will ask me what I'm working on, and I don't know how to even begin to describe what will eventually become this book. The questions from these students are a lot more manageable.

But then one girl with a puzzled look on her face asks something unexpectedly on-topic: "Why do these people want to be the king?"

It's a good question. But I pause, because I realize I'm not actually sure how to answer it. If I wanted a simple, classroom-friendly explanation, I could tell her that lots of friends like to have inside jokes with one another, or that it can be fun to imagine a totally different life for yourself than the one you have. But I can tell that won't answer what she's really asking, which is: Why do they want to be the king of *this* island? Of all the places in the world, why Redonda? And that's a bit more complicated.

When it was first conceived, the Kingdom of Redonda was a bit of shared fantasy between a father and his only son. The island was a local landmark but held no political, economic, or cultural value. Regardless of how seriously Matthew Sr. took his claim, it really was there for the taking. Inside jokes, however, have a shelf life, and this one had multiple opportunities to peter out naturally: the crowning ceremony, the death of the father and instigator. It took a desperate M.P. Shiel, half a world away and nearly half a century into his writing career, to finally unearth this anecdote from his childhood—and that was the point when the kingdom's meaning changed. Now, instead of a shared joke about a familiar place, Redonda became an exotic symbol of potential and reinvention. For John Gawsworth, saying he was king of an empty island was a tall tale that played well in the pubs. But his vision of Redonda was also a form of wonder and wish fulfillment. King Juan I created an intricate fantasy realm that was insulated from the multiple harshnesses of reality, a place devoid of war and class and injury and poverty, a place where literature was revered above all else, and a place where friendship (as codified through mock-formal titles) was agreed to in writing and could never be rescinded. By the time Wynne-Tyson and Marías got involved, the kingdom had taken on a life—and a mythology—entirely its own. Redonda the island had become an afterthought. The kingdom, then, wasn't colonizing an existing place so much as generating a new one, which operated in a parallel dimension that only occasionally overlapped with the original. It was like telling someone you owned a painting of a soup can and them asking you how the soup tasted.

And yet the island itself wasn't *totally* irrelevant, because when people got sucked into the story of Redonda, what they were responding to was this particular mythology, with these particular roots: the escapist fantasy of a man who believed himself a descendent of kings, but who was stuck in a racially oppressed colony instead. No matter how many islands there are in the world named Redonda — and there are a lot of them — the story belongs exclusively to this one. Other mythologies may well develop on their own, like the one being pushed by the Argentine postmaster. But the Caribbean Redonda will always be unique, with a unique sense of humour, a unique string of rulers, and a unique story that will continue to grow for many years to come. All it takes is a willingness to suspend your disbelief a little.

That's some of what I'm thinking, anyway. But it's an awful lot to try to explain to an eleven-year-old. "I think," I say to her, "it's because the story started here. And they just wanted to be part of it."

That afternoon, an academic and volunteer with the literary festival offers to give me and another visiting writer a tour of Montserrat in her car. Jean Handscombe takes us up our steepest path yet to the volcano observatory, with its panoramic view of the surrounding hills and valleys, then all the way down to the edge of the exclusion zone. This is as far as civilians are allowed to travel, and the dirt roads along the way are eerily quiet. The jungle has already reclaimed much of the abandoned houses, with trees and foliage snaking

Redonda as seen from Montserrat.

through broken windows, leaving it unclear where human settlements end and nature begins. Back when the evacuation notice first came down, Handscombe says, people had to leave most of their belongings behind — including their domesticated pigs, whose descendants now run wild and feral in the surrounding woods. Then the trees disappear, and we get our first good look at what is left of Plymouth. It's a disturbing and incongruous sight, an expanse of uneven grey like gravel in the world's largest parking lot. Underneath the hardened ash and mud, I try to remind myself, are the encased remains of the entire capital — and along with it, all physical traces of the childhood of M.P. Shiel.

We get back in the car and drive down to Fox's Bay, a beautiful black-sand beach on the west side of the island. We're the only people in sight — and staring back at us from across the sea, once again, is Redonda. It's the clearest view of the island I've had yet, and I can't stop looking at it.

"I think I'm going to go for a swim," I say.

The others hardly have a chance to turn around before I strip down to my underwear and sprint into the crashing waves. I've never touched the Caribbean before, but the warm, salty waves are inviting and comfortable, with none of the shock I normally associate with ocean water. I take several big strokes in the direction of the island then stop and tread water for a minute, staring out at Redonda and trying to imagine Shiel in my place. Even though he left Montserrat as a teenager, he knew these waters. When he looked across at this odd little island, distant enough to hold its mysteries but close enough to feel like a chunk of home, what did he think?

At the very least, he was intrigued enough to sail over and climb to the top. And soon, so will I.

AT LEAST I think I will.

In the totality of the Kingdom of Redonda's existence, few involved have paid attention to the state of the actual island. Those who have did so from a distance. Which is why almost nobody connected to the legend has realized that in the span of just a few years, Redonda has undergone a dramatic transformation. The island best known for its infertility is now coming back to life, thanks to a group of conservationists armed with rat poison, yoga pants, and pool noodles.

When the Redonda Phosphate Company abandoned its mine in the late 1920s, it left behind buildings and machinery. But it also introduced two foreign animal species to the island: goats and rats. And for most of the ensuing century, these two species multiplied freely while devouring everything in sight. Redonda was once home to a variety of bird and lizard populations, including several species endemic to the island, but the invaders drove them nearly to the point of extinction. Some species were wiped out entirely. Redonda's natural vegetation, meanwhile, was eaten down so close to the nubs that new seeds couldn't develop, let alone take root. As the abandoned equipment rusted in the sun, this once-lush island slowly turned brown.

The scope of the damage, plus the island's remoteness, led many to conclude that Redonda could not be saved. There also wasn't much in the way of political will, as many in Antigua had little time for the concept of conservation. The feeling among locals was that if you were already wealthy, maybe you could afford to advocate for trees and lizards. But for most people, the fate of a distant island that nobody could even get to was not something worth fretting over.

That attitude started to change in the late 1980s, when a group of concerned Antiguans formed a non-profit called the Environmental Awareness Group. One of the group's leading voices was Desmond Nicholson, a historian who had previously helped restore Nelson's Dockyard, a famed British naval base in English Harbour that had fallen into disrepair, and which, thanks to his efforts, went on to become a UNESCO World Heritage Site. The EAG's first project was restoring nearby Great Bird Island, which was also overrun with rats; they have since done the same for more than a dozen other islands in the area. Throughout that work, Redonda was always the EAG's dream project, because of its size and visibility—and finally, in 2016, a group of volunteers set up a camp on the island's plateau and got to work.

The first step was relocating the wild goats, which had grown to a herd of approximately sixty. Volunteers went in prepared with snares, but after two full months of work, they'd only managed to capture a single goat: a buck they affectionately named Juan, after King Juan's Peak, the highest point on the island.[†] The others couldn't be induced, no matter how much food or fresh water was left out for them. After a two-week break to think things over, a larger group of workers reconvened on the island and this time were more successful, slowly rounding up the rest of the goats, one by one. They were then transported off of the island in small groups via helicopter. To keep the goats calm during the twenty-minute flight back to Antigua, each animal was placed in a plastic bag up to its neck, with a hood (made of old yoga pants) placed over its eyes and foam sheaths (made of pool noodles) over its horns.

While the goats were being relocated, workers also had to figure out how to eradicate the roughly six thousand black rats that had infested the island. By now the conservation group had grown to include representatives from other organizations, including Fauna and Flora International (whose vice presidents include David Attenborough). Still, the task was formidable. One onsite expert said that Redonda had the highest concentration of rats she'd ever seen; the EAG's coordinator, Shanna Challenger, reported having trouble sleeping on the island because she kept getting woken up by the thumps of rodents landing on the canopy of her tent. The Redonda rats were also voracious. Workers would walk the length of the island setting poison traps, and by the time they returned to empty them, other rats had already started eating

Like many Redondan landmarks, this peak was given its name during Morse and Wynne-Tyson's trip to the island in 1979. Nicholson accompanied the group on that trip and helped ensure that the kingdom-related names they came up with—including Shiel's Summit and Centaur's Cave—have now passed into general use.

their dead brethren. To reach the island's most inaccessible corners, the EAG flew in special mountaineers from England to scale cliffs and distribute yet more poison.

By the spring of 2017, after several months of painstaking work, Redonda was officially declared goat- and rat-free. Before it took any further action, however, the EAG decided to wait and see what kind of rewilding would occur naturally. Group members were optimistic, while also keeping in mind that Redonda had been subject to nearly a full century of destruction by multiple invasive species. How much energy did the island have left? Plenty, it turned out. Just as the creatures of Great Bird Island had seen their numbers rebound, so, too, did Redonda's native species, including tree lizards, pygmy geckoes, and the distinctive all-black Redondan ground dragon. After just one year, land-bird populations on the island had increased tenfold. The grasses, bushes, and trees, meanwhile, had all regrown faster than even the most optimistic projection. The EAG conducts annual studies listing the different types of vegetation growing on Redonda. In 2016, at the outset of the project, there were seventeen. Three years later, there were eighty-eight.

I had emailed the EAG before my trip in the hopes that I might be able to tag along on their next trip to Redonda and witness the rewilding in person. I wasn't sure how much they knew about the kingdom and was initially unsure whether I should even bring it up, in case they felt it demeaned or distracted from their work. But that wasn't the case at all. "Have you been in contact with any of the kings, then?" Challenger asked me over Skype, with mock-hurt in her voice. "How come none of them have contacted us?" They'd all been too busy with the map to realize what was happening to the territory.

Less than a month before I was set to arrive, however, the bad news arrived. It turned out there was only one company on Antigua that rented helicopters — and it had just gone out of business. Without access to a helicopter, even EAG workers couldn't get out to the island to do their monitoring work. Which meant I, too, was out of luck.

This was a crisis point. What was the point of going all the way to the Caribbean if I couldn't actually get to Redonda? Spinning in dejected circles in my office chair, I tried to think of any way the news could be reframed as a positive development. I even started mentally composing a write-around, just to see whether there was any way to make it not sound ridiculous. *In a way, given its history of absentee monarchs, perhaps it's fitting that even regular civilians can no longer visit Redonda ...*

In desperation, I emailed John Duffy, chancellor to King Michael the Grey. Duffy was the one who had informed King Michael of his surprise accession to the throne in 2009, and I knew he still lived in Antigua. I asked him if there was any way he could help.

Sure enough, Duffy said he had a connection. His name was Chris Harris, and he had sailed all around the Caribbean in a fifty-two-foot boat that used to belong to the Royal National Lifeboat Institution. When I reached Harris, he said my timing was perfect. He was free the week I was in town and offered me the services of the *Sea Terror II*.

Just as quickly as my plans had threatened to unravel, everything seemed to be coming back together. That's when Harris told me that the reason he was familiar with Redonda was because he was, in fact, its king. It was kind of a funny story, really. Had I ever heard of a guy named King Bob the Bald?

A MERE ROCK 22

A WHITE VAN sits idling in front of Antigua's National Sailing Academy. It's more than an hour before dawn, and English Harbour is still cloaked in darkness. I grab my backpack and close behind me the front door of the academy's modest lodgings, which is where I slept a handful of fitful hours the previous night after flying back from Montserrat. The passenger door of the van swings open, and Harris's girlfriend, Megan Fallon, greets me with a hearty "Good morning!" At the wheel is King Christopher of Redonda.

"Did you hear?" he asks. "Redonda's in the news."

As a matter of fact, I did. The night before, I read an article from Antigua's *Daily Observer* bearing the headline: "Wanted man surrenders after hiding out on Redonda." According to the story, a twenty-four-year-old policeman who was wanted in nearby Saint Kitts and Nevis had gone missing for more than a week before unexpectedly showing up in the Antiguan capital of St. John's and turning himself in to local police. In between, he evaded authorities by camping out on Redonda. During our short drive over to Galleon Beach, Harris, Fallon, and I try to figure out how such a hide-out would work. Redonda has so little navigable terrain that, had our itinerary been off by a day or two, it's likely our paths would have crossed.

Harris parks the van, and the three of us climb into a small dinghy and paddle over to the *Sea Terror II*. In its previous life, this vessel was an emergency rescue boat in the Orkney Islands, off the coast of Scotland. It's survived all kinds of inclement weather, compared to which today should be, well, smooth sailing: clear skies, little wind, and a high in the mid-thirties Celsius. As its name indicates, this is actually Harris's second boat. He bought the original *Sea Terror* in the 1990s, but a few years ago it mysteriously detached from its mooring and hit the rocks, just a few feet from where its identical sister ship is now anchored. As we pull up to the *Sea Terror II* and climb aboard, Harris points straight down into the water. The sun is now coming up behind us, and I can just make out the silhouette of a hull below. It's actually quite rare, Harris assures me, for a boat to sink here. "I guess I was the one for this decade."

Once we're onboard, roles quickly assert themselves. Harris is the skipper. Fallon is his second in command. And I am unhelpful, unsure even where to stand, and sometimes actively impeding the many small tasks that need completing before we can leave. At one point Harris puts a hand on my shoulder and says diplomatically, "Why don't you go have a seat in the lounge?" By 7 a.m. we're finally off, cutting through the surf and pointed due west. There's no turning back now. It's Redonda or bust.

It takes approximately four hours to sail there from Antigua, which gives our captain-king plenty of time to come out onto to the deck and survey his territory. Harris is a stocky, thoroughly tanned man in his late fifties, with light-blond facial hair covering his chin in the shape of an anchor.

He's wearing boardshorts and a pair of Oakleys, plus his Redondan crown, which a previous girlfriend made for him out of leather, shells, and black coral. Fallon joins us a few minutes later, and I ask her what she thinks of it. "The crown came out early in our relationship," she admits. "He doesn't wear it *that* often. But it does suit him."

Chris Harris with his crown and staff.

Harris also has with him his royal staff, which doubles as a practical seafaring tool: a rusted, two-hooked blade that can reach down into the water and clear out the propeller in case it gets caught on something. He has a sword, too, which at one point he goes down below to retrieve. It's something he picked up while travelling in the Sahara Desert, years ago, but its sheath is finicky. Harris spends a minute trying various grips in the hopes of pulling the sword free. But it won't budge, and eventually he puts it away again.

In front of us, Redonda is still a speck on the horizon. As we look out at the island, a rainbow, of all things, suddenly appears in the sky, with one end pointing directly and unmistakably at our exact destination. "It's a bit like a fairy tale, isn't it?" Fallon says. "As I stand here next to a grown man in a crown."

King Christopher's claim to the Redondan throne begins in 2005, but his sense of adventure dates back much further. In the 1980s, he was a motorcycle enthusiast and courier in

London, and later moved to Berlin, where for ten years he sold T-shirt designs to shops across Europe through a clothing company he called Terror. Harris then headed off to the Caribbean, where he lived off of his clothing residuals while running a beachside bar on the small island of Carriacou, at the southern edge of the Lesser Antilles; his customers there knew him as "Captain Terror." But when 9/11 happened, the word "terror" went from edgy to unsellable overnight. The clothing money dried up, and Harris moved to Antigua, where he started a new company called Lazy Bones Beanbags, which makes squishy but durable lounging chairs for boats.

That's where he met Bob Williamson. "He was a very cool guy," Harris says. "We probably met in our former lives." In fact, the two men figured out that when Harris was in London, earning a living as a courier, Williamson was working out of Dean Street in Soho, and his office was one of Harris's regular clients. Neither remembered a specific meeting, but when they reconnected in Antigua, the pair got along immediately. "We would sit at [local café] Skullduggery's, drinking coffee and talking shit for hours," says Harris. "Anyway, push came to shove and I decided to declare war on him."

I ask for details on what happened, and Harris pauses. "Um ... I think that I wasn't happy with his running of the kingdom. He's never been there—I don't think any of the pretend other kings have been to Redonda." I point out that King Bob did, in fact, visit Redonda in 1998, and that this was the basis of his claim to the throne. But, I add, it's true that he never climbed to the top. "Yes," Harris says slowly, "that's right."

King Bob accepted Harris's challenge to his throne and gave him three tasks to complete in order to prove himself worthy. One, steal his crown. Two, climb to the top of Redonda. And three, publish an account of the trip. Harris decided to do the climb first, and brought with him Zach LeBeau, a writer friend whom he knew from Carriacou, and Harris's pet pit bull, who was also named Terror. When the trio reached the Redondan plateau, Harris planted his flag — the good old-fashioned skull and crossbones — and gave the island a new name to go with it: the Kingdom of Terror. Next was stealing the crown, which Harris was able to accomplish without much trouble, as Bob had a habit of leaving it on the floor next to his chair at Skullduggery's. But there was an issue with the final task. Production was about to start on the sequel to *Pirates of the Caribbean*, and King Bob's boat, the *St. Peter*, was again tapped to make an appearance. By this point Bob was too old to get the boat in working order himself, so he hired Harris to do it for him.

"He said, 'Look, let's hold off on the challenge, because I need you to get my boat ready,'" Harris says. "For a large wad of cash I was bought off, temporarily." But even after the filming was completed, Harris and Williamson never returned to the task-in-progress. By then Bob's health had started to seriously deteriorate, and he was back and forth between Canada and the Caribbean to receive medical treatment. Then one year he left and never came back. "In all honesty, I didn't finish the challenge," Harris says. But after Williamson died, he "naturally assumed" the crown.

"Wait," I say. "So you never actually published anything about climbing to the top of the island?"

No, Harris admits. But he *is* an author, he says, because Williamson was quite clear about that being a prerequisite for the throne. Way back in 1986, Harris wrote an article for a magazine published by Kawasaki about riding his motorcycle from England to Ghana. He claims he showed a copy of this story to Williamson, and King Bob decreed that was good enough.

Since that initial ascent, Harris has only been back to Redonda once, in 2018. I ask him why he returned. "I re-established my claim," Harris says. "Which you'll see."

"Do you still call it the Kingdom of Terror?" I ask, starting to feel uneasy.

"Yeah. You'll see!"

In front of us, Redonda is growing larger as it comes into focus. Not just that: it changes colour. When we first set out that morning, the island appeared to be the same monotonous dusty brown I recognized from all the old photographs. But as we come within a dozen or so miles, Redonda's plateau is revealed to be covered in a thin but bright layer of green — a direct result of the Environmental Awareness Group's work. The island's cliffs also differentiate themselves, with a flaky volcanic texture and colours ranging from a rich purple to a light heather grey. Other areas are streaked white with seabird guano. From our position on the deck we can also make out hundreds of boobies and frigate birds flying overhead in slow, lazy circles — and for every bird in the air, there are at least ten more resting in the nooks of the island's fearsome cliffs. Redonda is still imposing, but it's now also teeming with life.

We sail around the south end of the island and anchor just off the leeward side, a few hundred yards from shore. Across from us is a small rocky beach, which is our only real place to land. From there, we'll have our choice of two steep gullies, each of which leads to the plateau above. That's what the maps say, anyway. From down here at sea level, we can't actually see the plateau yet, only the lip that serves as its supposed entranceway.

The three of us climb into the dinghy. Harris says he doesn't feel like re-hooking up its engine, so instead he pulls out a couple of oars, which he and Fallon use to steer us within

Redonda as seen from aboard Sea Terror II.

a couple of feet of the shore. We stop short of some large rocks sticking out of the water, and I leap out onto the nearest one. Harris does the same. This leaves Fallon alone at the bow of the dinghy, tentatively holding both oars. I only now realize that Harris didn't tell her ahead of time that she was going to have to solo paddle the hundred feet or so back to the *Sea Terror II*. She looks terrified as she considers the difficulty of the task before her. If the wind picks up or her technique falters, she could easily be blown out to sea. Harris, however, seems unconcerned, and gives her a short reassurance before turning away. He starts ambling away across the rocks, even as the sound of Fallon's cries drifts over to us as she starts rowing back to the boat. From what I can see, the dinghy is starting to spin in a circle.

"Are you sure she's OK out there?" I ask. "It looks like she's really struggling."

He turns around to look, briefly. "She struggles with being my girlfriend." I force out a half-laugh, uncomfortably aware that Harris is my only way back to the Antiguan mainland.

Now that I'm actually standing on Redonda, I start to recognize landmarks from my research. There's a nook in the cliff face next to us large enough to shelter two or three people from the sun—this must be the place where King Bob the Bald hid out during his invasion in 1998. To our right, meanwhile, are a few bricks stubbornly mortared to the rock: the last surviving traces of the Redondan post office. This is also the same landing spot that Shiel and his father would have used when they came to the island for the crowning ceremony. Their advantage was that they were able to use the phosphate company's pulley system to conveniently lift themselves up to the plateau. The pulley's buckets were used to transport guano, and later phosphate ore, but I've seen photos showing as many as four workers crammed into a single bucket, hitching a ride to the top. These days, visitors to Redonda have two ways of reaching the plateau: make friends with someone who owns a helicopter, or find a way to climb a few hundred vertical feet of volcanic rock and dirt. Looking up in the direction of the plateau, Harris and I agree that the right-most gully is our best option, both because of the shape of the path and because it looks to be mostly in the shade. It's time to climb. But before we do, I open a zippered pocket in my backpack and pull out a ceramic saltshaker in the shape of a goose.

Weeks earlier, when I had informed King Michael the Grey of my plans to visit Redonda, he agreed to grant me his permission from afar, so long as I paid his royal fee: a pinch of salt, thrown over my left shoulder, with my tongue pressed firmly into my cheek. I'd picked up the shaker at a Canadian antique mall, on the grounds that this entire trip had the makings of a wild-goose chase. The salt inside, at least, was local, swiped the night before off of the condiment table at

Antigua's weekly, island-wide barbeque party. Now, standing on the shoreline, I hold my shaker up to the circling boobies above and announce my intention, in as loud a voice as I can muster over the wind and waves, to pay King Michael's fee. I pour the salt into my hand and toss it over my shoulder; the wind immediately picks it up and returns it, with speed, into the back of my neck. As I'm doing this, Harris stands a few metres away with his back pointedly turned. He has no interest in acknowledging the ritual of a rival. By the time I put my shaker away, Harris has moved past the wind-tattered government sign alerting us to the presence of rat poison on the island and is already up over the first ridge. I put on the gloves he's provided — a yellow handknit pair that were intended for gardening — and follow.

A few minutes into the climb, it's become obvious that the path is much steeper than I'd first thought. It also requires more concentration and strategy when it comes to choosing my next hand- or foothold. The soil here is so dry and loose that even some of the larger, sturdier-looking rocks pull out of the ground at the slightest provocation. If I dig a foot in carelessly, or even at a slightly incorrect angle, a tiny avalanche spills down the hill behind me, threating to bring me down with it. Harris and I come up with a system: if the person in front accidentally upsets anything large enough to injure, he will immediately yell down so the person behind has time to move out of the way. I think back to descriptions of Morse and Wynne-Tyson's expedition, where they talked in passing about "dislodged boulders," and wonder whether this was an exaggeration after all. Forty years later, the hike to the plateau has become even more complicated due to the explosion of new greenery on the island. Even here in the gully, I'm surrounded by grass and bushes that come up to my knees. This makes hiking feel more akin to fighting through quicksand and also has the effect of disguising the oddly shaped rocks sitting underneath, leading to more than one twisted ankle en route.

Halfway up the incline, Harris and I find a place to stop and gather our breath. My shirt is soaked through, and I'm covered in dust and dirt. But already, our view to the west is incredible, nothing but clear, vibrant blue all the way to the horizon. Plus, I can now see that Fallon has made it safely back to the boat below. I'm in the middle of rambling to Harris about how thrilling it is to be so cut off from human civilization when his cell phone rings. It's a Lazy Bones customer, he says, covering the mouthpiece, so he should probably take it. Then we set off again, and ten minutes later we manage to clear the lip of the ridge and enter the plateau. I'm the first one up, and my first thought is to race over to the small patch of shade provided by the remains of the nearest building. After a few seconds Harris's head pops up over the ridge as well. "Fucking hell," he says, squatting down next to me. "Where's that breeze, anyway?"

Even as I struggle to catch my breath, it is clear that we have arrived at a unique moment in Redonda's history. Rusted machinery still dots the landscape, including a hulking metal spool from the old pulley system that's bigger than I am. But most of these scraps are now obscured by thriving wild grasses that are already several feet tall. I'd hoped that at some point in the trip I might catch a glimpse of a Redondan ground dragon, and before I can even get back to a standing position, a half-dozen of them emerge from behind the rocks to say hello. These creatures have had so little human contact in their lives that they don't know to be scared. One is bold enough to scamper right across the top of my sneaker.

An abandoned building on the Redondan plateau.

Another gently pokes Harris's shoe with one of its own little feet, as if trying to figure out what this strange new paw is made of. For the first time in a century, the island's future appears brighter than its past.

Once I've gulped down some water, I get up to look around the plateau. As the only real navigable section of the island, it's smaller than I'd imagined and not really all that flat. Around me are the remains of a half-dozen stone buildings that were once part of the workers' camp: there's a water cistern, what appears to be some kind of oven, and several group residences. To my left is a hill that leads past scores of nesting seabirds up to the manager's house, another water cistern, and a series of further incremental summits, the highest of which, I happen to know, sits exactly 971 feet above sea level: King Juan's Peak. When I come back to our resting spot, I find Harris inspecting the entrance point we've just passed over. He reminds me of the story of the fugitive cop who recently hid out on Redonda. "I think I saw a pretty fresh footprint back there," he says with a grin.

Harris has been here before, so he's content to rest and enjoy the view. But I want to take a run at the peak. Unfortunately, my timing is off. If we'd sailed out and slept onboard the boat the night before, we might have been able to get up to the plateau before the sun reached its apex. Instead, it's mid-afternoon in the Caribbean, and the sun is not just punishing but directly overhead. I've already drank more than half of the water I brought along, and it takes me fifteen minutes just to stumble my way up more pointy volcanic rocks to the manager's house, which has been reduced to some shattered stones strewn atop a concrete floor. A few feet away sits the second water cistern. I walk around to the other side of the tank, where someone has spray-painted a large cartoon symbol that looks like a combination of a sun and a throwing star. It's accompanied by two unmistakeable words: "TERROR KINGDOM."

Oh no.

I know that Redonda isn't an unspoilt paradise. I know that the mine was a massive human intrusion onto a natural ecosystem, set up to turn a profit and abandoned the moment it could no longer do so. But this feels different. And I can't help but feel outraged on behalf of all the people who've spent so much of their time and energy trying to reverse the effects of that human footprint. I think of the scientists with the Environmental Awareness Group, working for years to remove the goats and rats left behind by a company that couldn't be bothered to. I think of the group of local archeologists who, I learned, are in talks to fully map and excavate the former mine site. And I think of men like Dr Barnes's grandfather, who actually lived here, and who might even have drunk water out of this very tank. To deface an artifact like this requires more than nerve. It requires the arrogance of a king.

I look up towards my next destination. From the way the hill is shaped, I still can't actually see King Juan's Peak from the manager's house. According to the map drawn up during the Morse–Wynne-Tyson expedition—a copy of which I have forgotten to bring with me—the hump up ahead is actually the first of three I'll need to clear in order to reach the summit. I keep hiking, but it's frustratingly slow, tip-toeing from one wobbling rock to the next. Plus, there are booby nests hidden amongst the bushes and rocks, and I've been warned not to mess with a startled, defensive mama bird. My pace slows to a standstill. The sun is, somehow, getting even hotter. My legs are aching, I'm thirsty, and my vision is starting to blur.

Despite publishing more than a million words of prose, M.P. Shiel only mentioned Redonda in his fiction by name once. His 1899 novel *Contraband of War* took place during the Spanish-American War, which was still in progress as the story was being serialized in *Pearson's Weekly*. In a chapter called "The Chase," one of Shiel's characters notices something odd while passing through the Leeward Islands. "Yonder," he says, "right ahead of us is Redonda ..."

> The island towards which they were hasting was a mere rock, standing up with craggy sides from the water, conical in shape, and uninhabited save by boobies, and three men who live on its summit for the purpose of collecting the guano of the innumerable sea-fowl which haunt its shrubless sea-wall. The three men are lifted and lowered from and to the sea by a basket-and-crane arrangement high up on the face of the rock. From the summit a view (which the present writer has twice enjoyed) is obtained for many a mile over the sea as far as the coasts of Nevis to the North, and Montserrat to the South.

I first read this passage early on in my research, years before I ever dreamed of seeing the island for myself. The thing that always struck me about it was the narrator's parenthetical aside, disclosing a personal connection to Redonda: *which the present writer has twice enjoyed*. In terms of story, there's no reason to describe the view from the top, since none of the characters is privy to it. An aside like this doesn't add anything to the scene. It might even distract from it. So why does Shiel include it? I now know the answer: because he can't help himself. The view from Redonda's summit is special *because* it is rare. That observation may not have suited the purposes of his story, but Shiel wrote it down anyway because he wanted his readers to know he had been there — even if they never would themselves.

Neither would I. Despite my best efforts, I never make it up to King Juan's Peak. I wish I could say that I did. But the path, the heat, and the lack of water are obstacles I just can't get past. It reminds me of something Harris said when we'd first met in person, back at a café in English Harbour. When I told him I was going to climb to the peak, he'd tried to warn me — not that it was impossible, but that the ascent could feel at times like an optical illusion. "Just when you think you've made it to the top, another bloody ridge appears behind it," he'd said, taking a swig of beer. "It never ends."

As I look around now, even the view from Shiel's Summit — the third-highest point on Redonda — is strangely disorienting. I'm surrounded by a bushy, sage-green hillside; to my immediate right is a booby sunning itself on a rock, totally unconcerned with human presence until we make eye contact, at which point it drawls, "Oh, no!" Just as Shiel had promised, I can see all the way across the water to Montserrat, home of Gingerbread Hill and Maxwell chattering about KFC

The view from Shiel's Summit.

and the entire buried city of Plymouth. To the east, I can even make out the edge of Antigua, where the night before I'd stood at a barbeque and stared out at the exact place I'm standing right now. Everything else is pure Caribbean blue.

It's beautiful and serene, the kind of view worth momentarily derailing your war novel for. But what's disorienting me, I realize, is that by standing on Redonda, my frame of reference for the entire trip has disappeared. Since arriving in the Caribbean, this is one of the first times that I can't see the island in the distance — because I'm here. So maybe it's OK that I forgot my map back in the hotel room. We managed to find the island without it.

Back on the plateau, I plunk myself down next to Harris in the shade of the manager's house. I feel lightheaded—a mixture of euphoria and dehydration—and put my discomfort with his graffiti to one side for now. I tell Harris I didn't make it to the peak. Wiping my forehead with the front of my shirt, I admit that this whole trip has been a lot more difficult than I thought.

"See, that's why I'm so defensive about my claim to the kingdom," Harris says. "When you've climbed it a few times, you feel you've earned it. These other blokes who've never been here—or who just took a helicopter—I don't think that quite cuts it."

In that moment, I can't disagree.

Your sweaty author.

ON THE WAY DOWN, Harris and I decide to take the other gully back to the shoreline. Both routes are now in the direct sunlight, and the incline on this one looks slightly more forgiving than the path we took up. But a few minutes into the descent, I accidentally press too hard on a rock the size of a watermelon. It dislodges, falling a couple of feet and landing with a *whap* directly onto the bone of my right shin. The impact rips the skin open, and my leg immediately starts to bleed and swell. Before I have time to register what's happened, a second, smaller rock thumps down behind the first one and tears a strip off the side of my other shin. This time the pain comes right away, intense and sharp. I manage to grab hold of the cliff face and yell down to Harris, who ducks to one side just as both rocks bounce past him all the way down to the shore. I take a deep breath, steady myself, and reach for the next rock—only for it, too, to pull effortlessly away from the soil.

Now a wave of panic rolls over me. My mouth fills with the sour taste of adrenaline, and I start to distrust even my own senses. I look down at my gardening gloves, the fingers of which are now shredded, and realize that in flailing against the cliff I've torn off most of two of my fingernails. I mutter out loud that I need to start thinking clearly, *right now*, because I don't have any other choice. We're still a long way from the shoreline, and the only way to get there is down. I force myself to take another breath, counting the seconds, slowly in and then slowly back out.

A few steps later, though, the same thing happens again. Another melon-sized rock comes loose and goes careening down the hill. I shout to Harris again, this time with added urgency in my voice, and he leans back against the cliff. But this rock is shaped more like a football and bounces the same way. It's picking up speed, too, and only at the last second does it ring itself along the curve of the cliff, like the corner in a pinball machine, passing behind Harris and missing the back of his head by just a few inches. A wave of smaller rocks comes pouring down the path behind it, coating him in more dust. For a few seconds, neither of us says anything. Harris and I are both breathing heavily, and both hurt: in trying to dodge that last rock, I saw him accidentally stub one of his legs into a different rock, opening up three long bright-red cuts. It's only now that I realize we don't even know that it's possible to get down this way. Every other Redonda trip I've read about has taken the other gully. There's a chance that we're attempting a route that simply is not viable. And there are still a few hundred vertical feet of rocks and bushes between us and knowing for sure.

As my guide, Harris is trying to stay calm, but every few seconds he lets out a low, guttural groan, which makes me think he's more injured than he's letting on. I call down, but he doesn't answer. Blood is now running freely down both of my legs, and I can't put any pressure on either wrist. My brain feels like it's pulling on both sides of the same rope: I feel at once focused and helpless, alert and out of control. Like Gawsworth, I'm a sworn city boy. I have no experience in situations like this; I'm wearing *gardening* gloves, for crying out loud. Most of my life has been spent in environments where nearly every element has been carefully engineered and approved, allowing me the luxury of taking it all for granted. But there are no city planners on Redonda. Crouched on the side of this cliff, I am forced to reckon with the fact that if I grab the wrong rock one more time, there is nothing to prevent me from falling. And if I do fall, I probably won't be able to stop myself until I hit the rocks below, in which case I'm going to need the kind of medical attention that is currently several hours away by boat.

For a moment, I'm furious at myself for being so naive. I spent so long searching for the grand truth about some stupid inside joke from a hundred years ago that I didn't even consider the possibility that I might be putting myself in danger by coming here. But, no, that's not quite fair. The Second Shielian Discovery Expedition, from 1979, was mostly made up of sedentary, middle-aged Brits — and they were fine! Why should it be any different now? The only thing I can think of is the goats and rats. Without them here to eat everything, Redonda's plant life is quickly returning to its former splendour. In the process, the few remaining paths for humans to get up and down are steadily being sealed off. Maybe this one already is.

Eventually, I hear Harris's voice again. "There's nothing to do," he says weakly. "We've got to keep going."

We make a new plan. The cliff face is the sturdiest thing to hold onto, so Harris and I cling to it as we take our first tentative steps, a few inches at a time. Part of me expects that first handhold to crumble in my hand. But it doesn't. Neither does the next one. Soon we fall into a careful, repetitive pattern of movement. The sun is just as unrelenting as it was up on the plateau, but even this small act of assertion on our part has changed my thinking; now I imagine myself as a solar panel, absorbing the sun's energy and converting it into new reserves of determination. Slowly, the shore below us transforms from a threat back into a destination. When we finally reach the waterline, Fallon is already there waiting for us in the dinghy. Harris and I get in without a word, and as soon as we arrive safely back at the *Sea Terror II*, I hurl my backpack onboard, strip off my clothes, and fall limply into the sea.

Then it's back to Antigua. On the way over, I'd asked Chris if we could circle around the north side of the island on our return so I could see features like Fletcher's Rock, an islet named after Wynne-Tyson's co-executor, as well as a large sea-level cave dubbed the World's End. But I find my interest in any further sightseeing is sapped. I take a couple of perfunctory photos without getting up off of the mattress I'm sprawled out on, but at this point, Redonda has shown me all that I care to see. By now its secrets are either revealed, or best left alone. I wouldn't go back to that fucking island if you paid me.

THE NEXT MORNING, I have a meeting with Natalya Lawrence, who coordinates the Environmental Awareness Group's offshore islands program. Luckily, she's agreed to drive down from her office in St. John's to the sailing academy, because limping out to one of the onsite picnic tables is about as far as I can move. Lawrence joined the EAG in 2010, where one of her first tasks was teaching locals what made Redonda special. Some Antiguans knew it as a goat-infested rock near Montserrat; others had heard it was a dying island, slowly falling into the sea. Some didn't even know it had a name. Along with Shanna Challenger, Lawrence spent months doing educational outreach about the history of the guano mine and its importance in the international shipping industry. Later, Challenger created an exhibit called "Redonda on the Road," and brought it to restaurants and fairs around the country. The pair's outreach is working: as of 2019, 96 percent of respondents agreed that Redonda should be a protected area, and when we spoke the Antiguan government was considering a proposal to do just that.

The first time Lawrence visited Redonda, she says her stomach lurched. This was years before the rewilding efforts began, and the island looked barren and desolate. "We described it as the face of the moon," she says. Since then she's proudly tracked the island's recovery, but without access to a helicopter, Lawrence and the rest of the EAG haven't been to Redonda for months. I pull out my phone to show her pictures from my climb the day before, and the first thing she does is ask me to zoom in on the grass so she can try to figure out how much it's grown since her last visit.

I ask her what role she sees humans having on the island going forward, if any. From a conservation point of view, doesn't it make sense to just ban us from Redonda outright, lest we accidentally reintroduce another invasive species and undo all of the progress the EAG has made so far? But Lawrence doesn't think a ban is realistic. Locals have always gone there to fish and gather birds' eggs, she says, and you can still find sun-bleached Redondan goat skulls in many Montserratian living rooms. Of course, this approach has its risks. "Even after the eradication," Lawrence adds, with disdain in her voice, "somebody went and put graffiti up on a tank by the manger's house." I don't say anything, only flush with second-hand embarrassment.

Later that afternoon, Harris, Fallon, and Harris's son Marlin drop by the sailing academy's café to swap photos with me and reflect on yesterday's trip. As Marlin swipes through his dad's iPad, Harris tells me he's been thinking about something I mentioned onboard the *Sea Terror II*. "I have to tell you, I'm suspicious of this trunk they say was found in Bob's boat," he says. "I spent more time in that boat during Bob's final years than even Bob himself."

"You mean you're skeptical that he named a successor?" I ask. "Or that he did it this way?"

Harris peels off part of the label on his beer bottle and flicks it to the ground. "This supposed piece of paper," he says. "I just don't know."

I thank him for going through all of this on my account and apologize, again, for nearly killing him with Redondan debris. He assures me it's just one more adventure to add to the list.

Soon afterwards, the café becomes the meeting place for the Royal Naval Tot Club of Antigua & Barbuda, which congregates every night at 6 p.m. sharp to celebrate British naval history and drink a generous-sized toast to Queen Elizabeth. The Tot Club is the group that organized the search for King Bob's successor in 2009 and later handled the transition to King Michael the Grey once Williamson's royal proclamation was found inside the *St. Peter*. Like the Kingdom of Redonda, the Tot Club is built around lighthearted rituals and a sense of dramatic grandeur: they have four different levels of membership, strict rules for which toasts are given on which days of the week, and a series of infractions — ranging from not drinking quickly enough to forgetting to take off one's hat — each of which is subject to a fine of one bottle of port.

I'm here as a guest of John Duffy, who pulls up in his Jaguar a few minutes before the night's toast begins. As the two of us walk back to join the others at a pagoda overlooking English Harbour, Duffy tells me he had no idea that Harris was one of the claimants to the Redondan throne when he first put us in touch. I relay Harris's story about the three-part challenge he said he received from King Bob in 2005.

"But he's not a professional writer!" Duffy says.

"Well, there was this one motorcycle story ..." I say. "Apparently Chris showed that to King Bob, and he said that was good enough."

Duffy points a finger a few inches from my chest and says, "Now *that's* the most suspicious thing you've told me yet." The truth is, Duffy says, for years King Bob refused to even discuss the possibility of naming a successor. Whenever Duffy would bring it up, Bob would abruptly change the subject. "I think," Duffy says now, "because in naming a successor, it was admitting he was going to die." When Bob did pass away, there weren't any instructions on what to do, which is why Duffy put out the call for applications for a new king. While that was going on, a cache of papers was found inside the *St. Peter*. Many of them were basically illegible, Duffy says, but as a whole they indicated that Bob considered Howorth, his old friend from the yachting world, to be a worthy successor to his crown.

"That's all fine," I say. "But what I still don't understand is what made King Bob finally change his mind and write up this official document, leaving it all to King Michael. Had he finally made peace with the fact that he was dying? Or was it something else?"

At this point I'm not even expecting an answer. These are the kinds of questions I've been asking people for years, always in the hopes of unlocking a fresh detail or two, yet resigned to the fact that this, too, is shaping up to be one more Redondan mystery that will never be solved.

But something about what I've said makes Duffy pause, his mouth open. Then he slowly smiles and says, "One day I'll tell you the truth about that document."

"What?" I say. "When?"

"Never," he says, and laughs.

Behind us, the rum bosun clears his throat to let us know it's time to begin. The rest of the Tot Club is gathered in a circle, each member holding two generously sized tumblers: one containing water and the other the club's homemade brand of rum. As Duffy and I have been talking, nighttime has once again fallen in the Caribbean. The boats in English Harbour are gently sloshing up and down on the waves of a soft black sea.

I should be furious with Duffy. Instead, to my surprise, this admission strikes me as the most hilarious discovery yet. Of course the document was forged. Of *course* it was! In a legend full of exaggerations, misdirections, and outright lies, what was one more fabrication? What could be more Redondan? The risk all along in getting involved in a story like this was taking it too seriously. I had come all the way to the Caribbean in pursuit of the truth, but in the process had lost sight of the most basic Redondan tenet of them all — something I'd once read in a picture book about a dragon who gets stuck inside a volcano. *Ride si sapis*, it read in Latin. *Laugh if you are wise.*

Finally, I did.

"Now," Duffy says, his eyes shining, "let's get you that tot."

APPENDIX 1

State Papers

REALM OF REDONDA

Upon the Occasion of the Birthday of
H.M. KING JUAN I,
He is Graciously pleased,
In Recognition of their Services to His Royal Predecessor,
H.M. KING FELIPE I,
to Welcome into the Intellectual Aristocracy of His Realm
—— with Succession to their Heirs Male ——

TO
THE ARCH-DUCHY OF REDONDA
MACHEN, Arthur Llewelyn Jones,

TO
GRAND-DUCHIES OF NERA ROCCA

GOCHER, Kate,
GOLLANCZ, Victor,
MILLER, Annamarie V.,

MORSE, A. Reynolds,
SHANKS, Edward Buxton,
VAN VECHTEN, Carl.

TO
DUCHIES OF THE REALM

ARMSTRONG, Ethel Laura,
BELL, Neil,
CARTER, Frederick,
CHESSON, W. H.,
" CONNELL, John ",
DERLETH, August,
DORO, Edward,
FERGUSON, Malcolm M.,
FLETCHER, Iain,
HENLE, James,

KING-FRETTS, Anne,
MASON, A. E. W.,
MEYERSTEIN, E. H. W.,
MYER, K. G.,
NAYDLER, Merton,
OWEN, Walter,
PHILLPOTTS, Eden,
POLDEN, DAVID C.,
" QUEEN, Ellery ",
RANSOME, Arthur,

RICHARDS, Grant,
ROBERTS, Walter,
ROWLAND, John,
SWINNERTON, Frank
THOMAS, Dylan,
TYTHERIDGE, Alan,
WALKER, James,
WALLER, John,
WHEELER, John,
WIGGINS, G. H.

Further His Majesty is Graciously pleased
to Confirm the following Appointments, Admitted under His Patents as Regent
in the Reign of His Royal Predecessor, with Succession to their Heirs Male,

TO
BLAKESTON, Oswell, The Duchy of SANGRO,
DURRELL, Lawrence, The Duchy of CERVANTES PEQUENA,
JEPSON, Edgar, The Duchy of WEDRIGO,
JOHNSEN, Buffie, The Duchy of NERA CASTILIA,
LINDSAY, Philip, The Duchy of GUANO,
MILLER, Henry, The Duchy of THUANA,
RAMSEY, T. Weston, The Duchy of VALLADOLIDA,
ROTA, Cyril Bertram, The Duchy of SANCHO.

Given Under His Majesty's Hand, His Court-in-Exile, Kensington
The Twenty-ninth Day of June in the Year of Our Lord Jesus Christ
One Thousand Nine Hundred and Forty-seven.

Chamberlain.

325

REALM OF REDONDA

Upon the Occasion of the Birthday of
H.M. KING JUAN I,
He is Graciously pleased,
In Recognition of their Services to His Royal Predecessor,
H.M. KING FELIPE I,
or to the Realm,
to Welcome into the Intellectual Aristocracy of Redonda
— with Succession to their Heirs Male —

TO
THE ARCH-EPISCOPAL SEE
MARTIN, John William,

TO
DUCHIES OF THE REALM

DAWSON, Arnold	GRAHAM, Stephen	MOULT, Thomas
DUFF, Charles St. Lawrence	HEATH-STUBBS, John	ROSS, J. Maclaren
DWYER, P. G.	KNOPF, Alfred A.	SAYERS, Dorothy L.
FRASER, George Sutherland	MEGROZ, R. L.	SECKER, Martin

TO
THE SOLE BARONY OF THE REALM
ARMSTRONG, Percy Francis Brash Newhouse

TO
THE ORDER OF SANTA MARIA DE LA REDONDA
(Grand Cross)
Her ex-Majesty QUEEN BARBARA (reg. 17 : ii : 1947 - 22 : iv : 1948)
Her Majesty QUEEN ESTELLE (reg. 6 : viii : 1948 -
MORSE, A. Reynolds, Grand Duke of REDONDA

TO
THE ORDER OF THE STAR OF REDONDA
(Knight Commander)

BLEILER, Everett	GOUGH, Michael	PALMER, Herbert
BLOCK, Andrew	GUPTA, Susil	PATMORE, Derek
COX, Nigel Roy	HARE, Kenneth	PIMM, Rev. M. H.
DITTON, Peter	HERBERT, Benson	RIDGWAY, Alfred
DOERFLINGER, Frederic	HERRING, Robert	SAMUEL, Edgar Horace
ELWIN, Malcolm	McQUILLAND, Louis J.	STEPHENSON, George
FRIEND, Stuart B. J.	MULLEN, Thomas Anthony	VISIAK, Edward Harold
GEORGE, Daniel	O'LEARY, John Joseph	WYNNE-TYSON, Jon

Further His Majesty is Graciously pleased
to confirm the following Appointments,
Cartographer Royal : DUFF, Charles St. Lawrence, Duke of COLUMBUS
Chief of Royal General Staff : CAMPBELL, Ignatius Roy Dunnachie,
Duke of CARMELITA
Grand Chamberlain : FRASER, George Sutherland, Duke of NERUDA
Historiographer Royal : LINDSAY, Philip, Duke of GUANO
Master of the King's Horse : TSCHIFFELY, A.F., Duke of MANCHA-Y-GATO
Master of the King's Musick : CLARKE, Cyril James Fernandez, Duke of TUBA
Minister Plenipotentiary to the French Republic : LEVAI, Georges,
Duke of SALINAS

Given Under His Majesty's Hand, His Court-in-Exile, Temple Fortune
The Twenty-ninth Day of June in the Year of Our Lord Jesus Christ
One Thousand Nine Hundred and Forty-nine.

State Paper : Two

Grand Chamberlain

REALM OF REDONDA

Upon the Occasion of the Birthday of
H.M. KING JUAN I,
He is Graciously pleased,
In Recognition of their Services to His Royal Predecessor,
H.M. KING FELIPE I,
to Welcome into the Intellectual Aristocracy of His Realm
— with Succession to their Heirs Male —

TO
THE ARCH-DUCHY OF REDONDA
(Confirmation)
MACHEN, A. Hilary Blaise, succeeding MACHEN, Arthur L. J.

TO
DUCHIES OF THE REALM
(Confirmations)
ARMSTRONG, P.F.B.N., Sole Baron, succeeding ARMSTRONG, E.L.
JEPSON, Selwyn, Duke of WEDRIGO, succeeding JEPSON, Edgar
(Creations)

BRIDSON, D. G.	METCALFE, John	SYMONS, Julian
BURKE, Patrick	PINE, L. G.	TAYLOR, Rachel Annand
FABIAN, Robert	POTTER, Stephen	TREWIN, J. C.
HARRISON, Michael	PRIESTLEY, J. B.	WEST, Rebecca
HOLLAND, Trudy Frances	SAVAGE, Henry	WILLIAMS, Robert

TO
THE SOLE MARQUISATE OF THE REALM
INMAN, The Hon. Philip

TO
THE ORDER OF THE STAR OF REDONDA
(Knight Commander)

ARMSTRONG, Robert	CROFT-COOKE, Rupert	PHILLIPS, Andreas
BARTON, Frank	HENRY, Leigh Vaughan	RANNS, Noel
BAYLISS, John	HOPKINS, Kenneth	RICHARDSON, Maurice
BISHOP, Morchard	NICOLL, J. A. G.	SWINGLER, Randall
BUDGELL, Robert Michael	PERKINS, H. Bowen	TOLLOW, Joseph William
COLLCUTT, Roy James	POLLOCK, George	WHITE, John Foster

TO
THE JUAN CROSS
(For Valour: Civil Division)
O'LEARY, William Joseph

Further His Majesty is Graciously pleased
to confirm the following Appointments:
Acting Grand Chamberlain: FLETCHER, Iain, Duke of URGEL
Commissioner of Police: FABIAN, Robert, Duke of VERDUGO
Commissioner of Tax Suppression: ARMSTRONG, Sir Robert, (K.S.R.)
Lord Chancellor: NAYDLER, Merton, Duke of LOGOS
Lord High Admiral: METCALFE, John, Duke of BOTTILLO
Master of the Chapel Royal: HENRY, Sir Leigh Vaughan, (K.S.R.)
Physician in Ordinary: PERKINS, Sir H. Bowen, (K.S.R.)
Postmaster General: WILLIAMS, Robert, Duke of BALLY;
and to permit His Cartographer Royal
DUFF, Charles St. Lawrence, to relinquish the Dukedom of COLUMBUS.

Given Under His Majesty's Hand, His Court-in-Exile, within the Precincts of
Nonsuch Palace, Ewell, the Twenty-ninth Day of June in the Year of Our Lord
Jesus Christ One Thousand Nine Hundred and Fifty-one.

State Paper: Three   Acting Grand Chamberlain

APPENDIX 2

Redondan National Anthem

To the State of REDONDA

NATIONAL HYMN

(O God who gave our Island soil)

LEIGH HENRY
(1949)

Largamente e maestoso

O God who gave our Is-land soil in trust for ev - er more; Grant
O grant that now our glor-ious dead - in - spire us in this hour; In

grace that by our faith and toil we hold our heir - loom pure. The
those who from our loins are bred im - bue their spir - it's power. O

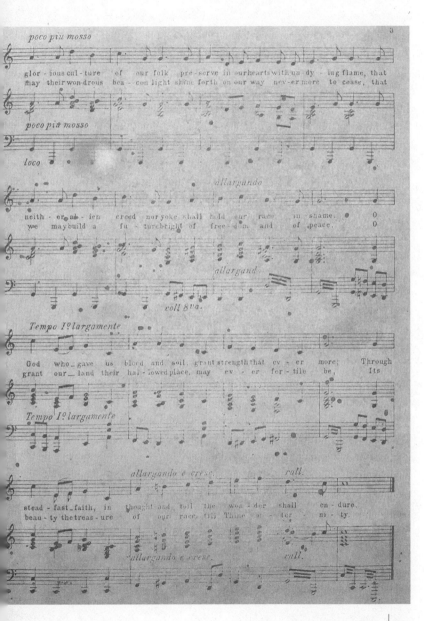

ACKNOWLEDGEMENTS

All books are written on the backs of other books, but this one especially so. My sincere thanks have to be offered first to the many Redonda historians and enthusiasts who have tried to make sense of the kingdom over the decades, including Harold Billings, Roger Dobson, Steve Eng, Alan Gullette, Henry Hutchison, A. Reynolds Morse, and John D. Squires. This work simply does not exist without yours. Equal, and equally heartfelt, thanks go out to those family members who scanned and mailed documents, sifted through personal archives, and otherwise helped facilitate my own research: Carol Billings Blood, Anne Eng, and Misty Peeler.

I spoke to several kings and one queen over the course of writing this book, which is not a sentence I expect I will ever be able to write again. Thank you to Steve Buist, Chris Harris, William Scott Home, Michael Howorth, Javier Marías, and Queen Josephine.

Thank you as well to the members of various Redondan courts, whose paths I was so pleased to cross: Stephen Chambers, Marius Kociejowski, Frané Lessac, and Marina Warner. The same is true of several descendants of previous kings: Richard Shiell (who has retained the second L), Tilly Vacher, and Tamara Williamson.

For their help with archival research, I am grateful to Richard Dana in Iowa, Reid Echols in Texas, and Jennifer Mason in Sussex. Gareth Wood helped clarify the royal correspondence between King Juan II and King Xavier. Silvia Sellán and Gabriel San Martín Fernández translated a key sentence from Marías into English.

I also had plenty of on-the-ground help in the Caribbean. In Montserrat: Gracelyn Cassell, Jean Handscombe, David and Clover Lea, everyone involved in the Alliouagana Festival of the Word, and the lower forms at Montserrat Secondary School. In Antigua: Shanna Challenger, John Duffy, Megan Fallon, Natalya Lawrence, and Christopher Waters.

This book also owes its existence to Dan Wells, who thought I was pitching him an entirely different idea but understood this one from our very first phone call. I've been equally thrilled to work with Vanessa Stauffer, Rachel Ironstone, Allana Amlin, Emily Mernin, and everyone else at Biblioasis. And to Natalie Olsen, this isn't one of our books but it might as well be. You nailed the design because you always do.

Part of this book was written during my tenure as a writer-in-residence for the Metro Edmonton Federation of Libraries. I also received funding from the Canada Council for the Arts. Sincere thanks to these organizations for the time and space, and the money that was used to purchase more of both.

I'm lucky to be friends with some astute early readers and co-conspirators, namely: Omar Mouallem, Jana G. Pruden, Naben Ruthnum, and the (Mostly) Western Narrative Nonfiction Writers Conference Collective.

Doretta Lau and Aaron Peck were the other members of the *Dark Back of Time* Twitter book club.

Finally, an embarrassingly big hug in front of all their friends to Bridget and Finn, my two favourite people on the planet. And, of course, thank you to Kate Gutteridge. If anyone asks, it was no big deal.

ABOUT THE AUTHOR

Michael Hingston is a writer and publisher in Edmonton, Alberta. He is the author of the books *Let's Go Exploring* and *The Dilettantes*, as well as the co-author of Harnarayan Singh's memoir *One Game at a Time*. Hingston's writing has appeared in *Wired*, *National Geographic*, *The Atlantic*, and *The Washington Post*. He is also one of the co-founders of Hingston & Olsen Publishing, makers of the Short Story Advent Calendar and other literary experiments.

NOTES

CHAPTER 1
"what had happened...Marías, *All Souls*, 105.
"a tiny island in the Antilles"...Marías, *All Souls*, 104.

CHAPTER 2
"appears to be...Quoted in Squires, "Of Dreams and Shadows."
"In seasons of drought, we...This and the following quote are found in Harding, "A Girl's Life on a Desert Island."
"Shiel has done so much better...H.P. Lovecraft, quoted on the back cover of Billings, *M.P. Shiel: The Middle Years*.
"an important artist" whose work...Van Vechten, *Letters*, 56–57.

CHAPTER 3
Matthew Sr. petitioned Queen Victoria...De Fortis, *Kingdom of Redonda*, 21.
"Try not to be strange."...Billings, *M.P. Shiel: His Early Years*, 89.
"You have kindled a...Shiel's letter to sister Gussie, quoted in *Middle Years*, 14–15.
"As is the *Yellow Book*...From a review of Shiel's *Prince Zaleski*, quoted in MacLeod, *Fictions of British Decadence*, 130.
"But why do you insist...Shiel to Gussie on her comparison of him to Conan Doyle, quoted in *Middle Years*, 34.
"legitimate son" of Poe's Dupin...This and the following quote are Shiel on *Zaleski*, in MacLeod, *Fictions of British Decadence*, 131.
"This, we sincerely hope, is...H.G. Wells, quoted in Billings, *Middle Years*, 35.
Shiel's stories "tell of a...Arthur Machen, quoted in Billings, *Middle Years*, 49.
an unnamed, "poisonous" French novel...Wilde, quoted in Ellmann, *Oscar Wilde*, 253.
"filthy" and refused to carry it...W.H. Smith company statement, quoted in *Oscar Wilde*, 323.
"Whether the Treasury or...Anonymous reviewer, quoted in Frankel, "General Introduction," in Wilde, *Dorian Gray: Uncensored*, 6.
"[The book] is poisonous...Wilde, quoted in Ellmann, *Oscar Wilde*, 321.
"the High Priest of the Decadents."...Anonymous story in the *National Observer*, Apr. 6, 1895, quoted in Ellmann, *Oscar Wilde*, 475.
"Poor chap!" Shiel wrote. "I...Billings, *Middle Years*, 33.
"find ugly meanings in...Wilde, *Dorian Gray*, 273.

"The Wilde scandal," writes academic...MacLeod, *Fictions of British Decadence*, 139.

Publisher John Lane decided to...Billings, *Middle Years*, 36–37.

CHAPTER 4

founded the Kingdom of Talossa...Wired Staff, "It's Good to Be King."

Glacier Republic, founded by Greenpeace...BBC Monitoring, "Chile: Activists 'Create Nation' to Protect Glaciers."

For a more literary example, consider...Details on Booth from Oliver Balch, "Richard Booth Obituary," *The Guardian*, August 22, 2019, https://www.theguardian.com/books/2019/aug/22/richard-booth-obituary and "Richard Booth, Self-crowned King of Used Books, Dies at 80," *New York Times*, August 28, 2019, https://www.nytimes.com/2019/08/28/books/richard-booth-dead.html?searchResultPosition=1.

CHAPTER 5

"[Y]ou could make as much...Louis Tracy, quoted in Billings, *Middle Years*, 47.

Shiel couldn't resist adding...Billings, *Middle Years*, 47.

length of 70,000 words to 150,000...Billings, *Middle Years*, 56.

two months before the first...Billings, *Middle Years*, 80.

is confident there were other flings...Billings, *Middle Years*, 69.

the couple was married in...Billings, *Middle Years*, 84.

asking for an advance on...Billings, *Middle Years*, 87.

she began lobbying for Lina...Billings, *Middle Years*, 87–88.

"If now a wave from...Shiel, *Purple Cloud*, 68.

first recorded instance of a literary "future history."...Critics of Shiel's work, quoted in Squires, "Rediscovering M.P. Shiel."

"an unconventional and horribly...*Sunday Times* review, quoted in "Note on the Text" in Shiel, *Purple Cloud*, xliv.

heavily borrowing from Villiers de l'Isle-Adam's...Billings, *Middle Years*, 74–75.

a "very beautiful" eighteen-year-old...Shiel, *Purple Cloud*, 116.

"an inveterate liar"...Machen, quoted in Billings, *Middle Years*, 30.

a man to whom "'right' and 'wrong'...Machen, quoted in Billings, *Middle Years*, 49–50.

Shiel later estimated he earned...MacLeod, "M.P. Shiel and the Love of Pubescent Girls," 357.

"his race is as great a mystery...Anonymous *Candid Friend* article, quoted in Billings, *Middle Years*, 123.

"a very great and holy place...Shiel, quoted in Billings, *Middle Years*, 125.

"was so well known that...Ransome, *Bohemia in London*, 255.

"the most dishevelled room...Ransome, *Bohemia in London*, 256.

"with a basin out of...Ransome, *Bohemia in London*, 256.

"You are thinking that it...Shiel, quoted in Ransome, *Bohemia in London*, 257–58.

"He loved theories above everything...Ransome, *Bohemia in London*, 262.

"I say, my wife...Ransome, *Bohemia in London*, 262–63.

"He could think of nothing else...Ransome, *Bohemia in London*, 263.

at least two different pseudonyms...Billings, *Middle Years*, 149.

wrote that *The Yellow Danger* was...Richards, *Author Hunting*, 103.

"the Spanish Squall."...Shiel, quoted in Billings, *Middle Years*, 160.

"You must remember, darling,"...Shiel, quoted in Billings, *Middle Years*, 161.

CHAPTER 6

he received a paltry £10...MacLeod, "Love of Pubescent Girls," 372.

"I was so pleased to...Mary Price, quoted in Billings, *Middle Years*, 203.

In a letter written from jail...MacLeod, "Love of Pubescent Girls," 358–59.

"She is still the same...Kenneth Shiel, quoted in MacLeod, "Love of Pubescent Girls," 375.

"You are a gang of...Shiel, quoted in Billings, *Middle Years*, 303.

"I like the light of the...Shiel, quoted in Dobson, *Library of the Lost*, 35.

[Shiel] passed me, panting, a...Ransome, *Autobiography*, 115.

CHAPTER 7

author's most "Shandean" novel...Wood, "Following the Precedent: Marías's Shandean Novel," in *Debt to Translation*, 97–138.

as a "false novel"...Quoted on back of the 2013 Vintage paperback edition of *Dark Back of Time*.

that "proceeds by digression,"...Marías, *Dark Back of Time*, 47.

"I believe I've still never...Marías, *Dark Back of Time*, 7.

returned to campus with "wagonloads"...Marías, *Dark Back of Time*, 65.

("Dear God," Marías thinks...Marías, *Dark Back of Time*, 100.

fictional Gawsworth" and "the real Machen"...Marías, *Dark Back of Time*, 66.

"pure Kiplingesque invention."...Marías, *Dark Back of Time*, 18.

"Any resemblance," the note reads...Marías, *All Souls*, 1; reproduced in *Dark Back of Time*, 247.

"more of a shopkeeper than an...Marías, *Dark Back of Time*, 237.

"(this book isn't that important...Marías, *Dark Back of Time*, 254.

"He lives in me to...Marías, *Dark Back of Time*, 126.

as "Gawsworth's room."...Marías, *Dark Back of Time*, 251.

The feeling that books seek...Marías, *Dark Back of Time*, 208.

"following the abdication of...Marías, *Dark Back of Time*, 303.

"REALM OF REDONDA" at the top...Marías, *Dark Back of Time*, 307.

"[I] limit myself to registering...Marías, *Dark Back of Time*, 253.

"If I did know everything...Marías, *Dark Back of Time*, 329.

"the individual, whatever his station...Shiel, *Purple Cloud*, 10.

"a circular clean-cut lake"...Shiel, *Purple Cloud*, 40.

and every kind of Arctic fowl."...Shiel, *Purple Cloud*, 48.

"liquid air"...Shiel, *Purple Cloud*, 25.

"wheeling with a shivering ecstasy,...Shiel, *Purple Cloud*, 40.

"the morbid searching out"...Marías, *All Souls*, 106.

CHAPTER 8

"the book boy,"...Gawsworth on his youth in a 1970 BBC documentary, quoted in Dobson, *"Hail, O King!"*, 5.

the nickname "the Duke."...Story in Eng, *Romantist*, 87.

more than one person...Eng, "Profile: John Gawsworth," 74, and Fletcher, "John Gawsworth," 206.

"In July 1931 a nineteen-year-old...Gawsworth, foreword to Shiel, *Science, Life and Literature*, 7.

"frenetically furious for 'Form in Art.'"...Gawsworth, foreword to Shiel, *Science, Life and Literature*, 8.

"The course of English Poetry...Gawsworth, ed., *Known Signatures*, 13.

"fake pastoralists, based in the city"...Eng, "Lyric Struggles."

"not poets at all but...Thomas, *Letters of Dylan Thomas*, 311.

"an accomplished craftsman,"...Quoted in Gawsworth, *Poems: 1930–1932*, 71.

dedicate poems to him...See, for example, Hugh MacDiarmid, "The Little White Rose," *Complete Poems* (Grove/Atlantic Inc., 1993), reproduced at https://www.poetryfoundation.org/poems/46800/the-little-white-rose.

"I think [Gawsworth] will soon emerge...Quoted in Gawsworth, *Poems: 1930–1932*, 70.

"magnetic fingers"...Gawsworth, "Magnetic Fingers."

"His memory for bibliography...Durrell, "Some Notes," 20.

"I was in the presence...Durrell, "Some Notes," 17.

lends the young poet-narrator five...Kavanagh, *Green Fool*, 346–47.

"only literary mate"...Kavanagh, *Complete Poems*, 348.

"literary admirers and acquaintances"...Durrell, "Some Notes," 18.

tradition they had left us."...Durrell, "Some Notes," 21.

volume of "literary confessions."...Shiel, quoted in Morse, ed., *Works of M.P. Shiel*, 13–14.

discover a surprising number."...Shiel, quoted in Morse, ed., *Works of M.P. Shiel*, 9.

"He would recruit unpublished tales...Jackson, quoted in Eng, *Romantist*, 87.

performing a Roman salute...de Montalk, *Unquiet World*, 147.

Woolf, who organized meetings...de Montalk, *Unquiet World*, 158.

Friends say he talked about...Edward Craig, quoted in Eng, *Romantist*, 89.

CHAPTER 9

We hereby proclaim that our most...Paraphrased by Gawsworth in Morse, ed., *Works of M.P. Shiel*, 12.

At Gawsworth's request, Shiel had...Jepson, *Memories of an Edwardian and Neo-Georgian*, 242n1.

"his prime word of contempt."...Fletcher, "John Gawsworth," 211.

"Most writers are too busy...Kenneth Hopkins, quoted in Eng, *Romantist*, 90.

a signature from Virginia Woolf...MacLeod, *Fictions of British Decadence*, 169.

"A mixture of ferocity and...Durrell, "Some Notes," 19.

Once, as a joke, Durrell suggested...Durrell, "Some Notes," 21–22.

"In those days one had to be...Durrell, "Some Notes," 19.

He bragged to the *New York Times*...Horwill, "News and Views of Literary London," 1938.

merely an expanded and slightly repurposed reprint...Eng, "Lyric Struggles."

"the counterfeit nineties diction...Eng, "Lyric Struggles."

"Do you not know that all...Gawsworth, "Carpe Diem," *Collected Poems*, 11.

I am a vampire of love...Gawsworth, "Advice of Juan," *Collected Poems*, 51–52.

"I have of late the rags...Gawsworth, "Reformation of Juan," *Collected Poems*, 52.

So I must be considered one...Gawsworth, "December 12, 1940," *Collected Poems*, 84.

"John, in fact, had a great...Fraser, *Stranger and Afraid*, 164.

"good but dangerous company."...Fraser, *Stranger and Afraid*, 165.

"But hist!" Gawsworth replied...Fraser, *Stranger and Afraid*, 163.

He talked, while he wrote, but...Fraser, *Stranger and Afraid*, 165.

"Gawsworth always seemed hovering...Fraser, *Stranger and Afraid*, 166.

"a world of outsiders, down-and-outs...Reporter on Fitzrovia, quoted in David, *The Fitzrovians*, ix.

"district of the mind" and...David, *The Fitzrovians*, 164.

"Gawsworth would be a standing joke...Thomas, *Collected Letters*, 332.

a "leftover, yellow towelbrain...Thomas, *Collected Letters*, 361.

"a violent man, fantasist...Stanford, *Inside the Forties*, 212.

"Was it in his eyes...Stanford, *Inside the Forties*, 213.

There are stories from these years...Stories from Stanford, *Inside the Forties*, 213.

jokes about misplacing his crown...*Sunday Referee*. "Author Is King of Isle."

pullies installed on the ceiling...Hutchison, *Realm of Redonda*, 24.

"What a formidable list...Shiel's letter to Morse, ed., quoted in *Works of M.P. Shiel*, 14.

found it "very interesting."...Wells, *Correspondence of H.G. Wells*, volume 4, 152.

Shiel, Gawsworth wrote, was "a master of...Gawsworth's obituary for Shiel in *The Times*, "Master of Fantasy."

"noted for ingenuity of plot...Obituary in *New York Times*, "Matthew P. Shiel, 82."

another "'one-book' man"...Edward Shanks compares Shiel to Melville in eulogy, quoted in Morse, ed., *Works of M.P. Shiel*, 161.

For a number of years his...Shanks's eulogy for Shiel, quoted in Morse, ed., *Works of M.P. Shiel*, 161.

"literally a Shiel collector."...Eng, "Profile: John Gawsworth," 80.

On his way home from the funeral...Story in Morse, ed., *Shiel in Diverse Hands*, 68.

His guests went along with...Sutherland, *Curiosities of Literature*, 43.

CHAPTER 10

"Court-in-Exile" in Kensington, State Paper...Reproduced in Morse, ed., *Works of M.P. Shiel*, 11.

all six recipients of which...De Fortis, *Kingdom of Redonda*, 25.

Whenever he encountered his old friend...Story from Eng, *Romantist*, 94.

"a lady novelist who briefly...Eng, "Profile: John Gawsworth," 78.

On the anniversary of the execution...Durrell, "Some Notes," 19.

"We are a motley lot...Durrell, "Some Notes," 22.

was surprised to see his own name...Letter to Squires, quoted in "Of Dreams and Shadows."

listed his hobby as "creating nobility."...Gawsworth, quoted in Eng, "Profile: John Gawsworth," 80.

much of the book's print run...Story from Eng, "Lyric Struggles."

a joke started to make its way...Eng, *Romantist*, 94.

remembered Gawsworth drunkenly emerging...This story and the following epithets Gawsworth used against his wife can be found in Holloway, *John Gawsworth*, 26–27.

When he was fired from a second...Story in Eng, *Romantist*, 100.

"milk, bread, bicarbonate of soda…Wynne-Tyson, *Finding the Words*, 168.

a Redondan national anthem…Wynne-Tyson, *Finding the Words*, 174; the full lyrics and audio of "O God Who Gave Our Island Soil" can be found at http://anthems.lidicity.com/o/rdd.html.

the first Redondan flag…De Fortis, *Kingdom of Redonda*, 25–26.

"an unaccountable mantle of obscurity"…Morse, *Works of M.P. Shiel*, xvii.

Shiel's "honeyed, frenzied madness."…Morse, *Works of M.P. Shiel*, xiii.

worried that Shiel's "royal heritage may…Morse, *Works of M.P. Shiel*, xiii.

"No finer service could…*Daily Mail*, "The King of Redonda Has Investiture."

John Heath-Stubbs, for instance…Story in Eng, *Romantist*, 95.

"KING JUAN ADVOCATES"…Thomas, "Two Epigrams of Fealty," reproduced in Freeman, *Dylan Thomas and Redonda*, 5.

"The legend was tailor-made…Wynne-Tyson, *Finding the Words*, 174.

"If one kept John's glass filled…This story and the following can be found in Eng, *Romantist*, 100–101.

"Of course I know you're…Story in Eng, *Romantist*, 91.

"CARIBBEAN KINGSHIP," it read…"Caribbean Kingship," *The Times*.

CHAPTER 11

"The entire absence of women…Gawsworth, quoted in Whitcomb, "What Women Don't."

"I will become plain…Gawsworth, quoted in Whitcomb, "What Women Don't."

"Perhaps Mr. Armstrong *is* entitled…Fawcett, "King of All the Seagulls."

"there is considerable money…Hipwell's attorney's letter, quoted in De Fortis, *Kingdom of Redonda*, 27.

"I was vulgarizing…As told to a reporter by Gawsworth, quoted in Eng, "Profile: John Gawsworth," 82.

When he met Lawrence Durrell's younger…Story in Eng, *Romantist*, 94.

"It happens to be in pawn…"Ex-Malayan Dulcie Has Become a Duchess," *The Straits Times*.

("He was in constant demand with…Roberts, quoted in Eng, Romantist, 101.

One bookseller remembered…Eng, Romantist, *Realm of Redonda*, 101.

John Heath-Stubbs felt was "disastrous."…Quoted in Eng, *Romantist*, 95.

what Wynne-Tyson "euphemistically" called…Wynne-Tyson, *Finding the Words*, 178.

singing the entire French national anthem…Story in Eng, *Romantist*, 101.

"unsurprisingly," wrote the Redondan historian…Dobson, *"Hail, O King!"*, 1.

referred to as "Queen SJ,"…Dobson, *Library of the Lost*, 102.

small pile of "mongrel ash," . . . Wynne-Tyson, *Finding the Words*, 179.

"Friends are seriously concerned . . . "The *Times* Diary," Dec. 4, 1969.

"He slept in our large . . . Fletcher, "John Gawsworth," 215.

"It is a real problem," Fletcher told . . . "The *Times* Diary," May 9, 1970.

"Tho' utterly broke," he wrote . . . Wynne-Tyson, *Finding the Words*, 181.

"an often-exhausting dynamo." . . . Irish novelist Kate O'Brien of Gawsworth, quoted in Dobson, *"Hail, O King!"*, 5.

"Now, I haven't an address . . . Gawsworth, quoted in Dobson, *"Hail, O King!"*, 11.

"I feel 999 years . . . A letter from Gawsworth to a friend after returning from war, quoted in Eng, *Romantist*, 93.

"As a professional anachronism . . . Eng, "Lyric Struggles."

at one point reported the name . . . "John Gawsworth, 58, Poet and 'King' of Tiny Island," *The New York Times*.

"The poet, John Gainsworth." . . . "The *Times* Diary," Dec. 24, 1970.

"We found ourselves playing up . . . Fraser, *Stranger and Afraid*, 165–166.

be remembered "as an excellent . . . Wynne-Tyson, quoted in Eng, *Romantist*, 102.

life since his friend's death "has . . . Fletcher, "John Gawsworth," 219.

CHAPTER 12

"Steve would be happy to . . . Email from Anne Eng, March 28, 2018.

"a large quantity of correspondence . . . University of Reading's John Gawsworth Collection, http://www.reading.ac.uk/adlib/Details/archiveSpecial/110014380.

"The Gawsworth collection is quite . . . Email from University of Reading librarian, July 2, 2019.

a hypocrite and "lousy Jew bastard." . . . From a letter dated February 28, 1948.

thanks King Juan for "the rich merriment" . . . In a letter from Machen to Gawsworth, dated July 10, 1947.

"Never assume anything . . . Robert A. Caro, "The Secrets of Lyndon Johnson's Archives," *The New Yorker*, Jan. 28, 2019, https://www.newyorker.com/magazine/2019/01/28/the-secrets-of-lyndon-johnsons-archives.

"What, after all, is any nation's . . . King Cedric, from the foreword to De Fortis, *Kingdom of Redonda*, 9.

CHAPTER 13

"reprehensibly unplanned drift." . . . Wynne-Tyson, *Finding the Words*, 16.

formed in fall 1954, "with no resources . . . Wynne-Tyson, *Finding the Words*, 21.

later called "suicidal" . . . Wynne-Tyson, *Finding the Words*, 16.

"A new imprint can establish...Frederic Warburg, quoted in Wynne-Tyson, *Finding the Words*, 109.

I had no formal training...Wynne-Tyson, *Finding the Words*, 21.

"No major newspaper gave...Wynne-Tyson, *Finding the Words*, 113.

referred to as "humane education.""...Wynne-Tyson, *Finding the Words*, 223.

"manipulative Performing Monarch act"...Wynne-Tyson, *Finding the Words*, 180.

"Our sovereignty, upon our...Shiel, quoted in Morse, ed., *Works of M.P. Shiel*, 12.

"If it is true that we...Fletcher, "John Gawsworth," 213.

a "graceful last gesture,"...Email from Loraine Fletcher, September 5, 2019.

CHAPTER 14

"The death of Gawsworth...Wynne-Tyson, *Finding the Words*, 186.

"No," said Somerville. "Not King...Morse, *Quest for Redonda*.

"apprehensive reminders that I...Wynne-Tyson, *Finding the Words*, 187.

"Our conjoint inward amusement...Morse, *Quest for Redonda*.

With the pending relinquishment..."Proclamation," in Morse, *Quest for Redonda*.

"totally free of beer cans"..."A Good Friday for Redonda," in Morse, *Quest for Redonda*.

This bad poet..."Fait Accompli," from Scrannel, *Snowballs*, 11.

"There is every indication...Wynne-Tyson, *Civilised Alternative*, 11.

"angry and sorrowful, but...*Times* review of Wynne-Tyson's *The Extended Circle* (1985), quoted in Wynne-Tyson, *Finding the Words*, 282.

"The rock was grey...Wynne-Tyson, *So Say Banana Bird*, 158.

"It would not have been difficult...Wynne-Tyson, *So Say Banana Bird*, 162.

"Instead of being remembered...Wynne-Tyson, *So Say Banana Bird*, 217.

"The queen is knocking up...Pitts, "The Dotty Dynasty of Redonda."

"Has things a bit out...Wynne-Tyson, *Finding the Words*, 190.

"The legend of Redonda...Wynne-Tyson, "Two Kings of Redonda."

"The pictures are splendid...King Juan II in the foreword to Jackson and Lessac, *Dragon of Redonda*, 3.

Laugh if you are wise...Wynne-Tyson does this himself on page 195 of his *Finding the Words*.

CHAPTER 15

her father had passed away...Telegraph Obituaries, "Jon Wynne-Tyson, Publisher of Varied Interests Who Founded Centaur Press."

"lifeblood to the professional...Roy Harley Lewis, *Antiquarian Books: An Insider's Account* (New York: Arco, 1981): 130–131.

CHAPTER 16

little Javier got used to...Marías, "The Invading Library," *Between Eternities*, 25.

"You've just started...Julían Marías, quoted in Herzberger, *Companion*, 5.

"When you think about it...Marías, "This Childish Task," *Between Eternities*, 140.

compared his young protege to...Juan Benet, quoted in Wood, *Debt to Translation*, 31.

a "goddamn Anglosaxonist,"...Marías, "Chamberi," *Between Eternities*, 43.

"morbid"...Marías, *All Souls*, 106.

"a man with a false name"...Marías, *All Souls*, 113.

hailed the book as "stunning"...Review of *All Souls*, in *Kirkus Reviews*, Nov. 1, 1996, https://www.kirkusreviews.com/book-reviews/javier-marias/all-souls-3.

"a dazzling example of...*Times Literary Supplement*, quoted on the back of Marías, *All Souls* paperback.

"the pieces began to...Wynne-Tyson, *Finding the Words*, 192.

"Perhaps I should come...Wynne-Tyson, quoted in Wood, *Debt to Translation*, 35.

"seemed to have a mysterious...Marías, *Voyage*, 23.

"James Denham" was Marías himself...As admitted to in Marías, *Dark Back of Time*, 143–144.

"I shouldn't be termed...Marías in BBC Radio, *The Island with Too Many Kings*.

"I had the feeling...Marías, "Tribute to Jon Wynne-Tyson," *Elysia*, 95.

CHAPTER 17

his writings about Redonda have...Dobson and Valentine, eds., *Redondan Cultural Foundation Newsletter*, no. 5.

spelling derived from...Marías, *Dark Back of Time*, 300.

Dark Back of Time mentions that Marías...Lesser, "Stranger than Fiction."

"between 1943 and 1945 in...Marías, *Dark Back of Time*, 128.

"What I want to point...Marías, "The Man Who Could Be King" (translation by Gabriel San Martin Fernandez, original to this book).

"can be located"...Marías, *Dark Back of Time*, 92.

"I'll have to name...Marías, *Dark Back of Time*, 322.

writers, artists, and other creative people...A partial list is available online at "Duques y Duquesas de Redonda," http://www.javiermarias.es/REDONDIANA/DuquesdeRedonda.html.

"It is to me a pleasant...A.S. Byatt in BBC Radio, *The Island with Too Many Kings*.

sketch of an imaginary...Frank Gehry's palace design, and links to the
other Redondan regalia, can be viewed online at http://www.javier
marias.es/REDONDIANA/palacio.html.

"We have hundreds of...Marías in BBC Radio, *The Island with Too
Many Kings*.

"renouncing their own voices."...Marías, quoted in Aida Edemariam,
"Looking for Luisa," *The Guardian*, May 7, 2005, https://www.the
guardian.com/books/2005/may/07/featuresreviews.guardian
review34.

I couldn't be bothered...Marías, *Berta Isla*, 379.

"Those subjects, or those...Penguin Books UK, "Javier Marías," YouTube,
https://www.youtube.com/watch?v=PqrGBof4VPs.

odds as high as ten-to-one...Alex Shephard, "Who Will Win the 2019
(or the 2018!) Nobel Prize in Literature?" *The New Republic*, Oct. 9,
2019, https://newrepublic.com/article/155316/will-win-2019-or-2018-
nobel-prize-literature.

"printed privately," the manager...Marías, *While the Women Are
Sleeping*, 62.

"Tell my two friends...Marías, *While the Women Are Sleeping*, 63.

CHAPTER 18

"I offered to kill these...Personal interview with Marius Kociejowski,
July 16, 2019.

"there was much pleasure...Kociejowski, "A Factotum in the Book
Trade," *The Pebble Chance*, 4.

"a measured hostility...Kociejowski, "Richard Stanyhurst, Dubliner,"
The Pebble Chance, 109 n1.

ridiculed in its time for...Contemporary review of and C.S. Lewis
response to Stanyhurst *Aeniad* translation both quoted in Kociejowski, *The Pebble Chance*, 111–112.

"It was such a big...Personal interview with Stephen Chambers, July
9, 2019.

"bringing to the High Table...Chambers, *The Court of Redonda*, 17.

she was likely the inspiration...Gleick, "Boo! (Scared Yet?)" *Time*.

"The book is not popular...Personal interview with Marina Warner,
Jan. 19, 2022.

"the most haunting thing...H.P. Lovecraft, quoted on publisher's
webpage for Shiel, *The House of Sounds and Others*, (New York:
Hippocampus Press, 2005), https://www.hippocampuspress.com/
lovecrafts-library/the-house-of-sounds-and-others-by-m.-p.-shiel.

children "naturally" don't enjoy...Wynne-Tyson, *Civilised Alternative*,
103.

CHAPTER 19

Never to pay any…Marías, quoted in Wynne-Tyson, *Finding the Words*, 193–194.

"Javier's 'accession' is just…Wynne-Tyson, "Foreword," in Holloway, *John Gawsworth*, 6.

this "irrevocable covenant" clearly stated…Squires, "Of Dreams and Shadows."

a proposed "Court Council…Hutchison, *Realm of Redonda*, 39.

Evening Standard, whose story…Reproduced in Hutchison, *Realm of Redonda*, 41.

"ex-king" and "Juan as was."…Gawsworth, quoted in Hutchison, *Realm of Redonda*, 41.

"By this time it was clear…Hutchison, *Realm of Redonda*, 42.

Roberts continued claiming…De Fortis, *Kingdom of Redonda*, 28.

reference to a sensational…William L. Gates, "A Memory of 'Instant John': On first Meeting the Poet

John Gawsworth, Third King of Redonda," The Redondan Foundation Facebook page, Jan. 14, 2019, https://www.facebook.com/redondan foundation/posts/the-lost-club-journala-memory-of-instant-john-on-first-meeting-the-poetjohn-gaws/2228623150798145.

"In London," Gates wrote…Quoted in Hutchison, *Realm of Redonda*, 47.

"regardless of colour, class…Hutchison, *Realm of Redonda*, 47.

"Shiel cannot be effectively…Morse, *Quest for Redonda*.

seagull with a broken…Gates, *Times of Redonda*, 5.

patron of an unusual pub sport…Hutchison, *Realm of Redonda*, 62.

"I must admit that…Gates letter to Morse, reproduced in Hutchison, *Realm of Redonda*, 55.

passed, according to a statement…"William Leonard Gates

2nd February 1934–2nd January 2019," The Redondan Foundation, http://www.redonda.org/home/DeathOfKingLeo.

"it had been John's…Wynne-Tyson, *Finding the Words*, 186.

claimed that Gawsworth had…Squires, "Of Dreams and Shadows."

Leggett outlined his claim…King Juan II, "Redonda: At the Heart of the Caribbean," 1996. Archived here: https://web.archive.org/web/19991009093554/http://www.geocities.com/SoHo/5900/index.html.

"following a bloodless coup."…Buist, "Laying Claim."

the "reincarnation" of Shiel…Review quoted in Morse, *Shiel in Diverse Hands*, 355.

The title of "King…King Leo, quoted in BBC Radio, *The Island with Too Many Kings*.

enriching, as he put it, "their emotional…Boshoff, quoted in Liesl, Hattingh, "Hennie Boshoff," *Dekat*, Dec. 9, https://lieslhattingh.files.wordpress.com/2010/01/dekat_dec09_1.pdf.

"Kids won't look into…Wynne-Tyson, letter to Frané Lessac, Aug. 21, 1986.

"I mean, one would know…*LIAT Islander,* "When Kings Fall."

the kingdom's first university…De Fortis, *Kingdom of Redonda,* 34.

"Nobody could describe…De Fortis, *Kingdom of Redonda,* 35.

Santa Claus, that "dangerous heretic…De Fortis, *Kingdom of Redonda,* 75.

"Perhaps I was always…Margaret Parry, quoted in Oldfield, "Hail Queen Maggie."

"We could have a…Parry, quoted in Oldfield, "Crowning a Caribbean Queen."

"My father and grandfather…Parry, quoted in Oldfield, "Crowning a Caribbean Queen."

CHAPTER 20

Williamson estimated Picasso spent…Eiloart, "Solo Pack Design."

"When he worked in London…Personal interview with Tamara Williamson, Apr. 23, 2019.

Not so very long ago I met…"A New King in the Caribbean!" unknown newspaper clipping.

"The day after tomorrow, sixty-five…Williamson, quoted in Finlay, *The As It Happens Files,* 94.

"I'm five foot six…Williamson, quoted in Finlay, *The As It Happens Files,* 94.

then issued his first royal orders…"The Man Who Would Be King of Redonda," *Design Week*; Williamson, "The Isle of Redonda."

"around $35 million USD…Williamson, "The Isle of Redonda."

"The smoke-free law…Pyatt, "Embassy No. 1."

"I'll look them up…Williamson, quoted in *The Sun,* "Pint-Sized Country."

"On August 27th my father…Email from Tamara Williamson to unspecified mailing list, Aug. 30, 2009.

King Bob had told him…Email from John Duffy to Tamara Williamson, Aug. 31, 2009.

"a little splodge…Personal interview with Michael Howorth, Jan. 19, 2018.

"'Gosh,' he said with…Email from Howorth to John Duffy, Dec. 3, 2009.

"Will you solemnly promise…Archbishop's prepared text in an email from John Duffy to Howorth and Terry Bowen, Dec. 9, 2009.

posed for Frances's camera…This photo of Howorth with de Lorenzo can be seen at "The King and the Prime Minister," The Howorths, Apr. 6, 2014, https://www.thehoworths.com/2014/04/the-king-and-the-prime-minister.

"it has a not inconsiderable reputation…Marías, "Only Air and Smoke and Dust."

CHAPTER 21

"a mountain-mass, loveliest..."About Myself," from Morse, ed., *Works of M.P. Shiel*, 1.

90 percent of the island's population..."Montserrat Hurricane—Sept 1989," International Rescue Corps, http://www.intrescue.info/hub/index.php/missions/montserrat-hurricane-sept-1989.

"On no island I have...Margaret Mead, quoted in Billings, *M.P. Shiel: His Early Years*, 35.

"The blacks—the natives...Morse, *Quest for Redonda*.

"For what is a king..."About Myself," from Morse, ed., *Works of M.P. Shiel*, 2.

After just one year...Some figures from Tim Knight, "Environmental transformation spells brighter future for Redonda's fantastic beasts," Phys Org, July 31, 2018, https://phys.org/news/2018-07-environmental-brighter-future-redonda-fantastic.html.

CHAPTER 22

"dislodged boulders,"...Wynne-Tyson, *Finding the Words*, 188.

The island towards which...Shiel, *Contraband of War*, quoted in Squires, "Of Dreams and Shadows."

BIBLIOGRAPHY

BOOKS

Billings, Harold. *M.P. Shiel: A Biography of His Early Years*. Austin, TX: Roger Beacham, 2005.

———. *M.P. Shiel: The Middle Years (1897–1923)*. Austin, TX: Roger Beacham, 2010.

———. *An Ossuary for M.P. Shiel*. Bucharest: L'Homme Récent, 2015.

Chambers, Stephen. *The Court of Redonda*. Cambridge, UK: Downing College, 2018.

David, Hugh. *The Fitzrovians: A Portrait of Bohemian Society, 1900–55*. London: Michael Joseph, 1988.

De Fortis, Paul, ed. *The Kingdom of Redonda: 1865–1990*. Upton by Chester, UK: Aylesford Press, 1991.

De Montalk, Stephanie. *Unquiet World: The Life of Count Geoffrey Potocki de Montalk*. Wellington, New Zealand: Victoria University Press, 2001.

Denison, Michael. *Double Act*. London: Michael Joseph, 1985.

Dobson, Roger. *"Hail, O King!": The Last Days of John Gawsworth*. Oxford: The Friends of Arthur Machen/Tartarus Press, 2005.

———. *The Library of the Lost: In Search of Forgotten Authors*. 2015. North Yorkshire: Tartarus Press, 2018.

Durrell, Lawrence. "Some Notes on My Friend John Gawsworth." In *Spirit of Place: Letters and Essays on Travel*, Edited by Alan G. Thomas, 17–23. London: Faber and Faber, 1969.

Ellmann, Richard. *Oscar Wilde*. New York: Knopf, 1988.

Finlay, Mary Lou. "There'll Always Be an England." In *The As It Happens Files: Radio that May Contain Nuts*, 93–96. Toronto: Knopf Canada, 2008.

Fletcher, Loraine. *Print/Capture*. Reading, UK: The Female Quixote Press, 2013.

Fraser, G.S. *A Stranger and Afraid: The Autobiography of an Intellectual*. Manchester: Carcanet New Press, 1983.

Freeman, Arthur. *Dylan Thomas and Redonda*. Swansea, UK: Ty Llen, 2003.

Gardiner, Charles Wrey. *The Answer to Life Is No*. London: Rupert Hart-Davis, 1960.

Gawsworth, John. *The Collected Poems of John Gawsworth*. London: Sidgwick & Jackson, 1948.

———, ed. *Crimes, Creeps, and Thrills*. London: E.H. Samuel, 1936.

———, ed. *Known Signatures*. London: Rich & Cowan, 1932.

———. "Magnetic Fingers: A Bibliophile's Holiday." In *Holidays and Happy Days*, edited by Oswell Blakeston, 129–146. London: Phoenix House, 1949.

———. *Poems: 1930–1932*. London: Rich & Cowan, 1933.

———. *Some Poems*. Privately printed, [1971].

———. *Ten Contemporaries: Notes Toward Their Definitive Bibliography*. London: Ernest Benn, 1932.

Grant, James. *The Narrative of a Voyage of Discovery, Performed in His Majesty's Vessel the Lady Nelson, of Sixty Tons Burthen, with Sliding Keels, in the Years 1800, 1801, and 1802, to New South Wales*. London: Thomas Egerton, 1803.

Grohmann, Alexis. *Coming into One's Own: The Novelistic Development of Javier Marías*. Amsterdam and New York: Rodopi, 2002.

Herzberger, David K. *A Companion to Javier Marías*. Woodbridge, UK: Tamesis, 2011.

Holloway, Mark. *John Gawsworth and the Island Kingdom of Redonda*. Oxford: The Lost Club and the Redondan Cultural Foundation, 2002.

Hutchison, Henry. *Realm of Redonda: A Definitive History of the Island-Kingdom of Santa Maria de la Redonda in the West Indies*. Norwich, UK: William L. Gates, 2004.

Jackson, Jan, and Lessac, Frané. *The Dragon of Redonda*. London and Basingstoke: Macmillan Caribbean, 1986.

Jepson, Edgar. *Memories of an Edwardian and Neo-Georgian*. London: The Richards Press, 1937.

Kavanagh, Patrick. *The Complete Poems*. Edited by Peter Kavanagh. New York and Newbridge: The Peter Kavanagh Hand Press and the Goldsmith Press, 1972.

———. *The Green Fool*. 1938. London: Martin Brian & O'Keeffe, 1971.

Kershaw, Alister, and Temple, Frédéric-Jacques, eds. *Richard Aldington: An Intimate Portrait*. Carbondale and Edwardsville: Southern Illinois University Press, 1965.

Kociejowski, Marius. *The Pebble Chance*. Windsor, ON: Biblioasis, 2014.

Maclaren-Ross, Julian. *Bitten by the Tarantula and Other Writing*. London: Black Spring Press, 2005.

———. *Memoirs of the Forties*. London: Alan Ross, 1965.

MacLeod, Kirsten. *Fictions of British Decadence: High Art, Popular Writing, and the Fin de Siècle*. New York: Palgrave Macmillan, 2006.

Marías, Javier. *All Souls*. Translated by Margaret Jull Costa. New York: New Directions, 1992.

———. *Berta Isla*. Translated by Margaret Jull Costa. London: Hamish Hamilton, 2018.

———. *Between Eternities*. Translated by Margaret Jull Costa. New York: Vintage, 2017.

———. *Dark Back of Time*. Translated by Esther Allen. New York: New Directions, 2001.

———. "Javier Marías' Tribute to Jon Wynne-Tyson, Juan II of Redonda." In *Elysia*, edited by Richard Grenville Clark, 95–98. Guildford, UK: Apocalypse Press, 2014.

———. "Only Air and Smoke and Dust." Translated by Eric Southworth. *La mujer de Huguenin*, by M.P. Shiel. Barcelona: Reino de Redonda, 2000.

———. *Voyage Along the Horizon*. Translated by Kristina Cordero. San Francisco: Believer Books, 2006.

———. *While the Women Are Sleeping*. Translated by Margaret Jull Costa. New York: New Directions, 2010.

Morse, A. Reynolds. *The Quest for Redonda*. Cleveland, OH: The Reynolds Morse Foundation, 1979.

———, ed. *Shiel in Diverse Hands: A Collection of Essays*. Cleveland, OH: The Reynolds Morse Foundation, 1983.

———, ed. *The Works of M.P. Shiel*. Los Angeles: Fantasy Publishing Co., 1948.

Nicholson, Desmond V. *Heritage Treasures of Antigua and Barbuda*. St. John's, Antigua: Museum of Antigua and Barbuda, 2007.

Nicholson, Desmond V., and Dyde, Brian. *The Place Names of Antigua and Barbuda*. St. John's, Antigua: Museum of Antigua and Barbuda, 2014.

Ransome, Arthur. *The Autobiography of Arthur Ransome*. Edited by Rupert Hart-Davis. London: Jonathan Cape, 1976.

———. *Bohemia in London*. New York: Dodd, Mead & Company, 1907.

Richards, Grant. *Author Hunting by an Old Literary Sports Man: Memories of Years Spent Mainly in Publishing, 1897–1925*. New York: Coward–McCann, 1934.

Rota, Anthony. *Books in the Blood: Memoirs of a Fourth Generation Bookseller*. Middlesex, England, and New Castle, DE: Private Libraries Association and Oak Knoll Press, 2002.

Scrannel, Orpheus [John Gawsworth]. *Snowballs*. London: E. Lahr, 1931.

Shiel, M.P. *How the Old Woman Got Home*. 1927. New York: Collier Books, 1961.

———. *Prince Zaleski*. 1895. London: Martin Secker, 1928.

———. *The Purple Cloud*. 1901. London: Penguin, 2012.

———. *Science, Life and Literature*. London: Williams and Norgate, 1950.

———. *Shapes in the Fire*. 1896. New York and London: Garland, 1977.

Sinclair, Andrew. *War Like a Wasp: The Lost Decade of the Forties*. London: Hamish Hamilton, 1989.

Smith, Bradley. *Escape to the West Indies: A Guidebook to the Islands of the Caribbean*. New York: Knopf, 1956.

Squires, John D. "Some Closing Thoughts on M.P. Shiel: Or, the Frustrations of a Putative Biographer." In *M.P. Shiel and the Lovecraft Circle: A Collection of Primary Documents, Including Shiel's Letters to August Derleth, 1929–1946*, edited by John D. Squires, 103–111. Kettering, Ohio: The Vainglory Press, 2001.

Stanford, Derek. *Inside the Forties: Literary Memoirs 1937–1957*. London: Sidgwick & Jackson, 1977.

Sutherland, John. *Curiosities of Literature: A Feast for Book Lovers*. New York: Skyhorse, 2009.

———. "Introduction." In *The Purple Cloud*, by M.P. Shiel, xiii–xxxviii. London: Penguin, 2012.

Tate, Tim. *Hitler's British Traitors: The Secret History of Spies, Saboteurs and Fifth Columnists*. London: Icon, 2018.

Thomas, Dylan. *The Collected Letters of Dylan Thomas*. Edited by Paul Ferris. London and Melbourne: J.M. Dent & Sons, 1985.

Van Vechten, Carl. *Letters of Carl Van Vechten*. Edited by Bruce Kellner. New Haven and London: Yale University Press, 1987.

Wells, H.G. *The Correspondence of H.G. Wells*. Edited by David C. Smith. London: Pickering & Chatto, 1998.

Wilde, Oscar. *The Picture of Dorian Gray: An Annotated, Uncensored Edition*. Edited by Nicholas Frankel. Cambridge and London: Belknap Press, 2011.

Williamson, Robert. *The Cruise of the Schooner Driftwood*. Toronto and Vancouver: Clarke Irwin & Company, 1962.

Wood, Gareth. *Javier Marías's Debt to Translation: Sterne, Browne, Nabokov*. Oxford, UK: Oxford University Press, 2012.

Wynne-Tyson, Jon. *The Civilised Alternative: A Pattern for Protest*. Sussex, UK: Centaur Press, 1972.

———. *Finding the Words: A Publishing Life*. Norwich, UK: Michael Russell, 2004.

———. "Foreword: As Prodigal as Byron, and as Lame." In *John Gawsworth and the Island Kingdom of Redonda*, by Mark Holloway, 3–6. Oxford: The Lost Club and the Redondan Cultural Foundation, 2002.

———. *So Say Banana Bird*. Sussex, UK: Pythian Books, 1984.

NEWSPAPER AND MAGAZINE ARTICLES

"Author Is King of Isle His Father Seized with Own Navy." *Sunday Referee*. October 24, 1937.

Bevan, Nathan. "The Welsh Composer Unmasked as a Secret Nazi Who Tried Helping Hitler Invade the UK." *Wales Online*. September 18, 2018. https://www.walesonline.co.uk/lifestyle/nostalgia/welsh-composer-who-unmasked-secret-15078392.

The Bolton News. "Hunt Is Over in Search to Find Caribbean Island Queen." May 28, 2007.

Buist, Steve. "Laying Claim to the Kingdom of Redonda." *The Hamilton Spectator.* Nov. 23, 2002: T07.

"Caribbean Kingship with Royal Prerogatives." *The Times.* June 21, 1958: 1.

Daily Mail. "The King of Redonda Has Investiture." June 30, 1951: 3.

Daily Sketch. "Poets at Dinner: Novelist King." October 20, 1937.

Drysdale, William. "A Visit to Montserrat." *The New York Times.* December 29, 1885: 4.

Eiloart, Tim. "Solo Pack Design." *New Scientist.* February 19, 1976: 412.

"Ex-Malayan Dulcie Has Become a Duchess." *The Straits Times.* May 31, 1959: 9. https://eresources.nlb.gov.sg/newspapers/Digitised/Article/straitstimes19590531-1.2.29.

Fawcett, F. Dubrez. "King of All the Seagulls." *Men Only.* November 1960: 58–60.

Gleick, Elizabeth. "Boo! (Scared Yet?)." *Time.* May 24, 1999. http://content.time.com/time/subscriber/article/0,33009,991046,00.html.

Harding, Dorothy. "A Girl's Life on a Desert Island." *The Wide World Magazine* 6, no. 36 (April 1901): 563–565.

Holmes, Richard. "Character Portrait." *The Times.* July 10, 1970: 13.

Horwill, Herbert W. "News and Views of Literary London." *The New York Times.* June 19, 1938.

———. "News and Views of Literary London." *The New York Times.* July 2, 1939.

King Michael the Grey. "The King and I." *Motor Boat & Yachting* (April 2010): 148.

Lesser, Wendy. "Stranger than Fiction." *The New York Times.* May 6, 2001. https://www.nytimes.com/2001/05/06/books/stranger-than-fiction.html.

"The Man Who Would Be King of Redonda." *Design Week.* Jul. 24, 1998. https://www.designweek.co.uk/issues/23-july-1998/the-man-who-would-be-king-of-redonda.

Marías, Javier. "The Man Who Could Be King." *El País.* May 22, 1985.

Newsweek. "Transition." June 30, 1947: 45.

The New York Times. "John Gawsworth, 58, Poet and 'King' of Tiny Island." Obituary. September 27, 1970.

———. "Matthew P. Shiel, 82, Author, Journalist." Obituary. February 18, 1947.

Oldfield, Stephen. "Crowning a Caribbean Queen." *Daily Mail.* June 1, 1993: 24–25.

———. "Hail Queen Maggie, Monarch of Redonda." *Daily Mail.* May 18, 1993: 3.

Pitts, Denis. "The Dotty Dynasty of Redonda." *Sunday Express Magazine.* September 23, 1984: 14–17.

PW en Español. "Javier Marías, Veinte Años Como Rey de Redonda." November 26, 2020. https://publishersweekly.es/javier-marias-veinte-anos-como-rey-de-redonda.

Pyatt, Jamie. "Embassy No. 1." *The Sun*. June 27, 2007: Home News, 23.

Squires, John D. "Rediscovering M.P. Shiel (1865–1947)." *The New York Review of Science Fiction* 13, no. 9 (2001): 12–15.

The Sun. "Pint-Sized Country." June 12, 2007: Home News 12.

Telegraph Obituaries. "Jon Wynne-Tyson, Publisher of Varied Interests Who Founded Centaur Press." *The Telegraph*. May 21, 2020. https://www.telegraph.co.uk/obituaries/2020/05/21/jon-wynne-tyson-publisher-varied-interests-founded-centaur-press.

The Times. "M.P. Shiel: Master of Fantasy." Obituary. February 20, 1947.

"The *Times* Diary." December 4, 1969: 10.

——. May 9, 1970: 8.

——. June 26, 1970: 8.

——. September 25, 1970: 10.

——. September 26, 1970: 12.

——. December 24, 1970: 8.

"When Kings Fall Out." *LIAT Islander*. July 1988: 62.

Whitcomb, Noel. "What Women Don't Know About Men." [unknown newspaper] [unknown date] 1958: 36.

Williamson, Bob. "A New King in the Caribbean!" *All at Sea* [unknown date]: 20–21.

——. "Schooner *St. Peter* to Be in *Pirate* Sequel." *All at Sea*. January 1, 2005. https://www.allatsea.net/schooner-st-peter-to-be-in-pirate-sequel.

Wynne-Tyson, Jon. "English Harbour, Antigua." Letter. *Daily Telegraph*. September 5, 1980: 14.

OTHER

BBC Monitoring. "Chile: Activists 'Create Nation' to Protect Glaciers." BBC News, Mar. 10, 2014. https://www.bbc.com/news/blogs-news-from-elsewhere-26520166.

BBC Radio 4. *Redonda: The Island with Too Many Kings*. Aired May 22, 2007. https://www.bbc.co.uk/programmes/b007j7t6.

Dobson, Roger, and Valentine, Mark, eds. *Redondan Cultural Foundation Newsletter*, no. 1, February 1994.

——. *Redondan Cultural Foundation Newsletter*, no. 2, February 1996.

——. *Redondan Cultural Foundation Newsletter*, no. 3, November 1996.

——. *Redondan Cultural Foundation Newsletter*, no. 4, January 1998.

——. *Redondan Cultural Foundation Newsletter*, no. 5, November 1998.

Eng, Steve, ed. "John Gawsworth—A Tribute-Anthology." *The Romantist* 6–8 (1986): 85–106.

———. "The Lyric Struggles of John Gawsworth." *Books at Iowa* 38 (1983): 29–45. https://pubs.lib.uiowa.edu/bai/article/id/28814.

———. "Profile: John Gawsworth." *Night Cry* 2, no. 3 (1987): 73–85.

Fletcher, Ian. "John Gawsworth: The Aesthetics of Failure." *The Malahat Review* 63 (1982): 206–219.

Gates, William. *The Times of Redonda*, July 1998.

MacLeod, Kirsten. "M.P. Shiel and the Love of Pubescent Girls: The Other 'Love That Dare Not Speak Its Name.'" *English Literature in Transition 1880–1920* 51, no. 4 (2008): 355–380.

Shiell, Richard, and Anderson, Dorothy. "Matthew Dowdy Shiell (1824–1888)." Revised September 2006. http://www.alangullette.com/lit/shiel/family/Shiell_Matthew_Dowdy.htm. Accessed September 8, 2017.

———. "Matthew Phipps Shiel (1865–1947)." Revised September 2006. http://www.alangullette.com/lit/shiel/family/Shiel_Matthew_Phipps.htm. Accessed August 4, 2020.

Squires, John D. "Of Dreams and Shadows: An Outline of the Redonda Legend with Some Notes on Various Claimants to its Uncertain Throne." Revised February 2011. http://www.alangullette.com/lit/shiel/essays/RedondaNotes.htm. Accessed August 4, 2020.

Stetz, Margaret Diane. "Sex, Lies, and Printed Cloth: Bookselling at the Bodley Head in the Eighteen-Nineties." *Victorian Studies* 35, no. 1 (1991): 71–86.

Williamson, Bob. "The Isle of Redonda." http://www.jalypso.com/redonda. Accessed December 13, 2010.

Wired Staff. "It's Good to Be King." *Wired*, Mar. 1, 2000. https://www.wired.com/2000/03/kingdoms.

Wynne-Tyson, Jon. "Two Kings of Redonda: M.P. Shiel and John Gawsworth." *Books at Iowa* 36 (1982): 15–22.

INDEX

Hunt, Leigh, 97
Hurricane Hugo, 283
Huysmans, J.K., 42–43

Jackson, Jan, 189
Jackson, R.F.A., 99
Jepson, Edgar, 102–03, 118
John, Augustus, 110
Jonson, Ben, 90
Jull Costa, Margaret, 18, 208, 219

Kavanagh, Patrick, 95–96
Kentish, Barbara, 99, 115, 236
King Cedric, 156, 254–55
King Charles I, 120
King Christopher, 301, 303
King Felipe, 112, 137, 161, 244, 250, 268
King George V, 89
King Guillermo, 250–51
King James III, 108
King James VIII, 108
King Juan's Peak, 193, 263, 298, 311, 313, 314
King Leo, 245, 249, 251
King Michael the Grey, 257, 273, 275, 276, 278, 300, 308–09, 322–23
King of Poland, 99, 101
King Xavier, 21, 78, 192, 210–11, 214–16, 219–21, 224, 226, 230–31, 233, 251
King's College, 37
Kingdom of Redonda Prize, 216
Kingdom of Talossa, 49
Knopf, Alfred A., 30, 126
Kociejowski, Marius, 224–27, 229, 233, 237

Lamb, Charles, 97
Lane, John, 40–41, 45
Lawler, Michael, 257
Lawrence, Natalya, 320–21
Lea, Clover, 284
Lea, David, 240, 284–88, 298
Leeward Islands, 23, 253, 256, 271, 274, 282, 313
Leggett, Max Juan Tonge, 249–50
Lessac, Frané, 189, 253

Lesser, Wendy, 212, 245
Lewis, C.S., 227
Lewis, Wyndham, 195
Liddle, Dick, 177
Lindsay, Philip, 119
Lippincott's, 42
Literary Digest, 169
Logroño, 24
London's Commonwealth Institute, 253
London's University College Hospital, 165
López Mercader, Carme, 221
Lovecraft, H.P., 30, 235

MacDiarmid, Hugh, 94, 95, 135
MacEwan, Ian, 216
Machen, 61, 91, 104, 105
Machen, Arthur, 30, 41, 60–61, 91, 95, 97, 104–05, 117, 135, 151–53, 158, 192–93, 196, 221
Machen, Hilary, 254
Maclaren-Ross, Julian, 110, 126
MacLeod, Kirsten, 45, 69
Mariscal, Javier, 215
Martin, George, 252, 285
Mead, Margaret, 285, 289
measles, 37
Mendini, Alessandro, 215, 235
Merchant Taylors' School, 89, 198
Metcalfe, John, 155
micronation, 48–50
Miller, Annamarie V., 118
Milton, John, 90, 122, 184
modernism, 30, 92
Montalk, Geoffrey Wladislas Vaile de, 100
Montlake, Sir Nicholas, 269
Munro, Alice, 216
Murphy, Jack, 177
Museum of English Rural Life, 148

Nabokov, Vladimir, 206
Napoleon, 56
New Cambridge Bibliography of English Literature, The, 213